Off the Beaten Path

*

Where to Vacation or Stay-a-While in America's Own Bargain Paradises

*

by NORMAN D. FORD

13th Revised Edition. © 1970 by
HARIAN PUBLICATIONS, GREENLAWN, N. Y. 11740
Trade Distributor: Grosset & Dunlap

Elbow Room, U.S.A.

Increasingly, as ribbons of concrete bring motorists to our remotest hamlets, the true escapist is turning to the wilderness. For crowds go only where cars will take them. Even during the height of summer, when our National Park highways are jammed with cars, complete solitude can be found almost anywhere a couple of hundred yards from a highway. The average American will not walk or undertake any outdoor physical exercise. As a result, a bounty of un-crowded and low cost vacation opportunities exists all over America, wherever cars cannot or do not go. Hiking, cycling, canoeing, pack trips, boat trips down the western river canyons or a vacation on a working dude ranch—all offer outstanding opportunities to escape the problems of the machine age and to enjoy a healthful vacation amidst America's grandest scenery. For more information, write to the follwing information sources:

Superintendent of Documents, Government Printing Office, Washington, D.C. 20402, offers the following publications: **Outdoor Rerceations in the National Forests**, 60¢; **Camping**, 20¢; **Backpacking in the National Forest Wilderness**, 15¢; **National Forest Vacations**, 45¢; **Appalachian Trail**, 5¢.

Ballantine Books, 101 Fifth Ave, New York, N.Y. 10003, offers the **Sierra Club Wilderness Handbook** 75¢.

The following clubs have information on wilderness hiking and on family and group trips through America's outdoors:

Sierra Club, 1050 Mills Tower, San Francisco, Calif. 94104.

Green Mountain Club, 108 Merchants Row, Rutland, Vt. 05701.

Appalachian Trail Conference, 1916 Sunderland Place N.W., Washington, D.C. 20036.

Appalachian Mountain Club, 5 Joy St., Boston, Mass. 02108.

Wampler Tours, Box 45, Berkeley, Calif. 94701. Operates all-expense trips to the outstanding wilderness areas of the West.

American Youth Hostels, 20 W. 17th St., New York, N.Y. 10011. Operates inexpensive bicycle and hiking trips; all ages welcome.

International Bicycle Touring Society, 846 Prospect St., La Jolla, Calif. 92037. Adult bicycle tours.

Windjammer cruises are operated out of Camden, Castine, and Sedgewick, Maine and St. Thomas, Virgin Islands. Write local Chambers of Commerce for addresses.

Canoe vacations. Write the state or provincial travel bureaus listed in Chapter 10 for Maine, Michigan, Minnesota and Ontario.

Wilderness Society, 729 15th St., N.W., Washington, D.C. 20005. Riding, hiking and river trips.

River running trips: Western River Expeditions, 1699 E. 3350 South, Salt Lake City, Utah 84106; Hatch Expeditions, 411 East 2nd North, Vernal, Utah 84078; Don L. Smith, North Fork, Idaho 83466; Mexican Hat Expeditions, Box 156, Mexican Hat, Utah 84531; Wild River Expeditions, Box 110, Bluff, Utah 84512; Grand Canyon Expeditions, 518$\frac{1}{2}$ F. St., Salt Lake City, Utah 84103; American River Touring Association, 1016 Jackson St., Oakland, Calif. 94607; Harris Brennan River Expeditions, 1575 Madison Ave., Ogden, Utah 84404; George White, Box 368, Midway City, Calif. 92655; Wonderland Expeditions, 3862 S. 825 West, Bountiful, Utah 84010.

Trail Riders of the Canadian Rockies, P.O. Box 6742, Station D, Calgary, Alta.; American Forestry Association, 919 17th St., N.W., Washington, D.C. 20006. Both operate inexpensive pack trips.

For addresses of working dude ranches and operators of wilderness pack trips, write to the state or provincial information bureaus (listed in Chapter 10) of Alberta, British Columbia, California, Colorado, Montana, Oregon, Texas, Washington and Wyoming.

TABLE OF CONTENTS

4

IMPORTANT: THIS BOOK CONTAINS NO ADVERTISING WHATSOEVER—PAID OR UNPAID. EVERY PLACE OR ESTABLISHMENT WAS SELECTED ON ITS MERITS ALONE WITHOUT BIAS OR COMPENSATION.

Paradise On A Shoestring

Who hasn't dreamed of visiting Mallorca, Spain and Mexico — the bargain paradises of the world—where you can live in luxury on a few dollars a day?

For most people, the cost and time involved in reaching these far away places are prohibitive. Are there no bargain paradises nearer home?

There certainly are. If you're fed up with bumper-to-bumper driving, with crowded beaches, neon signs, TV, telephones, traffic jams, parking meters and high prices, this book is the answer. Here are scores of Old World islands, mountain Utopias, and hideaway villages where you can spend a week, a month, or a lifetime far from the bustle of cities and the worries of civilization. All but one are on United States or Canadian soil and you can reach the majority in the family car.

North America's shoestring paradises are made for escapists. Maybe you just want to get yourself and the family away from it all for a week or two. Or perhaps you're looking for a low-cost place to spend the summer or the winter in an ideal climate. Or you may want time: time to paint or write or think or rest in a place where your budget will spin out for months. However long you plan to escape, you'll find the answer within these pages.

Don't expect many of the place names to be familiar. With few exceptions, each place was chosen because it *is* unknown, unspoiled and unusual.

This is a guide to off-beat America, to quiet backwaters where life has stood still since the earliest days. Without leaving United States or Canadian soil and the familiar comforts of North American food and plumbing, you can spend an utterly *different* vacation in quaint corners of Brittany, Scotland, Scandinavia, Ireland and Spain. And you can do it at costs which often approach the bargain prices of more distant lands.

Today, right now, there's an island where two can spend a week on a picturesque salt water farm beside the sea for $70 *including three full homecooked meals a day for both*. There are places where Scotch sells at $2.50 a bottle, gin for $2, lobsters are $1 a pound and a haircut *and* shave will set you back exactly $1. And there are places, right in the United States, where you can buy a six-room home on a beautiful island for just $5,000.

Of course, prices vary across the country. Costs are higher in some regions than in others. But in each part of North America you'll find we've pinpointed the most alluring off-beat beauty spots where costs are well below average.

Town or village, mountain or desert, art colony or camper's paradise, island or lake—whichever you prefer—you'll find plenty of variety. There's a paradise for every taste, an environment to suit every personality, a setting to heal every tension, strain and worry.

Once an escapist, always an escapist. If you're contemplating retirement and commonplace suburban living seems dull, why not retire in a bargain paradise? Or on an island? Hundreds of imaginative, individualistic Americans have retired to the very same places described in this book. To help you choose, we give specimen retirement housing and rental costs for each suitable place.

Wherever you live, you'll find a choice of bargain paradises within easy reach. You won't need passports, visas or shots nor will you have to buy expensive steamer tickets to half way around the globe. With one exception, familiar dollar bills are legal currency, there are no dangerous foreign diseases, and efficient American or Canadian doctors, hospitals and drug stores are close at hand. Only the paradise themselves will be foreign or unusual.

And if you doubt that, read on.

Caution: while every care has been taken to ensure that prices and facts are correct, this information must of necessity be assembled prior to publication and no responsibility can be assumed for changes which occur afterwards. We have no control over hotels raising rates, going out of business, changing ownership, or altering their accommodations subsequent to publication of this book.

Abbreviations used in this book

CoC   Chamber of Commerce
o.w.   One way
r.t.   Round trip.

BETTER HEALTH: OFF THE BEATEN PATH

As pollution of our air, food and water becomes an increasingly important health consideration, America's out-of-the-way places offer an additional bonus: freedom from the smog, the noise and the growing tensions that plague our cities and metropolitan areas. Fresh fish and unfrozen meats and poultry raised without synthetic hormones and fresh fruits and vegetables free of toxic sprays and chemical fertilizers—can still be had at some of our islands and villages. And away from the perplexing modern world of belching auto exhausts, nerve wracking telephones, disturbing TV programs, and sophisticated appliances that need costly repairs, one can still lead a natural way of life where abundant outdoor exercise can be enjoyed. Statistics prove that people live longer in America's small towns and the death rate from such killers as lung cancer, emphysema and cardio-vascular diseases is barely half that found in our big cities.

CHAPTER 1

Six Island Outposts of
Old World Europe

North America, and particularly the United States, is truly a melting pot of world nationalities. With few exceptions, the foreign languages, traditions and customs brought by our European ancestors were quickly assimilated into our own North American culture. But long ago a few remote northeastern islands were each settled by one predominant European race. Cut off from the progressive mainland, these people continued to live as they had in Old World Europe. While their native France, Scandinavia, Scotland or Ireland acquired railways, factories and electric lights, these people went on using the horse and cart, the spinning wheel, and oil lamps. Their very isolation accentuated racial characteristics. They continued to lead a way of life and to speak a language which today are found only in the remotest corners of their respective native lands.

Here are six such islands where you can visit "Europe" on your summer vacation. You can drive your car straight onto two of the islands and the others are easily reached by connecting boats or ferries.

ST. PIERRE ET MIQUELON. Few people know it, but only 12 miles off the coast of Canada is a tiny transplanted corner of France where French francs are legal tender and dogs haul bakers' carts piled high with long French loaves. The French tricolor still waves over the eight rocky isles of the Territoire des Iles Saint-Pierre et Miquelon.

It's only an hour's flight from the North American mainland but this bit of France in the New World is so foreign you need a passport to land. You'll be met by a gendarme in fluttering cape and then you're free to stroll the narrow streets of St. Pierre, the capital.

St. Pierre—rows of brightly painted but salt-shabby French houses lining gray hillsides—could be anywhere in Brittany. Sturdy citizens in jaunty black berets and blue smocks stroll the quai, against a backdrop of old fashioned shops bulging with Parisian products. And in Place General de Gaulle or in flower bedecked Square Joffre, the chatter of lively French conversation mingles with the flavor of delectable French cooking in the cool evening air.

With the exception of two brief periods of British occupation, the islands have been French since 1635. But their settlement dates from comparatively recent times. Nowadays, they're primarily a base for French trawler fleets which sail into their harbors each year en route to fish the Grand Banks. For this reason, France maintains the islands' 5,500 people on a welfare-state basis. Though most of the men are fishermen, shopkeepers, or government employees, their actual income totals only one fifth of their needs. France subsidizes the remainder. It was a different story during prohibition.

In the dry years, St. Pierre served as a bootleg base for the entire northeastern United States. Still lining the waterfront are huge concrete warehouses which once poured liquor into the holds of fast rum-running ships. St. Pierre still has low excise taxes and liquor is cheap. In the numerous general stores—one to every 40 inhabitants—you can buy Scotch at $3-$3.50 a fifth, Burgundy at $1.50-$1.75, and good Bordeaux at 45¢ a liter. Every store is a groaning emporium of internationally famous goods: delicately-stitched Parisian "Lancel" handbags or the "en satin Beauvais" evening bags are only $10, beautiful leather wallets $3.80-$6. The much prized French kid gloves run from $3-$6 a pair, cognac—Napoleon, Hennessey, Courvoisier, etc.—is $3.50-$4 a fifth, champagnes, like Pommery, Moet et Chandon, or Mumm Cordon Rouge $3.50-$4, and American cigarettes sell for 23¢-27¢ a pack. At the existing exchange rate of 250 CFA francs per dollar, Swiss watches sell from $18 and silk scarves for $1.20. Name brand perfumes like Lubin "Nuit de Longchamp" or Molinard's "Chanel" range from $2.50-$3.50 for a bottle that would cost four times as much on Fifth Avenue.

You'll find curiosities aplenty: quickest way to locate anyone is to call them by 'phone. Regardless of the time of day, the operators have an uncanny knowledge of everyone's whereabouts. As on most small islands, you select your taxi driver when you arrive and play the bill the day you leave. So far, no one has ever been overcharged. And though St. Pierre has no traffic problems, a local ordinance requires each car, truck and taxi to sound its horn at each intersection until 8 p.m. French *matelots* in red pom-poms neck with island girls while chaperones look on undisturbed and there's even a small but brisk smuggling trade with Newfoundland.

The continental atmosphere extends across the islands' 93 square miles. Stern, grim and rocky, St. Pierre, the smallest and most barren, is nonetheless criss-crossed by pleasant walks and drives. There are scooters for rent and taxis if you feel less energetic. From hilltops, most of which are shrines and surmounted by large crosses, you can view magnificent landscapes and sea-carved panoramas. Beside the roads, small fenced vegetable gardens surround each weathered cottage.

Once a week, the M.V. *Langlade* puts out from St. Pierre for the neighboring isles. A fascinating legend accompanies the name of every cape, rock, and islet that you pass. Le Nid a L'Aigle, Anse de La Carcasse, Etang de Mirande, Anse de Voiles Blanches, and Ile aux Vainqueurs are just a few among scores of curious, flavorful island place names. First stop is usually Ile aux Marins, near St. Pierre, a fishing settlement so picturesque that artists and photographers devote weeks to it.

Then you're at Miquelon, the largest island and site of the colony's second settlement, a village of some 550 fishermen and their families. In the church is a painting presented by Napoleon III and you can see

EVEN IN A PARADISE: CAMPING CUTS COSTS

Camping is the very cheapest and often the best way to enjoy America's off-beat beauty spots. No longer need you associate camping with rain, mosquitoes, poison ivy, and comfortless Army cots. Camping is different today. That's why it's the fastest growing pastime in America. Twice as many families now camp out as ten years ago and their numbers are growing by leaps and bounds.

In or near most of the places described in this book you will find some of North America's more than 3,500 public camp-grounds equipped with piped water, outdoor fireplaces, toilet facilities, wooden tent floors, and parking space. Scattered across the country in the most scenic parks, on the seashore, in mountains or forests, beside rivers or lakes, these campgrounds are yours to use either free or at nominal cost. In addition there are tens of thousands of unimproved camp-sites where you can set up house at the drop of a tent peg.

The majority of public camp-grounds are in state or national parks and forests. You can also camp at most national monuments and federal recreation areas. All these organizations issue free literature briefly describing each camp-ground and its facilities. For camp-grounds in state parks and forests write the State Park Commission at the capital of the state you intend camping in. For a list of other state-maintained camp-grounds, write the Department of Conservation at state capitals. Availability of National Forest camp-grounds is described in the booklet *National Forests*, which you can get for 45c from the Superintendent of Documents, Government Prtg. Office, Washington, D.C. 20402. For camping information in the national parks, monuments, and federal recreation areas write the Director, National Park Service, U.S. Department of Interior, Washington, D.C. 20402. Excellent free literature on Canadian camp-grounds is issued by the information bureaus of each province.

Now for equipment. Today's campers sleep luxuriously in lightweight summer sleeping bags supported by comfortable air mattresses. These and modern gasoline stoves have taken all that's rough and rugged out of camping. You can cook at ease on a 2-3 burner instant-lighting stove and if you add a folding oven and grill you're headed for gracious living. Campers are a friendly lot and nightly barbecues are standard fare.

What will all this cost? For the average family you'd better reckon on a basic outlay of $200. (Since you'd spend that at a hotel on the average 14-day vacation, your outlay is returned on your first holiday.) But if it's your initial attempt at camping, you can rent an outfit for much less. Most dealers will apply the rental to purchase price if you buy later.

Umbrella tents are easiest to erect, have sewn-in floors, and can be purchased at Sears Roebuck or Montgomery Ward. Summer weight sleeping bags sell in surplus stores for about $10 each. Plastic air mattresses come at $4-$7.50, better quality rubberized ones $10-$20. Coleman or American 2-burner stoves sell for $15-$18, with 3 burners $21-$27; stands are $5 extra. A gasoline lantern will cost $11-$16. Both Sears and Montgomery Ward offer good quality portable ice boxes at $17-$22. In addition you'll need a folding table and chair for each person, a nested cooking outfit and 12" skillet, and a picnic set purchased or made up at home. All this fits nicely in the rear foot space or trunk of the average car.

What will camping save? Depending on how you shop and where you are, the average family of four can vacation under canvas for as little as $5-$7 a day. For automobile touring, your daily costs including 350 miles of car operation should average no more than $17-$18 for four, possibly less. (Tip: if touring, investigate the tents which fasten to your car, accommodate up to five, and cost from $20). A complete guidebook to camping equipment and outdoor cookery called Outdoor Holiday Fun Guide is available free from the Coleman Co. Inc., Box 1762, Wichita, Kan. 67201.

the grave of the Baronne de L'Esperance, wife of the governor of Acadie. But Miquelon's chief charm is its adjoining isle of Langlade reached by a jeep drive across acres of wild strawberries and a sandy isthmus. Langlade is covered with trees and deep grass and refreshing little brooks. Its curving, sandy beach reaches for miles.

Anywhere in the islands, you can swim or fish from powered dories and in St. Pierre see the weekly movie or watch traditional Basque dances on Sunday nights, when everyone whoops it up with champagne. Otherwise the islands offer nothing but quiet relaxation away from TV, night clubs, traffic jams, and newspapers. Only on July 14, France's traditional Bastille Day, is there any organized entertainment. Then St. Pierre dons paper hats and waves French flags at a round of races, soccer matches, and Old World contests, terminated by a torchlight parade and a Grand Ball at the Governor's House. But life is far from dull. For 40 days, from Christmas to Lent, citizens abandon work to enjoy the impromptu Mardi Gras celebrations in St. Pierre's streets. Each week sees 3-4 dances at the two halls in town or at the "Country Club" two miles out, and spirited *futbol* matches are frequent events.

Thanks to the trickle of tourists who visit the island in summer, you can now rent a motorcycle at $1 an hour to tour St. Pierre. En route, you can see the cemetery and mausoleum, Galantry Light and Savoyard Beach with its Club Nautique which you can join for $1. There ars also round-the-island tours by taxi or jeep.

Because the French spoken on St. Pierre is as pure as that of metropolitan France, the University of Toronto operates a summer school there during July and August with classes in French language and culture. During these same months, a French cultural center offers lectures on French literature and art; and the latest French films are shown at local *cines*.

A twice daily event throughout the year, however, and perhaps the most enticing of all the islands' attractions, is mealtime—dinner and supper. Whether you stay at a modest *pension en famille* or at a comfortable hotel, wine is served free with every meal and good, unpretentious French cooking is standard fare. Mouth-watering delicacies include island cod, herring and scallops prepared in traditional Basque or Breton style with delicious Béarnaise sauce.

Two of these meals plus a continental breakfast of *croissants* and coffee are yours at a cost ranging between $5.30-$7 a day at *pensions* and $6.50-$11 at hotels, room included, of course. In midsummer it's wisest to make reservations. Hotels include the Ile de France, the Central Hotel, Hotel Robert, Hotel Dutin, Cafe Francais, and the Hotel de la Rade, all on St. Pierre. Miquelon also has several *pensions* (and how you'll love those deep featherbeds, standard in every island *pension*). Inside, every home is warm and snug and equipped with American appliances.

Reliable summer weather comes to St. Pierre only from July 21 until September 15. Even then, the mercury never exceeds 80° and occasional days may be foggy. The rest of the year means cold, winds, and fog. Yet even in winter these gale-beaten islands possess a savage beauty—a therapy of magnificent stimulation to help you realize the insignificance of worry and care.

Nothwithstanding a slight rise in excise taxes, luxuries are cheap, most commodities very reasonable. A man's haircut, for instance, costs only 75¢. Though the islands maintain a rusty guillotine, it hasn't been used for over a century, and no one can recall when the last crime occurred. St. Pierre has a Catholic cathedral, the other islands have Catholic churches. An efficient hospital serves St. Pierre and there are several qualified French physicians.

Strictly speaking, orders from Paris say you must have a passport to visit St. Pierre, but in practice the easy-going islanders will let you land without one on payment of $1.10. If you have a passport, however, bring it. You will be permitted to land without charge.

St. Pierre is accessible by air or sea. You take the French government's boat M.V. *Ile de St-Pierre* sailing twice weekly from North Sydney, N.S., fare $40-$50 r.t., duration 15 hours each way. For exact sailing dates airmail an inquiry to Joseph Salters and Sons, North Sydney, N.S.; or the Flotte Administration des Iles Saint-Pierre et Miquelon, Territoire des Iles Saint-Pierre et Miquelon. Cars can be garaged at the departure point or you can bus to North Sydney from New York for $42.00 o.w. Too, the M.V. *Spencer II* operates thrice weekly between St. Pierre and Fortune, Newfoundland, a 3-hour voyage costing $7.50 o.w. Connecting taxis convey you from Fortune to St. John's. For current air service and fares write Air St. Pierre, Hotel Ile de France, Saint-Pierre.

More information: Tourist Bureau, Saint-Pierre, Territoire des Iles Saint-Pierre et Miquelon.

CAPE BRETON ISLAND, NOVA SCOTIA. It's hard to believe, but within 600 miles of Boston, you can vacation in a Scottish Highland village among misty glens and brooding moors. Over good roads and without even boarding a ferry, you can drive your car straight into the heart of New Scotland to Nova Scotia's eye-popping seascapes: the island's Cabot Trail takes you into a yesteryear world of remote Scottish and Acadian villages where more Gaelic is spoken, more kilts are worn, more bagpipes and highland games played than in Scotland itself.

Among Cape Breton's vapor-mantled lochs, you'll see smart stepping, tartan-clad lads and lassies practicing the sword dance and the highland fling for the big Gaelic Mod held each summer at St. Ann's. This corner of bonny Scotland is more Scottish than Scotland itself. You'll hear the soft ring of spoken Gaelic and encounter baffling place names like Beinn Bhreagh and Skir Dhu. You'll see red cheeked lassies busily spinning native wool on ancient spinning wheels and weaving wonderful hooked rugs and plaids on creaking handlooms. You'll be met by big, friendly, raw-boned men in tam o' shanters and wherever you wander, the swing of the sporran and the skirl of pipes will never be far away.

Excepting, of course, in Acadian villages. Dotted among the highland clans, these cheerful French hamlets add a bonus of contrast to the steadier temperament of the Highland Scottish. Predominantly Catholic and often with a dash of Irish thrown in for flavor, these villagers have all the quick volatile wit and fiery temperament of their dark haired ancestors. Regardless of race, all are embarrassingly hospitable with all the long-cultivated social graces which are invariably accentuated by comparative isolation. "Nowhere has more character been produced per square mile," an island hotelier told me. He wasn't exaggerating. These Acadian and Scottish people are as durable as the granite Cape Breton hills.

The scenery of northern Cape Breton staggers the imagination. Age-old grayed parapets thrust up a thousand feet from the surf and sand, and fiord-like inlets cut through the wild hilly interior. Long ago this region became one of Canada's National Parks. But Cape Breton teems with beauty spots. Almost splitting the island, the green-framed, silvery Bras D'Or Lakes create a thousand interior miles of island-speckled salt water coast. All over the island, majestic waterscapes and timber-wrapped hills mingle in astonishing beauty with the ever changing colors of sea, sky, and mountain.

Ile Madame: unspoiled corner of L'Acadie

For a picture of the France of long ago, turn off Cape Breton's Highway 4 at Grande Anse and drive over the bridge spanning Lennox Passage onto timeless Ile Madame. Named for a queen of France, Ile Madame holds all the magic of yesteryear. Until Word War II, island women still wore Norman kirtles. Artists and photographers go into ecstasies over quaint Arichat village, one of the oldest settlements in North America.

French to the core, Arichat clings to its storied past. One general store is 200 years old and a fish firm, still in business, was looted by John Paul Jones. A century ago, Arichat flourished as Nova Scotia's largest port and faded paintings of island ships still adorn the sitting rooms of ancient houses lining the old World village streets. The harbor is considered the world's fifth best and the island abounds with picturesque scenes. The full sweep of the mighty Atlantic breaks on Ile Madame's outside beaches, providing some of Nova Scotia's finest swimming. Beautiful coves, trout-filled lakes and snug harbors are everywhere on this 6 x 20 mile fragment of old time Acadie.

But there's little activity today. Wherever you go, the perpetual peace typifies the calm, deliberate life of the people. Tourists are still a novelty and local fishermen gladly take you on codding trips without thought of financial return. Anywhere on inland lakes, you can borrow a boat without charge. Beachcombing, clamming and crabbing are intriguing pursuits, there are berries aplenty, and frequent old time Acadian square dances and festivals for a change of pace. The small family-run Ile Madame Motel provides accommodation together with wholesome breakfasts, lunches and dinners.

Activities, food, weather, and accommodations are similar to those of mainland Nova Scotia (described later). But shopping is even more fun. You'll find wonderful hooked rugs from $5, and matching home-spun sweaters and skirts at $15 a set. Ten dollars will buy a local scene in oils and you can also buy Indian baskets from $1. Local restaurants serve such island delicacies as oatmeal bread, oat cakes and Ingonish salmon and, if you're lucky, you may also get to taste the world famous Margaree lamb. As in mainland Nova Scotia, you should reserve accommodations ahead in summer.

Picking Utopias in Cape Breton is like looking for the most heavenly corners of paradise itself. But, anyway, here's our choice.

Baddeck, on the Bras D'Or Lakes, is a tiny village of tranquil beauty and one of the world's outstanding scenic gems. In the heart of Gaelic Cape Breton, Baddeck lies only 12 miles from the St. Ann Gaelic Foundation. Within the harbor is Kidston Island with fine bathing beaches; and numerous scenic drives radiate in every direction. Several tourist homes and housekeeping cabins charge only $7-$8 per couple per night. June, September and October are the most relaxing months.

Big Bras d'Or, remote and off the Cabot Trail, is surrounded by beautiful scenery and is exceptionally popular with bird watchers. Rates at its Mountain View Lodge are most reasonable.

Cape North is an escapist's dream, the most northerly point on Cape Breton, among the National Park's finest seascapes. There are deep sea and stream fishing, mountain climbing, and swimming. Highland Lodge and McDonald's Mountain Lodge here charge $5-$8 per night per couple, meals extra. Housekeeping cabins are $7-$8 daily.

Ingonish Beach, a colorful village nestled under awesome cliffs, is *generally considered to be the most beautiful town on the entire Atlantic Coast of North America.* Costs are a bit higher here but it is well worthwhile. From the moment you arrive, a rare beauty surrounds you. Ingonish, split into two bays by gigantic Middle Head, is an extrava-ganza of nature. And always above looms the stark magnificence of Cape Smoky, its sheer thousand-foot cliffs eternally shouded by drifting cloud. Predominantly Highland Scottish and the home of Gaelic culture, Ingonish lies among granite-carved coves and rocks at the entrance to Cape Breton National Park. Unfortunately, Ingonish's beauty has made it quite popular. So, to avoid crowds, go only in September or October. Tartan Terrace Inn and the Spruce Guest Home are reasonable while Skyline Motor Court is commendable for its island hospitality. House-keeping cottages at Cape Breton Highlands Bungalows are $10 a day off-season.

Marble Mountain is a divine beauty spot 250 feet above sea level overlooking the island-sprinkled waters of the Bras D'Or Lakes. On moonlit nights, Marble Mountain is truly ethereal. There are bathing, boating, both fresh and salt water fishing, pleasant walking trails and square dances. Prices are not high. You can stay at Mr. Alistair Mac-Phail's Hillbrook Farm for $65 a week off-season, meals included (which means home cooking, lots of cream, good fish dinners, and free boats for fishing).

Margaree Valley. Few people can resist falling under the spell of this poetic, elm-dotted valley. Winding down through steep mountains, the sylvan valley of the Margaree River opens onto a superb sand beach at Margaree Harbour. Along its length, dozens of smaller valleys lead off, each a replica in beauty of the main vale of Margaree. You can stay at the Harbour Lights in Margaree Harbor, or at McDonald House over-looking the river, for $12-$15 double daily—with meals, or in house-keeping cottages at $20 a week. Another budget spot is Kilmuir Place in Margaree Northeast with full board at $56 single weekly.

Pleasant Bay lies in the Cape Breton Highlands where three rivers empty into a glistening bay. Until 1927, this village was inaccessible by road. Today there's still an air of Old Scotland. Fish and lobster are plentiful. Bathing is exceptionally good. Local motels and cottages provide comfortable accommodation.

Whycocomagh, a cozy hideaway village huddles under Salt Mountain beside the Bras D'Or Lakes. In one of Cape Breton's loveliest regions, Whycocomagh is hemmed in by mountains and deep glens. It's a strictly Gaelic town with an historic church. Nearby is an Indian reservation, source of its name. You'll find first-class bathing, boating, fishing, and hiking, and the sunsets are breathtaking. At Ainslie Village the housekeeping cottages rent for $40-$48 a week; those at the Village Inn $10 per day.

Old World Cape Breton Island is easily reached from mainland Nova Scotia. You simply drive east on Highway 4 and cross the new cause-way at Cape Porcuyne: gateway to the Bras D'Or Lakes and Cabot Trail.

More information: Nova Scotia Travel Bureau, Box 130, Halifax, N.S., Canada.

MAGDALEN ISLANDS, QUEBEC. Fifty miles out in the Gulf of St. Lawrence is a group of utterly fascinating, different, and colorful escapist isles where tourists seldom go. Yet a comfortable overnight ferry exists to transport you and your car, and causeways and sand dunes linking most of the larger Magdalen Islands allow you to visit them all in the family car. Les Iles de La Madeleine are a crescent of wind-swept, surf-rimmed islands with some of the most exquisite beaches in the Northeast. Towering red sandstone cliffs rise abruptly from glistening white sands. Cattle graze precariously on green clifftop pastures and two-wheel horse carts clip-clop along salt-sprayed island roads. Sturdy houses, built foursquare to withstand winter gales dot the treeless landscape with gay red and green patches of roof. Age-old white fences mark the boundaries of farms and the beaches are littered with dories drawn up to safety each night by teams of straining horses.

The Madeleines are very French and very scenic. Weird wind-carved red rocks line the shore and you'll discover deep caves and tunnels cut by thundering surf. In La Baie de Plaisance the cliffs are so curvaceous, islanders call them Les Demoiselles—the damsels. Tall lighthouses cap points like Brion Island and Le Rocher aux Oiseaux—Bird Rock, the isolated cliff home of thousands of gannets and sea birds.

In these untouristed French-speaking isles you'll encounter customs handed down from Acadian days and French hospitally that is both warm hearted and expansive. Small hotels and *pensions* set some of the finest tables in this hemisphere and you are treated as a member of the family rather than as a guest. One island, Entry, is populated by English-speaking survivors of a British shipwreck.

Jacques Cartier discovered the Magdalens in 1534. In 1787 they passed into the hands of Sir Isaac Coffin and the French population mined gypsum until 1903, when the islands were sold to the Magdalen Islands Corporation. Now they're an outlying part of Quebec Province, which in 1950 gave the islanders a new economy in the shape of fish factories and inter-island highways. If you don't take your car you'll find taxis for sightseeing. You can fish for cod, herring, or mackerel, take a boat trip to Bird Rock, and swim in cool but not chill sea water.

Cap aux Meules (Grindstone) on Grindstone, the largest island, is the most central place to stay. Here is the 15-room Aberdeen Hotel, the small Central and the Motels Boudreau and Logemont Arsenau. Over on the west coast of Grindstone are the Hotel Fougere and the Motel Madeleine, both at Etang du Nord. On Amherst Island, most southerly of the 30-mile causeway-linked chain, you can stay at the Thellab or at the Seagull Hotels, both in Havre Aubert, a fascinating village below a great red cliff topped by a huge white cross. Then in the center of the archipelago there's the Maisonette Ton Nid at Havre aux Maisons. All are small, require advance reservations in summer, and charge $120-$140 weekly for two with meals. Too, in almost every village you'll find equally comfortable *pensions* charging similar rates. And no doubt, you could also arrange to stay with fishermen's families on smaller islands with intriguing names like Wolf, Entry, and Grosse Ile (also English speaking). Wherever you stay, you'll find lobster canneries and herring smoke-houses to visit and your hosts will point out oddities like the wooden bonnets built over haystacks to keep them from blowing away. Movies start in the larger villages at ten p.m. and there's a modern 100-bed hospital in case you fall ill. Cool, sunny weather predominates from mid-July until September, after which the climate quickly turns cold.

Quickest way to reach the islands is via Eastern Provincial Airways' twice daily flights from Charlottetown, Prince Edward Island, fare $29.00 r.t. With a car, you must go via a steamer of the Magdalen

Islands Transportation Company, Ltd. (head office Pier C, Pictou, Nova Scotia) sailing every few days from Pictou or Charlottetown. Overnight fare for a two-berth cabin is $10 per person each way with meals available at $1.35-$2.15 each. Second class costs $7.30 with meals at the same price. Your car is carried on deck at a cost of $20.25. Advance reservations are needed.

More information: best sources are the steamship company, airline, and the hotels.

BEAVER ISLAND, MICHIGAN. Thirty-two miles out in the middle of Lake Michigan is a green island lifted bodily from Donegal. The 3-hour voyage from Charlevoix, Michigan, aboard the *Beaver Islander* costs only $3.00 and when you step ashore in Paradise Bay a huge sign greets you in Gaelic with "Cead Mile Failte"—a Hundred Thousand Welcomes. Huddling beside the crescent harbor is the tiny town of St. James, until recently a thriving fishing village. But the ravaging lamprey eel ended commercial fishing, the island's chief livelihood. Nowadays, the fishing boats are beached, the huge net reels empty, the fish boilers rusting in the harbor. Occasional empty houses and boarded-up farms tell of families who have moved to the mainland. But this economic decay has not spoiled Beaver Island. Now, more than ever, commercialism is entirely absent and the faint "ghost town" overtones accentuate the flavor of Old Erin that clings to the village.

From St. James, the narrow, winding King's Highway circles the island through tunnels of swaying north woods forests. Tall birches and maples crowd unbroken miles of white beaches in every direction.

Beaver Island, the only monarchy ever to exist on United States soil, was once ruled by King Strang, an outcast Mormon. After the Mormons were banished in 1856, Irish emigrants from Donegal and Aran joined the handful of French settlers and Chippewa Indians. America's Emerald Isle has changed little since. Through the long winter months when ice seals the harbors, a small plane is the sole link to the mainland for its 200 inhabitants. Sturdy horse-drawn sleighs are still used for winter transportation. Its isolation has kept timeless Beaver Island one of the most quaint, beautiful, unspoiled, and uncommercialized island Utopias in North America. There hasn't been a crime since 1900.

With a rented bike you can explore its 35,000 travel-folder acres, visit the Dominican Convent, the white lighthouse, and the high sand dunes lining the western shore. You'll see scores of white tailed deer, and inland are seven blue lakes teeming with bass, pike, and bluegill. Lake Michigan abounds with trout, salmon, bass and pike. Beaver Island also has a sporty 9-hole golf course. Otherwise, you can rent a boat for $3.00 a day or $15 a week and row out for picnics on neighboring islands with such fascinating names as Gull, Hat, Squaw, Trout, and Whiskey. Evenings you may drop into Archie LaFreniere's Shamrock bar or the Beachcombers for beer and island stories or see one of the occasional movies shown at the Parish Hall.

If you enjoy your springtime late, or autumns that are a tapestry of flaming fall colors, you'll find Beaver Island delightful in May and after Labor Day. You'll have the whole island to yourself at rates well below those of summer. But even in July and August, prices are not expensive. The King Strang Hotel charges $4 a night up, motels charge $8-$8.50 double and family housekeeping cabins rent for $50-$85 a week. All rates are lower in spring and fall. Delicious apples, berries and superb mushrooms are yours for the picking, fish free for the catching and most island foodstuffs cost less than on the mainland. You'll also find scores of delightful campsites.

For a permanent summer cottage or even a year-round escapist home, there is plenty of inexpensive wooded land on high, scenic bluffs overlooking Lake Michigan and on sheltered inland lakes. Some 50 families already have cottages here. Beaver Island has REA electricity, a modern medical center, fine public grade and high schools. If you retire here, there are good opportunities for summer businesses or for jobs at resorts.

Before going, write the Beaver Island Boat Co., St. James, Michigan, for current ferry schedules. Fare is $3 o.w., $5.50 r.t. and $10 each way per automobile; advance reservations for autos are advisable. You can also fly from Charlevoix in 15 minutes.

More information: Beaver Island Civic Association, St. James, Mich. 49782.

ISLE OF ORLEANS, QUEBEC. Within two days' drive of most north-eastern cities, and within sight of Quebec City itself, is an Old World island idyll, an outpost of medieval Europe in La Nouvelle France. With its high-peaked Norman roofs, ancient manor houses, historic churches, and massive stone-built farms, Quebec's Isle of Orleans presents a delightful panorama of unchanged rural French Canadian life.

You'll meet artists, of course, and at weekends the six villages resound to the gay chatter of outlanders who have cottages here. But no influx of tourists, and they appear only in summer, can ever change the island's gentle tempo. This is the land of the *habitant*, Québécois of French and Norman descent—gay, lively and courteous French Canadians with roots deep in the soil which their ancestors have plowed for three hundred years.

Time-worn farmhouses look out over the blue St. Lawrence and rich fields carpet this verdant, tree-clad island. When Jacques Cartier discovered it in 1535 he called it *Ile de Bacchus* for the wild grapes which grew everywhere. In hoary churches, some of the oldest in Quebec and richly decorated with wood carvings, the marks of Wolfe's cannon balls can still be seen. Spinning wheels and outdoor ovens are still in daily use, and ice cut from the river supplies refrigeration.

Regardless of its other charms, a stay here would be worthwhile for the food alone. French cooking is taken for granted, of course, but wait till you've tasted those long French loaves sliced while still warm and spread with rich country butter and *fromage raffiné*, a gourmet cheese

On a New World Island: Old World France

Imagine living at an inn called the Auberge de La Roche Pleureuse on a tiny St. Lawrence River island where all the picturesque charm of traditional French Canada has been by-passed by progress. You'll find this unique hostelry (the name means Weeping Stone Inn) at the top of Cap aux Pierres, a stony cape overlooking the enchanting scenery of Ile aux Coudres, the blue St. Lawrence River, and the nearby Laurentian Mountains. Though it's only two miles from the St. Lawrence's north shore, Ile aux Coudres hasn't changed much since it was first settled in 1741. Outdoor ovens and spinning wheels are still commonplace and the island is dotted with quaint old stony houses, windmills, and ancient gabled farms. With your car, you can drive the island's 15-mile road through an unbelievably peaceful countryside to two tiny villages, St. Louis and St. Bernard, and there are miles of winding country walks. Wherever you go, you'll discover cordial Old World hospitality and visitors are welcome at every farm and *habitant* home. The islanders will show you where Jacques Cartier held the first mass on Canadian soil in 1535 and the painting in the church at St. Bernard depicting the event.

Since we first wrote it up, the Auberge de La Roche Pleureuse has become so popular that a motel with pool and tennis courts has been added. However, all the inn's rustic charm and its reputation for *bonne cuisine canadienne* have been preserved and at the inn, rates were still recently only $60-$75 per person per week, three gourmet meals a day included. If you prefer a smaller hostelry, you'll find the Hotels St-Bernard, du Cap aux Pierres, and du Capitaine, with rooms as low as $5 per couple. To reach Ile aux Coudres, drive northeast from Quebec City on Highway 15 to Les Eboulements Wharf (or go by Canadian National Railway) and take the frequent car-carrying ferry across. More Information: Auberge de La Roche Pleureuse, Ile aux Coudres, Quebec, Canada.

---

whose secret is known only to a few families and, jealously guarded, is handed down from generation to generation. The island's strawberries and plums are famous across Canada and the thick maple syrup ranks as a spread second to its cheeses.

As an atmospheric place to write a book or paint, or merely to step into 17th Century France without venturing far off the beaten path, the Isle of Orleans is ideal. Our favorite village is Sainte-Famille—certainly the most picturesque—with a 17th century church, weathered houses over 300 years old, and magnificent views of Cape Tourmente, St. Joachim and Ste. Anne de Beaupre. Plain accommodations are available at Au Repas and Morency Cabins for about $5 while a modern motel charges $12 for two. Other places to stay are available at Ste. Petronille St. Laurent and St. Jean.

Wherever you stay, however, you simply must dine, at least once, at L'Atre, two miles east of Ste. Famille. Here an island artist serves delectable French-Canadian meals in a farmhouse that hasn't been altered since 1680. In fact, the meals are cooked on the hearth in front of you. To preserve the atmosphere of the past, cars are not permitted on the grounds of L'Atre and, instead, visitors are taken to the farmhouse in a horse and buggy.

You can easily reach the island via Highway 15 from Quebec. En route to the slender bridge spanning North Channel, you can visit Montmorency Falls and Ste. Anne de Beaupré shrine.

More information: Department of Tourism, Fish & Game, Tourist Branch, Parliament Bldgs., Quebec, P.Q.

WASHINGTON ISLAND, WISCONSIN. How would you like a trip to Scandinavia for $1.20? If that sounds unbelievable, drive to the tip of Wisconsin's picturesque Door Country peninsula and board the ferry for Washington Island. Pay your $1.20 and settle back for the enjoyable 45-minute cruise across Death's Door Strait. Pretty soon, you'll sight your destination, a rugged, rocky island with cliffs like medieval castles and a primeval forest reminiscent of Finland. A few minutes later you step ashore into a secluded corner of Old Scandinavia. Washington Island is America's oldest Icelandic settlement, 26 square miles of yesteryear dotted with quaint churches, cheese factories, shipyards, and timbered community houses among patches of woodland and ancient stone walls.

Originally the home of the Pottowatomi Indians who were wiped out almost to a man when their canoes swamped in a storm on Death's Door Strait, Washington Island was first settled by Scandinavians in 1850.

New Adventure in Leisure Cruising: Renting Houseboats

How would you like to skipper your own boat for a week and cruise clear lakes and beautiful rivers far from crowds and turmoil? At new "botels" all over the country, you can rent a 25'-40' houseboat for $150-$250 a week and do just that. In Florida, you can take your houseboat through the tarpon-jammed waters of the Everglades and Keys or up serpentine jungle rivers; you can sail the Mississippi, the St. Lawrence, the TVA dams and Kentucky lakes. Wherever you go, your houseboat supplies recreation and entertainment as well as lodging.

The outboard-propelled boats come equipped with galley (sink, stove, icebox and cabinets), a dinette with closets, a toilet and one or more staterooms with beds or bunks. The average houseboat sleeps four and rents for $200 a week which, plus an additional $25 per person for groceries, drinks and gas, works out to about $75 a week each for a party of four (occupying a boat worth between $3,200 and $9,500 not including the motor). Names and addresses of botels can usually be had from Chambers of Commerce at waterside towns or by writing the State and Provincial Information Offices listed in Chapter 10. The Canadian Government Travel Bureau, Ottawa, also has information on houseboats in Canada.

Isle of Yesteryear: Ile aux Grues

For a restful change of pace on a tiny St. Lawrence River isle populated by only 65 families, head for Montmagny, 40 miles downriver from Quebec City, on the St. Lawrence' south shore. From here, a ferry departs in summer for a two hour cruise through the incomparably beautiful South Shore Archipelago to Ile au Grues (Crane Island). Five miles offshore and accessible in winter only by plane or ice canoe, Ile aux Grues remains an untouched outpost of traditional French Canadian life. Among its historic landmarks are an old church, an ancient manor and a comfortable inn called L'Auberge des Dunes, which provides rustic comfort and good country cooking at very reasonable cost. The dining room is built up on an anchor board facing the inn and French-Canadian cooking is the speciality. Located opposite Cape Tourmente, a landmark for over 60,000 migrating snow geese each fall, Ile aux Grues offers outstanding goose hunting in season. More information: Auberge des Dunes, Ile aux Grues, Montmagny County, P.Q.

You'll learn more of the island's history at Jens Jacobsen's Island Museum at Little Lake. And you can explore ruined Indian villages along the shore and follow sandy trails to Mountain Wayside Park to see fossils 200,000 years old.

Bring stout walking shoes. These Icelanders love to hike. They've created miles of hiking trails through hills and valleys: to the top of Mount Misery; to Boyer's Bluff, where you can view 100 breathtaking square miles of lake, land, and bay; to cave-like formations on Little Mountain; and to photogenic Jackson Harbor, the island's fishing village. You can also tour the island by car. Whichever way you go, you'll discover that Washington Island possesses a beauty all its own.

Miles of gently sloping sand beaches, some with dunes, provide secluded swimming in scores of bays and just offshore are tantalizing islands where you can stage a fish boil on evergreen-scented shores. Rowboats rent for $15 a week. Painting is popular and summer plays are produced at the Barn playhouse. Try to be here for the midsummer Scandinavian Festival and smorgasbord when the island is decorated in colorful rosemaling designs; folk music and costumed dances are daily events; and at the smorgasbord, as many as 1,000 people are served such specialties as *kringle, abelskiver* and *rollepolse*. Because Washington Island waters are Federal property, no license is needed to fish for the jumbo-sized walleyes, bass, pike and perch. Too, just offshore is picturesque Rock Island State Park, a haven of beauty easily reached by boat. Here you'll find excellent skindiving with numerous wrecks to explore.

Throughout the summer, Washington Island basks in a cool refreshing climate. Hayfever is unknown. There is no central town. Stores, homes, churches, and resorts are scattered among groves of cedar all over the island. Costs are inexpensive: comfortable housekeeping cottages rent in summer for $40-$90 a week or you can stay at a choice of immaculate inns, with three huge meals daily, at $135 per week for two. Because real estate is cheaper than on the mainland, a small colony of retired people have settled on the island and their numbers are growing each year. The island has a doctor, a library, well stocked stores, taverns, garages, movies, bowling alleys and just about every other civilized comfort that a retired couple would require. During winter, everyone joins in a steady round of parties and dances in which oldsters of 85 dance the Flying Dutchman as vigorously as youngsters of eight . . . and no wonder. For Washington Island is the only place in the U.S. where men consistently live longer than women. A local physician believes this is due to the island's freedom from smog, noise and tension; its pure foods; and its natural way of life with everyone taking ample exercise. It's wonderfully wholesome place to retire and no one need ever feel lonely.

To reach Washington Island, drive up Wisconsin's Door County peninsula to Gills Rock, where the Washington Island ferry leaves twelve times daily, fare $1.20 per passenger, cars $2.75 each way.

More information: Washington Island Tourist Bureau, Washington Island, Wis.

CHAPTER 2

Shangri-Las, U.S.A.

> H ere are five widely varied communities, shut off from the
> outer world by mountain barriers, where you can spend a
> summer vacation in a pretty fair facsimile of the James Hilton
> original. Each is an amazing surprise package. And each is entirely
> different from the rest.

HAVASU CANYON, ARIZONA. Fifty miles west of Arizona's
Grand Canyon Village, in a labyrinth of perpendicular red rock walls
and towering pinnacles, America's smallest Indian nation leads a blissful
existence at the bottom of a deep, incredible canyon. No wheeled
vehicle has ever penetrated this forgotten Shangri-La. The post office
in Supai village on the canyon floor is the only U.S. post office still
served by pack train. Few outsiders have ever ventured into the Land
of the Havasupai Indians. But if you're willing to walk eight miles, or
make the trip on horseback, you can spend an unforgettable vacation in
this canyon paradise.

Though you can go in from Grand Canyon over the rough Topacoba
Trail, the recommended approach for visitors is to turn off U.S. 66
seven miles east of Peach Springs, Arizona, and drive 65 miles of graded
dirt road to Hualapai Hilltop. For 8 miles from Hualapai Hilltop, the
trail winds down through deepening canyons, emerging suddenly over
a brief rise into the lush greenness of Supai village on the valley floor.
You may walk or ride down the trail.

Either way you descend a precipitous 3,000 feet into a small verdant
valley 3 miles long and a quarter of a mile wide, dramatically sealed off
from the outside world by sheer red sandstone walls 2,500 feet high.
Within its 500 acres of breathtaking grandeur, Havasu Valley packs the
remotest Indian culture on this continent, three magnificent waterfalls,
one higher than Niagara, a green-blue river with deep cool pools, fruit
orchards and bright green fields of corn, hidden caves and primitive
hogans, and two lodges for visiting tourists.

Scores of years ago raiding Apaches drove the Havasupai Indians
into this canyon Utopia. The Indians have been there ever since. Their
name, Havasupai, meaning "People of the blue-green waters" comes
from the blue-green, travertine-rich waters of Havasu Creek, flowing
strong and clear the length of the valley. Nowadays 150 Indians live
at Supai, their hogans and cottages dotted among willows and cottonwoods, and under towering cliffs beside the river. Havasupai women
weave the finest baskets in Arizona and their men excel as horsemen
and hunters. You'll like the Havasupais. Friendly, peaceful Indians
dressed in motley store clothes, they possess a subtle humor and a care-

free outlook. Despite the fact that the valley is entirely theirs, they welcome strangers and all visitors are automatically invited to their festivals and rodeos. Many curious social customs survive. For instance, several times daily men gather in small dome-shaped sweat lodges similar to a Finnish *sauna;* and a continuous wailing accompanies an Indian's death.

Lay in six times as much color film as you normally use. Havasu Canyon is a photographer's heaven. Two enormous red monoliths soaring above the village dominate a multi-colored panorama of bright green fields, fantastic red cliffs, and azure blue sky. Two miles below the village, Havasu Creek plunges over the three most photographed waterfalls in the West. First comes Navajo Falls, then the 180-foot cascade of Havasu Falls, and finally the awe inspiring torrent of Mooney Falls, a sheer 210-foot drop. Among the damp green mosses and ferns lining the glens are the handspikes and ladders of old time prospectors. You can climb them to reach hidden caves behind the falls. Deep turquoise-blue pools below each cascade provide wonderful swimming among rocks laced with weird underwater tapestries of travertine deposit.

Best time to schedule a stay in this wondrous valley is between April 1-May 20 and September 15-November 15, when the weather is at its finest. In spring, Havasu is an unbroken carpet of flowering orchids, cactus, and crimson keyflowers. But if you don't mind dry, daytime heat you might arrange a stay to coincide with the Indian's peach festival in August. The Havasupais invite neighboring Walapais, Hopis, Navajos, and Mojaves to celebrate their harvest with an All-Indian Rodeo. At night, after a barbecue, tribal dances to native drums and chanting continue until dawn.

You can camp under the stars (no fee) at a camp-ground provided with tables, benches, and toilets. Or you can stay at one of two lodges. The older lodge has plain rooms and a common kitchen for cooking; rates are $7.50 a day for two. The newer lodge consists of cabins built of native rock with double beds, bathroom facilities, and a moderately well equipped common kitchen; rates are $5 a day single and $7.50 double. Besides a post office, church, school, and Indian agent's office, Supai has a small Tribal Enterprise Store where you can purchase staples and canned goods. Apricots, peaches, squash, melons, figs, apples, pears, and pecans are grown in the valley and always plentiful. Supai has telephone communication with the outside world.

Provided you can hike or stay on a slow moving horse for a few hours and don't expect tiled baths, you may safely plan to vacation in Havasu. There are no risks whatever. But it's well to remember you'll be dealing with a primitive Indian people who lead tranquil lives out of touch with the modern world. Don't descend into the valley before phoning Supai to advise them you are coming and when you arrive, respect the privacy of the Indians. Bear in mind, too, that these people seldom see money and don't begrudge the 50¢ you are asked to pay for permission to take photographs. (For $1 more you can fish for trout).

One way to visit Supai without the bother of making arrangements is through the 6-day spring and fall trips conducted by celebrated mountaineer-naturalist Joseph C. Wampler. Costs are $160 all inclusive from Kingman or Peach Springs, Arizona, and if you want to stay longer than six days (most people have difficulty tearing themselves away from Havasu's beauty, says Mr. Wampler) you can remain in the camp for $12 a day, which includes three first class meals. For full details, write Mr. Joseph C. Wampler, Box 45, Berkeley, Calif. 94701.

On your own, the route through Hualapai Hilltop is best. You can arrange for an Indian to meet you there with a horse and to bring you back up again for $18; or you can walk down and ride up for $16.

More information: Havasupai Tourist Enterprise, Supai, Arizona 86435.

MARFA, TEXAS. Unlimited miles of haunting desert scenery and mile-high buttes and mesas surround Marfa, a West Texas ranching center so unchanged that the movie *Giant* was filmed there. Though near Big Bend National Park and locally popular with hunters, glider enthusiasts and religious groups, Marfa has yet to attract tourist hordes.

In fact, if you studied a map and tried to find the most remote community in the continental U.S.—in an area least likely to be the target of enemy bombs and one with mild, sunny winters and cool, breezy summers—you might easily narrow your choice down to Marfa. In fact, that's exactly how we discovered the place. Looking for an inviting Shangri-La, we first selected the Big Bend Country of West Texas, a high, cool, sunny area with unlimited elbow room. Then, studying a map of this vast area, we decided on the community of Marfa, population 3,000.

We weren't disappointed.

As a contender for one of America's "Shangri-La's," Marfa is surrounded by some of the most primitive and rugged scenery in the nation. Located only an hour's drive from the Rio Grande and Mexico, about half the population is of Mexican descent. We found several streets of older adobe homes that belonged South of the Border. Two cultures live side by side and both Spanish and English are spoken on the streets. Marfa couldn't be situated farther from the pressures and problems of big cities. The nearest city, El Paso, is at least 200 miles distant and the closet megalopolis is at least 450 miles away.

Occupying a mesa in the Davis Mountains, Marfa is satisfactorily far from strife and turmoil. Yet it isn't isolated from the good things of life. The well kept homes and neat gardens of retired ranchers line the wide residential streets and some of the hilltop homes are genuine showplaces. Carefully tended flower beds in the streets surrounding the curiously American Gothic courthouse lend mute testimony to Marfa's strong civic pride. Yet to outsiders the name Marfa—a Russian derivative—is almost unknown. Only to glider pilots is Marfa a "household" name. For here each summer, graceful sailplanes soar silently through the sky, roaming the limitless airspace and riding the cool breezes created by a meteorological phenomenon known as the Marfa Dew Line Front.

Its 4,800′ elevation saves Marfa from enervating summer heat while its southerly location—on the same latitude as Daytona Beach, Florida —results in a mere five days of snowcover each winter. In this high, cool region where 90 peaks exceed a mile high, Marfa enjoys a healthful and invigorating climate with cool, breezy summers, mild sunny winters and the most transparent of air.

With your car, you can spend day after day exploring some of the least known country in America's Southwest. Scenic highways lead to Big Bend National Park, to the Mexican border town of Ojinaga, to historic frontier cavalry forts in the Davis Mountains and to weathered ghost towns like Terlingua and Study Butte. The drive along the Rio Grande on Route 170 is exceptionally beautiful. You'll find quiet paved farm roads for bicycling and Big Bend National Park is one of few places in America that offer winter hiking and horseback riding. From Ojinaga, bargain priced Mexican pullman trains leave for Chihuahua and for Mexico's tropical Pacific Coast over the most spectacular rail route in North America.

Because of the sailplane season, pressure is heavy on Marfa's accommodations in late June and early July. But the rest of the year, you can choose between staying at a modern air conditioned motel with heated pool for around $9 double or at the charming old Paisano Hotel on the main street. And at the Old Borunda Cafe, a historic eaterie in one of Marfa's oldest frame houses, you'll find some of the best Mexican cooking north of the border.

If you find Marfa as homey and nostalgic as we did and you decide to stay longer, furnished apartments are generally available from around $75 a month while unfurnished homes were recently renting from $75. Marfa has three real estate agents and attractive retirement homes sell from $8,500. Naturally, such statements are subject to change, particularly if high interest rates create a nationwide housing shortage. At somewhat higher costs are attractive hilltop sites immediately north of town. But land costs are far lower than in most American cities. The same goes for living costs. Don't look for opera or yoga classes. But if you're seeking a homey Southwestern town that hasn't changed very much since the 1930s, Marfa could be *your* Shangri-La.

More information: CoC, Marfa, Texas 79843.

EUREKA SPRINGS, ARKANSAS.

EUREKA SPRINGS, ARKANSAS. Tucked away in a deep valley among the Ozarks' highest peaks is a charming 19th century town so amazingly unique, it's called the "Believe It Or Not" resort. From valley floor to mountaintop, Eureka Springs is built on 20 hills in a series of 230 winding streets, few of which cross. Some streets wind a sheer 1,000 feet above others and seen from the air reveal an unbelievably intricate maze of 16 snaking S bends, 50 hairpin Us, and 51 abrupt Vs.

Scores of houses front onto one street and back onto another 60 feet

below, so that what looks like a one-story cottage from above turns out
to be a four-story mansion from below. An enormous statue of Christ
with an armspread of 65 feet overlooks the town and there's even a
church you enter through the belltower. Fifty-four miles of cut stone
retaining walls prevent the tiers of houses from sliding down precarious
hillsides. Until they bulldozed off a knob recently, there wasn't even a
flat spot large enough for a baseball diamond. Within a mile of the
Post Office are 100,000 trees of 115 different varieties, and within the
city limits 63 flowing springs gush healthful waters. There are 1,137
more within a 7-mile radius. Families living in the same house at
different levels get mail delivered at different hours and the town's first
lawsuit occurred when a woman threw water out her back door straight
down a neighbor's chimney. The longest straight street is only 300 feet
and when you ask for an address, residents point up or down.

This "Little Switzerland of America" really is different. It's busy
from Memorial Day through Labor Day, but at other times you'll find
it a haven of peace and contentment among the cool, green Ozark hills.
Whether you stay for a week or a year you'll discover a friendly and
courteous Ozark citizenry with kind and gentle manners, which is
exactly what you'd expect of this unhurried, restful place. Quaint curio,
antique, and gift shops merge harmoniously with Eureka Spring's
easygoing flavor. Crime is unknown. And doors are never locked in
"Stair Step Town."

Its Victorian flavor and tranquil way of life attract many people
anxious to get away from the strife and crime of the big Middle
Western cities. Prices are reasonable and living costs moderate. Even
during the height of summer, when both the local Passion Play and the
Inspiration Point Art Colony's summer concert sessions are in full
swing, hotel rates are far from excessive. For as little as $28, a couple
can spend a full week at the flavorful New Orleans Hotel in town, a
revamped old time hostelry with antebellum balconies and individually
decorated rooms. Warm-hearted Millie Martensen, the hospitable owner,
runs the hotel like a Danish inn. Most evenings Millie has a get-together
to introduce visitors to local residents over Danish pastry and coffee.
There's even elevator service direct from the parking lot to your room.
Yet in this homey Ozark inn, the *best* room with private bath costs only
$60 a week for two at the height of summer—with country club guest
cards thrown in.

For a longer stay, rentals are usually available *except in spring and
summer*. Rates are naturally much lower than in big cities. But you
may have to wait a while to find exactly the apartment you desire.
From time to time, a few quaint and roomy older homes also come on
the market. Most newcomers, however, prefer to build their own homes.
Some do the entire building themselves. Union restrictions are practically non-existent and building permits are easily obtained. Not too
long ago, one retired couple we know bought a beautiful ten acre hilltop
in town for $3,000 and, doing all their own work, added a four
bedroom home for under $9,000. Taxes are less than $150 a year. Of

course, you'd have to pay more today. Yet costs are well below those in big cities.

The "Crazy Quilt City," as it's often called, lies smack in the heart of the Ozarks and it's an easy skip to visit the Ozarks' big springs and fabulous onyx caverns, big lakes like Norfolk and Taneycomo, the Shepherd of the Hills country, the beautiful White River, and Inspiration Point. Closer at hand you can visit Hatchet Hall, the former home of temperance fighter Carry Nation. There are scenic walking trails galore, saddle horses at $1 an hour (less by the day) for exploring scores of miles of rambling trails, two swiming pools, and two mirror-like lakes for all water sports. Artists set up easels in every picturesque corner and you can hobnob with professionals or listen to homespun Ozark yarns while you paint. Every summer night there are outdoor musicals, moonlight operas, and hillbilly shows. Square dances are held all year to the old-time strains of banjo, fiddle, and guitar. For Eureka Springs is the folk lore and square dance capital of the entire Ozarks; not to be missed are the Ozarks Folk Festival in mid-October and soon after, the Bare Foot Ball. And no review of things to do would be complete without mentioning the mouth watering local delicacies: catfish, cornbread, hot biscuits, and huckleberry cakes and pies, all served in local cafes at uninflated prices.

At Eureka Springs' 1,460-1,804-foot elevation, you'll find blue skies and warm days in summer with cool, clean mountain breezes every night. There's no smoke or dust and even in midwinter, little or no snow. Uncrowded spring and fall are ideal for an escapist vacation when the air is bracing and nights crisp but seldom cold. You will find no racial problem here.

If you'd like to linger longer in this changeless Shangri-La, and money is the problem, here's a tip from a friendly Chicagoan now retired here. Midsummer tourists, he says, just can't find enough keepsakes and souvenirs to take home. Anyone who cares to can make quite good money making and selling novelties, paintings, bird houses, baskets, and dolls, or unearthing antiques and relics. There's a good sale for walnuts and huckleberries, wild canned blackberries, and jams and jellies; you can pick fruit and nuts by the bushel in the surrounding hills for free. You can also earn good money by raising hogs and selling hickory cured hams, or sorghum and molasses. And if you need land, you'll find it in abundance in this poor man's paradise at $350-$600 an acre. As this was written, also, almost anyone could find unlimited summer work in hotels and restaurants at good rates of pay.

For anyone who doesn't mind climbing hills, this Swiss-like village was made for retirement. All city facilities—gas, electricity, and water—are Class "A"; there is a modern 28-bed county hospital, and three doctors. And the retirees—who include many artistic people—organize interesting study and cultural groups during the winter months.

More information: CoC.

STEHEKIN, WASHINGTON. When Fred and Jo Ann Thompson left Chicago for their summer vacation they had no idea where they would go. "We just planned to keep going till we found the place of our dreams," Jo Ann told us. "For us, that had to be a real Shangri-La, a deep blue lake encircled by rugged mountains as far from civilization as we could comfortably get." The Thompsons drove west to Washington State and by chance turned down U.S. 97 to the town of Chelan.

"Chelan lies at the foot of 55-mile-long Lake Chelan," Fred explained. "It looked promising but lacked the exact qualities we sought. There were too many motels and the rolling hills were considerably short of being dramatic. Next morning, for a change, we took a boat cruise the length of the lake. Exactly 4 hours and 45 minutes after leaving Chelan we steamed into a Shangri-La that exceeded our wildest expectations. Its name is Stehekin and the only way to get there is by boat or chartered plane."

The Stehekin Ranger District is a mountain hideaway far removed from the bustle of the world at the primitive head of deep, blue Lake Chelan. Misty waterfalls plunge sheer down from glacier-fed trout streams into clear lake waters which mirror some of the most stupendous scenery on this continent. Panoramas of timbered peaks reach away on every hand. On sandy beaches in cedar-scented coves the Thompsons discovered the remote place they had driven so far to find. Shaggy mountain goats and deer and bear stalked in plain view among rocky bluffs in the forests of pine and fir.

"Lake Chelan is 1,500 feet deep," Fred said. "We swam in water at 75° and the fishing is unbelievable." Tackle-busting silver trout, cutthroats and rainbows swarm in the lake and in streams. Jo Ann sketched the radiant Rainbow Falls (312 feet high) and Fred spent hours photorecording wild animals, picture-postcard Agnes Gorge, painted Indian rocks, and the thrillingly scenic Horseshoe Basin country where sheer thousand-foot precipices loom high overhead.

"We even became rock hounds," he went on. "We felt so fit we hiked along trails beside the lake that led to forgotten mining claims and diggings." The couple found an amazing variety of different rocks and minerals. And Jo Ann collected exquisitely shaped driftwood along the winding shores.

Neither of the Thompsons was troubled by pollen or mosquitoes. Summer officially lasts from June 1 till Labor Day. Before and after these dates, some hostelries charge lower rates. Residents say the fall months are a tapestry of color and it seldom gets cold before the end of November.

But at the height of summer, their two weeks in this mountain lake paradise cost the Thompson exactly $128 plus the same groceries they'd have eaten at home. For $60 a week they rented a comfortable housekeeping cottage with modern plumbing, and a boat of their own went with the cottage. Half a dozen small lodges and cottage colonies supply accommodations. At Morse's Resort Cabins, $10 a day still gets you a housekeeping cottage with rowboat tossed in and similar, or slightly higher rates, apply at other places. For plusher living, try the Swissmont Lodge or Stehekin Lodge Resort, which offers comfortable rooms or housekeeping cottages. Two cafes serve meals at reasonable prices. And now that Stehekin has become the southern gateway to the North Cascade National Park, a 28-mile road runs from the settlement through the heart of the glacier area. Camping is good at Stehekin River.

You can reach Chelan by car or Greyhound bus; by rail take Great Northern to Wenatchee and continue by bus. From Chelan, a mail boat provides daily service to Stehekin, fare $6.50 r.t.

More information: Lake Chelan CoC, Box 216, Lake Chelan, Wash. 98816.

CAPITOL REEF NATIONAL MONUMENT. If you'd like to sample a unique desert vacation in some of the most brilliant and colorful scenery in the world, head for Utah's Capitol Reef National Monument. Today it's on a paved highway but until the late 1930s, the area was practically unknown.

Originally called Wayne Wonderland, the "Reef" is a great buttressed sandstone cliff reaching 20 miles across the heart of an awesomely scenic area carved by water and wind into fantastic rock towers, domes and pinnacles. From the monument road, 40 miles of foot trails lead to massive rocks big enough to shade an ocean liner, to yawning chasms, a natural bridge, petrified forests, Indian hieroglyphics and cliff dwellings. Everywhere are brightly colored and intricately eroded cliffs, fantastically tilted rocks and deep gorges, and canyons weirdly sculptured by wind and rain. The remotest canyons were the last hideouts of old line Mormons with plural wives.

Despite the steadily increasing number of visitors, the Reef is still a place of peace and quiet. You'll find complete relaxation amidst its extraordinary scenery and friendly hospitality among its few families, descendants of Mormon pioneers.

Best time to visit the Reef is between March 30 and October 30; spring or fall are ideal. On foot and with your own car, you can explore such unbelievable places as Grand Wash, its 1,000' walls only 16' apart; the 1,200 year old petroglyphs at Golden Throne; and the self guiding trail to the Natural Bridge which, with the printed brochure, introduces you to the monument's natural history. You'll fare a lot better if you're fond of walking. If you can't get about on foot, jeep tours will take you into the most remote sections of the monument at $60 a day for three people. Photography and rock hunting opportunities are outstanding.

Least expensive way to linger here is to camp at the 53-unit campground near the Visitor Center. Water is available and stores can be purchased at neighboring towns. Trailer spaces also exist. Attractively inexpensive is the small Gifford Motel at nearby Fruita which recently offered a kitchenette unit for two people at only $36 a week. Then there's atmospheric Sleeping Rainbow Guest Ranch, which charges $208 weekly for two people with all meals. You'll also find Capitol Lodge and several other small motels and cafes at average rates.

To reach the monument, leave U.S. 89 at Sigurd, Utah, and follow State 24 for seventy-two miles to monument headquarters: or leave US50 at Green River and follow State 24 for 97 miles.

More information: Superintendent, Capitol Reef National Monument, Torrey, Utah; for accommodations at Fruita, write via Torrey, Utah 84775.

Poor Man's Paradise: Pennsylvania's Northern Tier

They aren't entirely untouristed but two beauty spots in northern Pennsylvania offer low costs and reasonable seclusion in a spectacular setting of primeval forest and mountain scenery.

Cook Forest State Park, near Cooksburg, is a 6,800-acre expanse of cathedral-high hardwood forest, one of the East's few remaining stands of virgin white pines. Miles of hiking trails lead through luxuriant rhododendrons and mountain laurel to glens green with ferns and bearded moss, and to sweeping mountain vistas. Between the great trees looming 150-200 feet high, the Clarion River flows the length of the forest. Despite its being well known locally, the park itself is hardly overcrowded and you can spend long days swimming, hiking, riding, canoeing, or observing the 100 species of birds in the deep, hushed stillness of the trees. Rustic log housekeeping cottages for 2-7 people rent for $20-$60 a week in the park, others outside the park at slightly higher rates. Camping costs $3 per week. More information: Cook Forest State Park, Cooksburg 1, Pa. 16217.

Pennsylvania's Grand Canyon, 50 miles long and 1,000 feet deep, embraces over a million acres of glacial canyon, deep stream-cut valleys, lacy waterfalls, shady glens, and awe inspiring views. Through its heart, between mountain peaks and walls of rock, runs the deep narrow gorge of Pine Creek—the "River of Pines." Once the home of warlike Seneca Indians, Pennsylvania's Grand Canyon is now the peaceful grazing ground of raccoon, deer, and bear. Scores of trails zig-zag through a mantle of pink and white laurel. You can also explore the entire area by car over switchback mountain roads. Accommodations range from low-rent cabins to pleasant, moderately priced motels. More information: CoC, Wellsboro, Pa.

The Warren area is another section of the Northern Tier which has an abundance of overlooked beauty and recreational facilities.

CHAPTER 3

The Islands Time Forgot

Fear of Indians drove the earliest English colonists to settle on islands along our eastern seaboard. New England's first white settlement was on Cuttyhunk Island, and Block Island has been settled since 1661. Later colonists landed directly on the mainland and the by-passed islanders, content with their New World Utopias, simply stayed on. The rest of the story is identical to that of the islands in Chapter I settled by isolated Europeans.

For centuries, the changeless sea has insulated these islands from mainland development. Up and down the coast you'll still hear the soft burr of West Country English and discover a setting and way of life preserved almost intact since colonial days. Ocracoke is at its best in spring or fall; the northern islands are most attractive in June and in September.

TANGIER ISLAND VIRGINIA. For $1 in fare, you can board the mail boat at Crisfield, Maryland, and take a one-hour cruise across the green-gray waters of Chesapeake Bay to one of the most astonishingly isolated and legendary islands in North America. Tangier Island, 3 miles long, 2 miles wide, and 2¹/₂ feet high, is an atmospheric community of old clapboard frame houses on narrow, picket-fenced lanes where scooter pick-ups are used to haul freight and women clad in sunbonnets and calico dresses carry gay parasols to shield them from the sun. Apart from the bristling TV antennas, the 20th century has scarcely touched Tangier. Bicycles, scooters, and a few small cars constitute the only traffic, and there are no lawyers, screeching police sirens or racial riots, and no parking problems. Rickety wooden bridges span the boat-dotted creeks which wind in from the sea and you will find good bathing on the southwestern shoreline. Weathered tombstones mark front yard graves where departed islanders are buried just below the surface because of seeping salt water a few feet down.

"How be ye?" friendly fishermen in long hip boots greet you. "It be a good day." Elizabethan English has remained a legacy in this neglected backwater since John Crockett and his family settled the island in 1686. Today, almost one-third of the islanders bear the prolific Crockett's name and most of the others are called Pruitt or Parks. Strongest influence in Tangier's isolation is the spired Methodist Church from which Sunday sermons—at least two—are relayed throughout the village by loudspeakers. Villagers live strictly by the Methodist *Discipline* and regard the mainland as a frenzied, immoral place where the population is eternally damned. Immediately they land their catches of crabs at Crisfield, Tangier fishermen race their swift boats back to the sanctity of their island stronghold. Until recently, Tangier's sole contact with the mainland was by emergency radio-telephone and many homes were without plumbing or electricity. Nowadays, however, you'll find normal telephone service and all the comforts of home with water supplied from a deep well system. Plans are afoot to build a small airstrip and an excursion boat operates an all day cruise to the island.

Whatever its drawbacks—and these include several ugly garbage dumps and a not inconsiderable population of flies and mosquitoes—photogenic Tangier possesses a unique charm of yesteryear. The duck hunting and fishing for trout, cracker, drum, spot, and rockfish are unusually good. Hundreds of white fishing boats fleck island waters by day but none ever land on the tiny uninhabited islet off Tangier's eastern tip. If you enjoy idyllic solitude wou will find it here.

The place to stay is Mrs. Hilda Crockett's Chesapeake Guest House, a white two-story island home furnished in Victorian style but cozy and comfortable and famed for its all-you-can-eat seafood meals. Rates are $10.40 per person per day, three superb meals included; advance reservations are advised. For a longer stay, occasional apartments can be rented from $25 a month and sometimes, homes or lots are for sale at very reasonable prices.

More information: try Chesapeake Guest House, Tangier Island, Va.

MONHEGAN ISLAND, MAINE. Monhegan, Maine's "Fortunate Isle," is a rich plum for anyone seeking the utmost in peace and quiet and unspoiled beauty. Ten miles out at sea and surrounded by crashing breakers, Monhegan is a rocky square mile of soaring cliffs, forest, moor, and meadows where the stars are your street lights and life continues at the unhurried, remembered tempo of a century ago.

Every well known marine artist in America has painted Monhegan's seascapes. You've probably seen its great surf-pounded cliffs perpetuated in canvas in major art museums, along with quieter paintings of its salt-encrusted fishing village strung with lobster pots and gaily painted buoys.

From January to June, Monhegan's 150 inhabitants toil day and night to supply the primest winter lobsters in this hemisphere. If you eat a lobster after June, it won't be from Monhegan. By rigidly enforcing a closed season and prohibiting the taking of short lobsters—something impossible outside this close-knit island community—Monhegan's fishermen have built up the richest lobster grounds on the Atlantic coast. There are no poor fishermen in Monhegan and no slums. The finest mahogany-built fishing boats in New England dance on the swell in the foam flecked harbor.

Monhegan has no electric light, no traffic, no juke boxes, and no movies. Soft kerosene lamps glow after dark and housewives prepare Maine's most delectable chowders over gas stoves or wood-burning ovens. You make your own amusements here. There are 17 miles of scenic trails to explore the island's 650 acres, which stretch 1½ miles in length and three-fourths of a mile in width. You can swim or fish among tidal pools speckled with limpet, winkles, whelks, and moon snails or you can spend long hours among the hushed silence of mast-like trees and green lichens in Cathedral Woods. Many a nerve-torn city dweller has discovered a new joy in living with the stimulus of sea and forest.

Artists come here to paint in July and August and then the lobstermen take fishing parties out daily, and there are daily boat trips around the island to view the long list of bird life, the gannets and petrels, and the seals and whales which sport offshore. Moonlight cruises are equally popular. Then, too, you won't want to miss being rowed over to beautiful Mañana Island nearby to visit with its hermit.

Despite haulage costs involved in bringing everything out from the mainland, you can spend a week on Monhegan for as little as $56. At the Trailing Yew, with an unobstructed view of harbor and ocean and an enviable reputation for home cooking and island seafood, rates are $112-$156 weekly for two with all meals. Plusher accommodations at the famous Island Inn average $100 per person weekly, meals included. You'll also like the Gull Inn, where full board costs $80-$112 weekly. Only 14 guests can be accommodated, neither radio nor TV is offered

---

Chebeague Island; historic New England

Every summer day ten boats leave Portland, Me., for historic Chebeague Island out in Casco Bay. And when you step ashore at the Old Stone Wharf or in Chandlers Cove, you're headed for a restful vacation on a serene, undisturbed island of 350 sincere and hospitable fisherfolk. The quaint Methodist church, built in 1855, with its soft wood tones and large crocheted copy of the Lord's Prayer above the altar, gives you a glimpse of island culture. Legends of pirate gold, ghosts and intrigue are still aired over lobster and beer by the descendants of men who sailed Maine's famous stone sloops. Chebeague islanders carried granite to build almost every breakwater and most of the famous public buildings the length of the Atlantic Coast. Nowadays, they live by trawl fishing, seining and lobstering.

Interesting paths criss-cross the island's 2½ x 5 mile expanse, winding through spruce and pine to beautiful old homes and cottages; others take you on breathtaking walks along stretches of rocky shoreline and smooth sandy beaches. Sometimes the sea mist enshrouds Chebaegue. But most days are sunny and you can play golf beside the sea on a 9-hole course with the sportiest water hole in New England, swim, sail and fish, or plan a clam bake with the inevitable lobster and hot buttered corn. Twenty-five miles of road serve Chebague yet there is no hectic traffic, not even a movie. Nor does its regular following of summer visitors destroy the island's precious quiet.

The place to stay is the Hillcrest Hotel, a cozy New England inn high on a hill, with a dining room famed for smorgasbord. Rates are $160 weekly for two people, including three superb meals daily, and the season runs from July 1 to Labor Day.

More information: Hillcrest Hotel, Chebeague Island, Casco Bay, Me.

---

and the proprietors caution that if you bring your own you'd better be sure that no one else can hear it.

There are also furnished housekeeping apartments and cottages, some of which are suited for year around living. Every breeze is a sea breeze on this deep-water island. In summer, Monhegan is 10° cooler than the nearby mainland. Spring and fall are milder than on the coast and you can almost smell the Gulf Stream when the mainland is piled deep with snow. In fact, some escapists live all year in the furnished apartments. There's a post office, church, gift shop, and general store, and phone and telegraph communication with the mainland. But not much else. If you need a haircut, for example, you must patiently cajole the local carpenter into doing the job.

Because cars cannot go there, Monhegan remains one of the least changed places in this book. People get about by bicycle and on foot. Only a few rickety cars are permitted on the island. Camping is not encouraged. Neon signs and juke boxes have yet to appear. If you're seeking a place with an isolated quality where the mood is of the sea and leisure is the only pastime, Monhegan will not disappoint you.

You reach Monhegan by a 75-minute, 12-mile scenic ride on the mailboat *Laura B.* leaving Port Clyde, Maine, each weekday morning. Fare is $5 r.t. and facilities include a parking lot for your car. In July and August, an excursion boat also sails daily from Boothbay Harbor, Maine, taking 105 minutes for the 18-mile cruise and charging around $7 r.t.

More information: address the accommodations mentioned, Monhegan Island, Me. 04852.

BLOCK ISLAND, RHODE ISLAND. Twelve miles out at sea, with a summer climate ten degrees cooler than that of the mainland, Block Island has been a favorite resort since the early 1880s. But despite its 5,000 summer visitors, the island remains a haven of serenity. Often called the Bermuda of the North for its great quiet and beauty, Block Island is 11 square miles of low, treeless hills webbed by stone walls that mark the boundaries of the island's small farms. Over 300 sparkling ponds dot the moorlike meadows; brown rocks and granite boulders stud the miles of paths that wind along the island's clay cliffs; and encircling much of Block Island are driftwood scattered beaches, some of the finest in New England.

Although cars can be brought over on the ferries, they're not encouraged. This is an island for walkers and cyclists. Signs often read: "No vehicles—walkers welcome." Hence the average motoring tourist doesn't reach Block Island and the place is thankfully free of billboards and hamburger stands. Thanks, also, to the extreme conservatism of its 500 individualistic Yankee fishermen populace, Block Island has successfully resisted change. You'll discover an unmistakable Victorian aura enhanced by the turn-of-the-century gables, cupolas and dormer windows that adorn the white frame homes.

When the hurricane of 1938 wiped out the fishing fleet, Block Island entered a decline from which it only recently emerged. Because of its insularity and remoteness from the problems of the automobile age, it now draws a clientele of upper middle class summer visitors, some of whom are buying land and building homes. Land recently sold at $1,000 an acre and for a little more, you could have yourself a site with a grand view of the hills, sea and sky.

The taciturn islanders are cold and reserved at first but once you're accepted, it's considered an insult if you pay a friendly call that lasts less than three hours. A good way to get to know the island and its people is to come here in May or between Labor Day and early November. At these times, you'll have the island practically to yourself. Rates, too, are bargain priced during these spring and fall off-season months. Even in summer, however, a dozen or more small hotels offer full board for two people at well under $120 a week, with lots of the island's famed lobster, swordfish and bluefish on the menu. Several sedate, Victorian flavored inns cluster around the old harbor, offering fine views of the fishing fleet. Elsewhere, efficiency apartments rent in summer for about $75-$85 a week and less than half that in spring or fall.

You'll begin by exploring Block Island: walking out to rocks like Settler's Rock, Mohegan Bluff and Clay Head; studying the gravestones in the island cemetery; visiting the lighthouse; and picnicking at Settler's Rock Grove. Beachcombing is rewarding along the great stretches of beach while island waters are superbly clear for skindiving and exploring underwater wrecks. As on so many islands, Captain Kidd is reputed to have buried treasure here and there are rumors that booty has been found. For more routine amusement, you'll find a golf course at Vaill. But the big enticement is the fishing. If you can afford the charterboat fees, you can fish in August for giant bluefin tuna and swordfish. But it costs little to fish in the ponds for perch, pickerel and bass or to fish the island's shores for cod, mackerel, pollack and stripers. And located as it is on the Atlantic Coast flyway, Block Island plays host to a plethora of birds. One group of birdwatchers counted 128 different species in a mere two days.

Although it gets below freezing in winter, Block Island's winter temperatures average ten degrees higher than those on the mainland and, as a result, the island offers an eminently suitable New England setting for retirement or restful living. Even in summer, it's scarcely overcrowded. But walk the clifftop paths on a spring day when white seagulls play tag in the green windblown sea mist and the meadows are bright with wildflowers . . . or stroll beside an aged rock wall in autumn when the whole island is ablaze with goldenrod . . . and you'll agree that few other places in America are so unhurried and relaxing.

Boats serve Block Island from Montauk, Long Island and from Galilee and New London; also in summer, from Providence and Newport. A light plane air service also operates. Boat fares are approximately $3-$5 r.t.

More information: Rhode Island Development Council, Roger Williams Bldg., Providence, R.I. 02908.

EAST PENOBSCOT BAY AND ITS ISLANDS, MAINE. A few miles south of Bangor, Maine, State Highway 175 leaves busy U.S. 1 for an undiscovered peninsula of untramelled natural beauty where the country hasn't changed since 1900. From the winding highway, leafy lanes lead down to white salt-water farms, azure coves with sandy beaches, and quiet lakes. On Penobscot Bay's east shore time is measured by the rise and fall of tides. Life is delightfully informal and uncomplicated and whenever you call at a cottage or farm, it's always coffee time.

Wherever you look seawards, there are spruce-covered islands—400 in all. Penobscot's islands are the quintessence of her rockbound coast. Toll bridges and small capacity car ferries have preserved their isolation from motoring tourist hordes. On islands like Vinalhaven, Swan's, and Deer Isle, you can still enjoy unique privacy amid the primitive beauty of quaint fishing villages, innumerable shore lines broken by dark fir-topped headlands, and sky, water, and cloud which mirror the most superb dawns and sunsets on this continent. Add the tangy salt smell of lobster and drying seaweed, or the cool, fresh fragrance of green moss and lichens inland, and you have some idea of the overwhelming beauty of these unhurried escapist isles.

The few summer visitors—well educated professional and business people and teachers who discover contentment here—are as congenial as the native islanders. Not a few visitors have come back to retire. Said a former accountant, now retired on Vinalhaven: "As an off-islander who retired here because I love it, I can testify that the people are about the most hospitable and friendly group that one can imagine. We found it a delightful vacation spot for many years and are now finding it a very happy and most interesting community in which to live year around."

For 300 years, island families have harvested the deep blue coastal waters and most natives are direct descendants of Maine's first settlers. "Ayeh, I feel distempered to cawst me net today," is how a fisherman typically words his intention not to go fishing. Their stern rugged life has developed a courteous, dignified and intelligent people of extreme independence, a unique philosophy, and, often, a subtle humor. Islanders abhor hurry but greet you on sight, and every stranger is accepted at face value until he proves otherwise.

There's absolutely no organized entertainment. Instead, you'll swim, fish, sail, or hike. Swimming is surprisingly warm in protected coves and also in inland lakes and abandoned quarries. Smack on the Atlantic flyway, Penobscot Bay abounds with birds and both the northern and southern bird zones overlap here. You can fish for cod, haddock, pollack and flounder, dig delicious clams, and pick bushels of blueberries for free. Scenic motor roads lead to a score of interesting spots: to Bar Harbor, Schoodic Point, Ellsworth's historic Black Mansion, the pottery kilns at Brooklin and Blue Hill, and to a dozen lighthouses, boat building centers, and lobster pounds. Golf and tennis are played at mainland centers, and there are summer theater productions at Surry and country dances at various towns. Boat cruises leave daily from Castine.

An island cook-out is something to remember. Picture yourself on a dark, spruce-covered granite ledge above the sea. With others, you'll prepare clams steamed in seaweed and lobsters boiled in kettles of sea-water, plus chowders and the ubiquitous island coffee. There'll be fresh garden peas and chicken, eggs, and rich cream; if an island cook is along, you'll also get hot breads and pies, cookies, cakes, and dough-nuts like those of Grandma's day. Almost identical meals are served in the less exotic but equally homey and nostalgic dining rooms of island lodges and guest farms.

Summer means mild sunny days and cool nights. Sometimes fog drifts in at night and early mornings can be misty. But otherwise Penobscot's summers are flawless and after rates go down on Labor Day, you can still find enjoyable weather as late as November. Even the winters are the mildest in Maine. And June is often delightful.

Rates for *some* but not all accommodations are exceptionally low. Typically, housekeeping cottages rent at $60-$85 a week or $400-$550 for the entire summer, which is not too expensive when shared among four. And a few small furnished homes can be found for $100 a month or $85 a month after September. Without meals, guest houses and hotels charge from $28 double a week and $22 after September and in season, with all meals, around $60-$80 per person per week. Most island hostelries are ancestral homes or atmospheric white salt-water farms built by old sea captains among the pines. And in almost all, after dark, you can rightly expect to find a huge fire of 3-foot logs glowing in an enormous fieldstone hearth. But many make no secret of being unpretentious hostelries off the beaten path. So don't expect tiled baths and vented heat. One final word: be sure to make reservations well ahead. Visitors aren't too numerous but neither are accommodations.

Just to give you an idea of rates and accommodations where you'll find ideal country living near the sea, here are some on the mainland. All rates were recent and included meals but are naturally subject to inflation and will undoubtedly be increased as time goes on. At West Brooksville, David's Folly, a salt water farm for informal living, charges $77-$84 single weekly; Hill Top House charges a modest $42-$49 single per week; and Sea Winds charges $50-$55 single weekly. At South Brooksville, Breezemere, a real Down East salt water farm, charges $60-$70 weekly with a free boat included. Other inexpensive hostelries in this area with varied accommodations are Hiram Blake's Camp at Cape Rosier and Blue Hill Inn at Blue Hill.

At Harborside, not far from where historic old Fort George overlooks the stately colonial houses of Castine is Bayside Lodge, with captivating views and rates of $43-$48 per person per week; and with cottages available at only $48-$65 per week. To sample an ancestral farm, try the superior living at Oakland House and Cottages at Sargentville, where rates are $63-$94.50 weekly per person with meals and a free boat thrown in.

Now for the islands.

Deer Isle, reached by toll-free bridge from Sedgewick, is a wonder-fully natural and unspoiled area of trees, birds, and flowers. Eighty miles of coastal road weave through hills carpeted by hackmatack and balsam, and pass endless panoramas of inlets, coves, islets, rocks and rural farms. On this fifth largest island off the Atlantic coast, quiet, beauty, and serene peace are universal. You'll see pink granite quarries, old fashioned woodcutters harvesting firewood, pulpwood and logs, and one of the most perfect fishing villages in the whole of New England.

That village is Stonington at the island's southernmost tip. Adjectives such as "quaint" and "picturesque" fail to describe the field day which awaits photographers and artists here. (Famous artists like Marin and Hartley, and LaMarr Dodd came here to paint.) From rocky hillsides, Stonington drops down through streets of weather-beaten fishermen's cottages and front yards piled with lobster pots and chequered buoys, to bustling wharves on the cool green waters of Isle au Haut Bay. Odors of cooking clams, boiled lobsters and halibut steak mingle with the tang of half-rotten kelp and clam shells. Every day, a fleet of 150 fishing boats work offshore. Only a few TV antennas and an occasional gaso-line engine remind you that you are not back in colonial seafaring days. Accommodation averages $35 weekly for two, meals extra; cottages can be had at $100-$125 a month; fine improved campsites run $15 a week.

Probably the best place to stay is Dr. Ralph Waldron's Goose Cove Lodge at Sunset. For $65-$90 a week single with meals, (some accom-modations are higher) you get free use of a 32-foot sloop plus nature hikes, bird watching trips, sightseeing excursions and illustrated evening lectures to help you understand Maine, all conducted by celebrated naturalist Dr. Waldron himself. Ruth's Tourist Home in Stonington also has some Down East flavor.

Swan's Island is an escapist's gem, an untouched and absolutely un-spoiled ocean outpost inhabited by simple fisherfolk. Apart from a few summer people, the entire island is yours. Eighteen miles of road and scores of footpaths lead to beauty spots like Goose Pond and forbidding Dead Man's Beach and to miles of other beaches—both stormy and sandy—as well as to lighthouses and exquisite picnic spots, all rich in old time beauty and salty charm. If you like, you can also search for Captain Kidd's treasure on nearby John's Island. Every islander is an official historian and loves to recall Swan's Island's stirring history over coffee and steaming home made doughnuts. Located on beautiful Blue Hill Bay, Swan's Island is rimmed by rugged granite shores and its lighthouse guards one of Maine's loveliest harbors. There are three small villages—Atlantic, Minturn and Swan's Island—each with its own post office, churches and stores. This is an island of rolling hills and deep forests with seals basking in the sun on the outer ledges—one of the loveliest and least spoiled islands in America today.

Though the island is remote, it isn't primitive. Nowadays, you'll find a good restaurant, a light plane strip and a beautiful camping ground for tents and trailers. Cottages and apartments rent for $35-$85 a week in summer, when available. For information about islands accommodations, write the Chamber of Commerce, Swan's Island, Me. 04685. You get there by daily car carrying ferry in 45 minutes from McKinley on Mount Desert Island, fare $5.75 r.t. car and driver, passengers $1.43 each.

Vinalhaven Island, reached by a delightful 90 minute ferry cruise through the island-studded Reach from Rockland, Me., is a charming community in a primitive setting of wild and eroded granite shores. Its dramatic beauty extends to a score of offshore islands with boundless picnic possibilities and if you're seeking a quiet, restful place, Vinalhaven offers much which is rare in this day and age.

A fair sized summer art colony annually gathers here. Favorite among their subjects are Carver's Harbor, busy from dawn to dusk with colorful lobster boats, draggers and seiners, and Vinalhaven town, color-filled with fishermen's shacks and lobster gear, which has stood still in time since the quarries closed years ago. Though it's up-to-date and self contained, Vinalhaven town is still separated from the world by its location and simple economy and it still retains its Victorian appearance and simple way of life.

In Spring, you can scoop smelt out of creeks with your hands and in summer you'll comb the beaches for twisted driftwood, stray lobster buoys, and odd shells. You can also skin dive in fantastic flooded quarries, join in sailing, races, shop for island made handicrafts, and attend a movie three nights each week. And if you fall in love with Vinalhaven, you'll find land for sale from $500 an acre, higher in the coves and on headlands. The island has a population of 1,257; communal facilities include electricity, good city water, an efficient volunteer fire brigade, good public library, a hospital and clinic and a physician. Sole drawback is the lack of a really outstanding beach.

Rustic cottages along the shore, with breathtaking views but no plumbing, rent for $50 a week in summer; more modern ones are $70 a week and up. Several guest houses offer summer rooms but you'll particularly enjoy the Islander Inn, which is open all year. Ten dollars a day pays for a comfortable room with a view of ocean or garden plus a hearty breakfast and a real Down East style dinner based on old Maine recipes and with all the hot bread you can eat. Far from Maine's hectic winter whirl of ski tows, headwaiters, dance orchestras and swimming pools, the Islander Inn is an attractive retreat even in the dead of winter. More information: Islander Inn, Vinalhaven Island, Me. 04863.

Delightful smaller islands dot the Maine seacoast and if you're willing to board in a fisherman's cottage, accommodation can usually be arranged. First, there's Isle au Haut, settled in 1772 and pronounced Eel-o-Ho, a 5 x 2 mile fragment of Acadia National Park south of Deer Isle. A portion of Western Head lies within the park territory and all island scenery is truly spectacular. A few fishermen live here all year and there are several summer homes linked by a narrow dirt road. Camping is not permitted, the only accommodation being in 12 large rental cottages, each available for the season by writing the Point Lookout Associates, Inc., Ile au Haut, Me. 04645. Daily mailboats, fare 75¢ o.w., serve the island from Stonington and Rockland, Me.

Another tiny off-the-beaten-path island is 800-acre Matinicus, 22 miles out at sea by ferry from Rockland, Me. Summer visitors are accommodated in the village. Since the ferry runs only thrice weekly in summer and twice weekly in winter, Matinicus is a "million miles" from the turmoil of the mainland. Only 60 people live on Matinicus but there are accommodations. Mrs. Harold Bunker rents cottages by advance reservations and both Mrs. Madeleine Ames and Mrs. Gladys Mitchell take in guests. More information: Mrs. Vance Bunker, Matinicus Island, Me. 04851.

Long Island in Penobscot Bay, settled in 1769, resembles Vinalhaven and is reached by ferry from Lincolnville on U.S.1. Large summer estates cover much of the island but small villages like Dark Harbor, Isleboro, and Pripet are summer resorts. Boatyards and sawmills dot the island's many lovely coves and bays. The island, also called Islesboro, has much to recommend it for retirement: artists, writers and musicians already living here provide a cultural background; many retirees go in for handicrafts—driftwood, shells and ceramics; the island has one of New England's finest 18-hole golf courses; and there are charming houses you can restore at low cost. Pendleton's Cottages at Dark Harbor rent for $60-$90 a week in June and September (they're big 2-4 bedroom cottages near the sea); there are also less expensive rentals and comfortable guest homes supplying full board. There are two splendid beaches and for sightseeing you'll find the interesting Sailors' Memorial Museum and the ancient lighthouse at Grindle Point.

Frenchboro on Long Island, close to Swan's Island, is another hamlet similar to Minturn on Swan's. Ferries serve Frenchboro from McKinley and Stonington. Moving north off Jonesport, the township of Beals on Wrass Island lies among magnificent scenery. You reach it via the toll-bridge from Jonesport. Wrass Island is 2 x 6 miles of deep pinewoods dotted with the freshly painted houses of its 800 fisherfolk inhabitants. You'll find several cottages and houses for rent and the postmistress can supply information on where to stay.

Increasingly popular for retirement with professors, doctors, and businessmen, East Penobscot Bay can be a paradise for the Harvest Years if you enjoy cold but not frigid winters. Haulage costs raise grocery bills slightly on the islands but lobsters cost only half as much as in New York City and crabs are inexpensive. Clams are free for the taking, so are delicious blue mussels, and most fish are priced at 45¢ a pound. Many an old six-room home away from the waterfront can be picked up for $6,000 and renovated cheaply by carpenters who are paid only $2.50 an hour. Unskilled labor can be hired for $2 an hour. There's a good hospital on the mainland at Rockland and fine schools, churches, and adequate public utilities everywhere.

More information: for the mainland, write East Penobscot Bay Resort Association, Blue Hill, Me. 04614; for Deer Isle write Deer Isle-Stonington CoC, Deer Isle; for Vinalhaven, address the Vinalhaven Development Association, Vinalhaven, Me.; for Islesboro, the Town Clerk, Islesboro, Me.; for Wrass Island, The Postmistress, Beals, Me.

OCRACOKE ISLAND, NORTH CAROLINA. Looking for an escapist island peopled by the descendants of shipwrecked sailors and buccaneers, where life moves with the tides and time has stood still for the better part of two centuries? Until 1957, Ocracoke Island on North Carolina's wild and desolate Outer Banks would have fitted your quest to perfection. You'd have found yourself in an utterly fascinating and entirely different maritime world of Elizabethan English, rolling porpoises, barefooted Bankers, lighthouse keepers, skeletons of once proud ships and 16 miles of wild, deserted beach. That was before a new road thrust out from the mainland and brought tourist cars to Ocracoke.

Even so, Ocracoke can hardly be called spoiled or overcrowded. Apart from a handful of new restaurants and tourist accommodations, Ocracoke still retains all the traditional flavor of the Outer Banks. Beside beautiful Silver Lake Harbor, villagers' white frame cottages line sandy, picket-lined lanes under color-splashed bowers of shady live oaks, crepe myrtle, yaupon and jasmine. There is no crime, jail, town hall, doctor or dentist and the first phone wasn't installed until 1956. Until recently, Ocracoke's 400 unhurried fisherfolk had few contacts with the outside world, and its primitive charm remains intact.

Ocracoke is a 16 by 1 mile sliver of windswept sand 19 miles off the Carolina Coast where sea, sun and sand have conspired to produce one of the last outposts of individuality in the North American continent. Until 1957, wild Arabian steeds roamed the shifting sands and prior to that year, no island car required a license plate. It all started in the 1700s when a shipwrecked Arab named Wahab reputedly married the daughter of Blackbeard's quartermaster, Howard, to start Ocracoke's first family. Whether legend or fact, both names are still common on the island today. For generations, the Bankers lived off salvage and shipwreck; many a beam in the island's houses once sailed the Seven Seas and island gardens are dotted with giant fish bones, mine casings, buoys and ancient graveyards.

"Aye, toime and toide, she don't wait on Owcracowk," is how older islanders describe life in typically Devonian accents. The residents are a friendly lot ready to stop and pass the time of day, and to spin yarns of big fish, shipwrecks, hurricanes, and the deeds of Blackbeard. You'll see Teach's Hole at Springer Point, where the pirate was beheaded. And when you hike along the beach, you'll learn about the ghost ship *Caroll A. Deering*, discovered abandoned off the island in 1923 with coffee boiling in the galley but not a man aboard or ever heard of since.

Arrival of a large yacht or unusual craft in Silver Lake Harbor is a major event. Down sandy lanes laid out with Old World irregularity, the villagers come to gather around the beautiful oval landlocked harbor beneath the tall white lighthouse built in 1823. Pretty soon you'll find yourself unerringly doing the same. For Ocracoke has few distractions.

Fishing, hunting, sailing, and swimming are all tops here. Channel bass fishing is the best on the Atlantic and any day, you can catch more blues, trout, and mackerel than you could eat in a week. Crabs and flounders fall an easy prey to your gig and you can rake up a bushel of clams or oysters in two hours in season. You can swim in the restless surf at the National Park beach on the Atlantic shore. Ocracoke's 16 miles of public beach are a treasury of driftwood and, in winter, the feeding ground for thousands of geese and wild duck. You can see wild horses, take in the weekly movie, and have a roisterous time at the Saturday night square dance. Fresh oysters, clams, crabs, and shrimp are featured on every menu and $2.25 buys a family plate dinner at island restaurants.

Near the Gulf Stream, with warm swimming from May to September, Ocracoke basks in a mild, breeze-fanned climate where figs and palmettoes thrive and snow is all but unknown.

Comfortable housekeeping cottages rent at the peak of summer for $75-$85 a week, much less at other times. You may also stay at a choice of inns, motels or hotels—none really expensive. Housekeeping costs are low with seafood abundant and cheap. But you must bring your own liquor.

Living without tension or pressure naturally assists longevity and islanders have been known to reach 117 years. And now that all modern conveniences are available, Ocracoke is ideal for quiet and peaceful retirement. Notwithstanding that the National Park Service has acquired title to most of the island, you can, with a little patience, find inland lots for as little as $1,000 and up. Carpenters, plumbers and electricians are paid only $2-$2.75 an hour.

Ocracoke has a registered nurse, daily mail delivery, general stores, seafood markets, REA electricity, local volunteer mosquito control, some paved roads and a recreation building for dances and social entertainment. In this old fashioned community where age is meaningless and everyone is young at heart, retired mechanics, carpenters, and electricians can generally count on finding work. Burial is a community expense; whenever someone passes away, every islander puts 25¢ into the burial association box towards the next funeral. Though there is now a fire department, only 3 homes have burned in the past 60 years and each time the villagers passed the hat and rebuilt the homes. Many retirees look at Ocracoke and leave. Others who catch its friendly feeling and stay, usually live better than those on the mainland. A few senior couples successfully harvest an abundance of seafood without cost. Homes were recently assessed at 40% of market value and taxed $13.50 per $1,000 assessed valutation.

Changes come slowly to timeless Ocracoke but the new paved road from Hatteras is threatening the island's isolated quality. Many mourn that the old time Ocracoke may pass the way of other Banks villages. But there is a strong desire to preserve the local flavor and though prices may eventually rise, they are sure to stay below average for a long time to come. Because almost all the island has become part of the Cape Hatteras National Seashore Preserve, Ocracoke can never be despoiled by commercialism. Thus to lovers of the old time Banks, the great storm of March 1962 was not entirely a disaster. For the damaging storm—which cut 1.500 acres from the Banks and made most maps obsolete—also halted the march of progress and prolonged the Banks' seclusion for, possibly, several more years.

An easy way to reach Ocracoke with your car is to drive down the All Seashore Highway, crossing Hatteras Inlet by free ferry. Alternatevely, you may put your car on the toll ferry serving the island from Atlantic, N.C.

En route, you'll pass Portsmouth Island, inhabited by only two permanent residents. Time has all but passed by Portsmouth, a quiet fishing hamlet on the Upper Core Banks settled since the 1700s. Today, it's almost deserted—an ideal spot to get away from turmoil and strife. There are no electricity, cars, horses or even wagons. All freight is moved by wheelbarrow, to and from the handful of freshly yellow painted island homes. A single phone supplies the sole link to the mainland.

More information: Civic Club, Ocracoke, N.C. 27960.

CUTTYHUNK ISLAND, MASSACHUSETTS. History books have made the name of Cuttyhunk familiar as the site of New England's first white settlement. But to the average American, the island itself is as unknown as the entire Elizabeth group, of which it is the principal island. Yet every day in summer the boat *Alert* leaves New Bedford for the two-hour voyage to Cuttyhunk Island. The few escapists who take the trip discover themselves turning back the pages of history. For Cuttyhunk Island retains all the unspoiled antiquity that existed before the automobile was invented.

For years it's been a popular hideaway for prominent people. And weekend trippers are still not encouraged. But any well educated person seeking quiet and rest, or perhaps a place to sketch or fish, can count on finding congenial company and hearty island hospitality.

Cuttyhunk, only 2½ miles long and three-quarters of a mile wide, is easy to visualize. From the lighthouse on its western tip, surf pounds at a sheer wall of perpendicular cliffs lining the southern shore. On top is one of the most beautiful walks in New England. From Lookout Hill, the path winds between white fences and shady willows to the edge of the cliffs for an unforgettable panorama of broad blue open ocean. The north and east shores are ringed by sandy beach. Cuttyhunk village, quaint and picturesque with a harbor full of fishing boats and a tiny white church, was once a famous whaling port. Today, this peaceful spot is the home of fishermen who supply a large share of New England's tastiest lobster.

Life is a lazy round of loafing at the fish docks, shelling, bird watching, and swimming in the boiling surf or in cool, quiet bays. You'll enjoy strolling footpaths along the cliffs, and lobster boils around drift-wood fires are a frequent diversion. For something more energetic, you can sample some of the best striped bass fishing in the Atlantic. Fishing is also good for bluefish, flounder and mackerel and, in midsummer, for swordfish.

Only 27 permanent residents or "Hunkers" live on Cuttyhunk all year and the local grocery store is simply a spare room in someone's home. An islander's front parlor also doubles as post office. Cuttyhunk has no neon signs, bars, golf or tennis courts, swimming pools, movies or restaurants but you will find modern lighting, water and sewer facilities. The 60 homes in the village, which cluster on a green hill above the harbor, average 80-100 years in age. And all the island's wild land is held by private conservationists to guarantee against commercial exploitation. Surprisingly, there's an excellent public library with 7,000 books; deer and wildlife abound; and the island ponds supply warm water swimming. Cuttyhunk has a nurse and air taxi service to the mainland in case of emergency.

Although rates are a bit higher than on most of our island paradises, savings in transportation will make up the difference. Lowest rates are those at the Allen House, which charges $91 a week single with meals and $35 for children, $98 weekly in a detached cottage. At the Bosworth House, noted for serving heaping platters of lobster, rates are $17 a day single with meals. Alternative accommodation can sometimes be had in fishermen's homes. The island is dry, so bring your own bottle.

The boat *Alert* leaves Pier 3 in New Bedford for the scenic 14-mile voyage through the Elizabeth Islands to Cuttyhunk daily between June 15 and September 15 and twice a week at other times.

More information: write the accommodations mentioned, Cuttyhunk, Mass. 02713.

SMITH ISLAND, MARYLAND. One of the best kept secrets in the realm of travel is the existence of this amazingly unchanged island in America's inland sea. Only ten miles out in Chesapeake Bay, Smith Island remains a haven of peace, contentment and quietitude.

It all began in the 17th century when a group of individualistic Dutch and English settlers quit one of our Utopias, Maryland's St. Mary's County (see Part II) and set out by boat to seek another. They settled on Smith Island, a low fertile chunk of land eight miles long and four miles wide, and established a completely independent community. For decades, the islanders resented any attempts at federal control and at one time were so autonomous that two of the leading citizens were referred to as "King." Even today, Richard and Solomon Evans are remembered as King Richard and King Solomon.

Dominant still are the original settlers' family names. About half of the people are called Bradshaw, Tyler, Evans, Marshall or Messick. For this is an old society, in which the 700 islanders have remained devout Methodists. To most of them, the word of God is still above that of any human being. As a result, modern change and bigness have by-passed

Smith Island. A haze of antiquity hangs over the three villages of Rhodes Point, Tylertown and Ewell. Each village nestles under huge shade trees beside the shore and the waterfronts are lined by white hulled boats and crab packing houses built on piles. Each village has its own church and the village streets are narrow lanes bordered by masses of hollyhocks and other flowers. It's only a short distance between the villages, though to reach Tylertown you must cross a creek by boat. Traffic is almost non-existent. Fewer than twenty cars are on the island. The entire population totals only 800. A canal serves as Tylertown's main street, with homes on one side and fish houses on the other. Flowers and vegetable gardens surround the neat white homes in each village and the narrow lanes are bordered by carefully tended hedges, rose bushes and hollyhocks.

While the men are away fishing, the women tend luxuriant home fruit gardens. Much of the produce is organically grown and Smith Island is justly famed for its delicious figs, pomegranates and fresh fruits and vegetables. Poultry is also raised without harmful hormones and an abundance of fish, oysters, terrapin and crab is sold straight out of boats. Each village has its huge crab floats where, before your eyes, thousands of crabs shed their shells daily and become the succulent soft shelled variety so prized by gourmets. Among local specialities is a fig preserve served on hot rolls. Dishes like this are standard fare at the island's four guest homes. (For reservations, write or phone Mrs. Bernice Guy, Mrs. Frances Kitching or Mrs. Evelyn Brimer at Ewell; Mrs. Lydia Marsh or Mrs. William Marshall at Tylertown; or Mrs. Ernest Evans at Rhodes Point.)

Nowadays, Smith Islanders have phones, electricity and a pure water supply. But pollution and commercialism have yet to arrive. The fertile soil and bay furnish an abundant life. And the hardy, religious fishermen are an exceptionally friendly lot. They'll show the British flag which flies over the grave of British veterans of the War of 1812. And for a nominal sum, they'll take you out fishing in their boats. A good beach lies within a short distance of each village and here you can bathe or picnic while the white sails of fishing boats and crabbers fleck the blue-green bay.

Proud and independent still, the islanders respect the simplicity of the past and make no effort to encourage tourists. Thus the only way to get here is via the once-a-day mailboat from Crisfield, Md. The boat sails daily at noon (except Sundays) and the voyage across Tangier Sound occupies about ninety minutes. No cars are carried and the mailboat does not return until the following day. All costs are low and if you have a book to write or want to escape the rat race, few places in America can offer more undisturbed tranquility.

In addition, if you're prepared to pay $12.50, you can join a summer excursion boat out of Crisfield which takes sightseers to both Smith and Tangier Islands and back in one day. The fare includes both a box lunch and a crab dinner.

CHAPTER 4

America's Cut Rate
Winter Riviera

If you can't afford Miami Beach, you can have a wonderful mid-winter vacation at these uncrowded warm spots where costs go down while the mercury stays high.

THE TEXAS TIP—LOWER RIO GRANDE VALLEY, TEXAS. How would you like a large winter vacation cottage in an orange grove for $30 a week? Down in the sun-drenched Lower Rio Grande Valley, where Texas touches Old Mexico, a dozen citrus-encircled resorts burst in winter with attractive cottages and large resort style apartments at $75-$125 a month. Five hundred miles south of Los Angeles and on the same latitude as Miami, the Valley boasts winter temperatures higher than in either city. In fact, you'll find the Valley the warmest, driest, sunniest, and lowest cost winter resort in the entire United States. And not only is it the nation's biggest bargain in winter vacations, but you also get to visit two countries for the price of one.

What the Valley lacks in mountains it makes up for with an international flavor, a flawless climate, and lush subtropical vegetation. Miles of exotic palms border highways traversing emerald citrus groves and ranches where strange Brahma cattle wade knee deep in clover. Bright, modern towns are gay with hibiscus, roses, oleander, orchids, and red poinsettias as large as dinner plates. Fruit trees flourish everywhere—oranges, lemons, ruby red grapefruit, bananas, tangerines, papayas, avocadoes, and dates—and sunshine is broken only by occasional drifting tufts of lazy Gulf cloud.

Like Florida's resorts, the Valley towns are also agricultural centers. Each town has a peaceful, farming background as well as an active tourist club organizing endless barbecues, dances, musicales, concerts, picnics, pot luck suppers, smorgasbord dinners, and fine arts programs seven days a week. Average cost to participate in all this is just 3¢ a day. From most Valley towns it's less than an hour's drive to powder-white Padre Island beach, where you can swim all year, sunbathe, and sample superb salt water fishing. There is fresh water fishing near all towns, excellent hunting for whitewing, doves, deer, turkey, javelina, duck, and geese (license $25) and you can go deep sea fishing in party boats at $6 per head. Because most Valley visitors are elderly Mid-westerners, senior sports such as shuffleboard, croquet, and horseshoes are universal. Each town holds a weeklong fiesta, you can study Spanish, attend college, and visit a long string of historical sights on both sides of the colorful Rio Grande.

From any Valley town you can drive across into Old Mexico in from

4 to 40 minutes for a fee of 25¢ per car and 10¢ per passenger. And you'll discover picturesque old Spanish towns like Reynosa and Matamoros with colorful plazas and markets, ancient churches, frequent fiestas, serenading mariachis, and Old World patios and homes. You can shop for superb silver, glassware, liquor, pottery, lacquerware, and leather at a fraction of United States prices. But your biggest surprise will be the low cost border night life. Reynosa, opposite McAllen, Texas, and the most colorful of border cities, has five large, sophisticated night clubs. High border wages draw Mexico's top entertainers, who present shows as fine as most in even the largest United States cities. You'll see two shows while dining because one show wouldn't give you time to devour the fantastic 8-course wild game dinners these night clubs serve. For $2.50-$3 (depending on how many quail you order) you get two main meat courses—vension, quail, turkey, duck, frogs legs, filet mignon, goat kid, or dove—plus six other courses composed of 14 other items. If you prefer, you can get an enormous cold plate for $1.50 while beer, daiquiris, and other Mexican drinks are half U.S. prices. Cockfights and bazaars are also here to see. For longer excursions into Mexico you can drive 150 miles to Monterrey, the republic's third city, or take a bus all the way to cosmopolitan Mexico City and back again for under $20 in fares. No wonder they call the Valley the winter tourist's last frontier.

Records show that the average winter visitor spends about $9 per day for everything. Although the climate is every bit as good as Florida's, rates are quite low. Pleasant housekeeping cottages and motel efficiencies go for $30-$40 a week; some are in orange groves and you can pick all the fruit you want for free. Rooms in private homes average $10-$15 a week for two. By the month, you can rent nicely furnished apartments for $70-$100, and furnished homes from $95 up. Groceries, fruits, meats and vegetables are often priced somewhat lower than in other states, particularly if you shop across the border in Mexico. Top grade Mexican cigarettes are only 11¢-12¢ a pack, large pineapples just 25¢ and three pounds of pecans $1.50. Papayas, vanilla, sugar, avocadoes and many other fruit and staple items can be bought across the border at bargain prices. Fuel averages $3 a month and you can hire a Mexican maid for $4 a day or $28 a week.

Perpetual sunshine and a climate drier than Florida's characterize the Valley's warm winters. Each January, physicians send hundreds of sufferers from rheumatism, asthma, hayfever, nervous and respiratory ailments, heart trouble, and sinus to regain their health in the Valley's curative sunshine. Winter cold spells are less frequent than in Florida, and shorter. Excepting in 1957 and in 1962, tourists have worn jackets on only four occasions each winter.

Summer heat makes the valley more of a bargain and less of a paradise. Yet if you don't mind dry heat, you'll find the same attractions as in winter, with rates some 40% less. One exception is Padre Island, which is a haven from summer heat and is crowded from June to September.

Each Valley town has its own special attractions, its own recreations, flavor, and appeal. You can obtain more information by writing to the CoC at each. But to give you some idea, here is a brief rundown on the most important.

Brownsville. Pop. 50,000. Largest, oldest and most charming of the Valley towns with a rich historical background and beautiful tree-shaded streets, Brownsville faces Matamoros—a night life center across the border—and boasts a fine library, golf course and active tourist program.

Edinburg. Pop. 22,000. A modern college town with smart stores and shops grouped round an enormous palm-lined parking area. There are adult college classes and tourists enjoy privileges at the exclusive Ebony golf course.

Harlingen. Pop. 41.207. A larger, young, modern city at the cross-roads of the Valley. You'll find an active tourist center providing shuffleboard tournaments, winter music concerts, and square dances, a large outdoor swimming pool, and an 18-hole municipal golf course.

McAllen. Pop. 36,000. The Valley's premier resort, a neat city of palms, and one of the most attractive towns in Texas. McAllen's tourist hall is the largest outside Florida or California and its program the most extensive in the Valley. You can swim, fish, hunt, bowl, play tennis or golf, and take part in choice of 38 other activities.

Padre Island. The $2½ million Queen Isabella Causeway (toll $1) connects the Valley with the firm white beaches of this pencil-thin island on the Gulf of Mexico. Extending 110 miles up the Gulf Coast, this is the nation's last remaining undeveloped tropical beach. To preserve it, the central 81 miles have been named a National Seashore—an unspoiled paradise of towering sand dunes and deserted beach. You'll find the south end developed but even here, lovely Isla Blanca County Park provides relief from the commercialism. You can camp in the National Seashore.

Port Isabel. If you like sea fishing you could try this oil and shrimp port on emerald Laguna Madre near Padre Island. Port Isabel still bears the flavor of a charming fishing village and its chief landmark is a lighthouse over 100 years old. Prices are slightly higher than in the Valley proper but lower than on Padre Island.

Raymondville. On a latitude with Fort Lauderdale, this smaller town offers shuffleboard, croquet, golf, and salt water fishing at Port Mansfield on Redfish bay. Prices are low.

Roma. If you're seeking a typically Mexican village in the U.S., with untouched natural charm, mellowed houses and lots of atmosphere, sample Roma, some 60 miles south of Laredo. It's so typically Mexican that the movie *Viva Zapata* was filmed here.

San Benito. Pop. 17,000. Called the "Resaca City," lively San Benito is cut by a beautiful tree-lined lake 400 feet wide, in which fresh water fish thrive. Salt water fishing is nine miles distant at Arroyo Colorado. The neighborly tourist center provides cultural activities and community concerts and plenty of get togethers. Prices are extremely inexpensive.

Weslaco. Only slightly smaller, with subtropical foliage, and friendly informality, Weslaco is a palm-lined town with a lazy, tropical atmosphere. The busy tourist club arranges a steady program of bingo, canasta parties, lectures, State and Canadian picnics, dances, concerts, and a major annual shuffleboard tournament. Opposite Weslaco is the lively Mexican town of Nuevo Progreso with an excellent restaurant.

All these towns are popular for low cost retirement. Average costs for heating a 2-bedroom home with gas is only $38 a year, electricity bills average $30-$84 annually, and water $40-$72. Seniors are often able to earn extra income through office and timekeeping work, retail selling or baby sitting. "I save nearly enough on fuel each winter to pay my rent," says Mr. G. D. of McAllen. "I can grow my own vegetables, fish or just lie around in the sun. My modest pension is quite sufficient here." Older 2-bedroom homes sell for $8,500-$11,000, new ones $9,500 up. At slightly higher costs you can build on Padre Island.

Caution: don't expect to occupy a plush air condioned luxury motel or apartment at the prices we've been talking about. Big deluxe motels with swimming pools average $14 a day and modernistic air-conditioned apartments are priced in proportion. But for plain, solid comfort, your money will go a good deal further than at other winter resorts.

More information: write the CoC's at individual towns. Also the Lower Rio Grande Valley CoC, Box 975, Weslaco, Texas 78596.

FAIRHOPE, ALABAMA. We must tell you about Fairhope—as utterly unlike other small towns as it is possible to imagine. Back in 1894 a group of Single Taxers seeking a place to prove Henry George's theory, thought they might as well do it in a setting of singular beauty. They chose a rolling, pine-covered bluff overlooking the eastern shore of historic Mobile Bay on the highest coastal land between Mexico and Maine. There Fairhope stands today, a serene little place with a rare old fashioned homelike quality where all the charm of the Deep South blends with the culture of an amazingly gifted and cosmopolitan population.

Shady lanes, some overhung with pecan trees, lead past the homes of craftsmen to the 125-foot heights of "Sea Cliff." Huge moss-hung live oaks crowd the miles of public beach and winding shoreline. Spacious, sprawling old houses dot the bay where the elite of Mobile spent their summers years ago. Every month in the year there are bright splashes of hibiscus, oleander, and roses. And in spring, Fairhope blazes with the flaming colors of red and orchid azaleas, dogwoods, camellias, yellow jasmine, and dazzling white magnolia.

Notwithstanding its steady summer resort trade, you won't find a single honky tonk or parking meter in Fairhope. Its surprisingly cosmopolitan stores are explained by the fact that Fairhope is one of the most cultural small towns in the South. Fairhope boasts the distinction of adept craftsmen in all major arts in its art colony. Not unnaturally, Fairhope has lured its quota of culturally-minded retired professors and Army officers.

For anyone over 40, Fairhope is a unique discovery where you can winter inexpensively in a balmy climate or find easy year around living in a relaxed, hospitable Southern setting. Materialistic standards are meaningless here: the man in stained khaki pants catching crabs off the pier is probably a former executive; and more likely than not the yachtsman working at an easel in the harbor is a retired schoolteacher.

Social life hinges around the yacht club (annual membership $35) and in winter there are weekly get-acquainted afternoon games and monthly pot luck suppers at the Tourist Club perched high above the murmuring surf. A theater group presents at least four plays each season while Mobile's concerts are only thirty minutes away. There are adult classes in metalcraft and pottery and a wide choice of adult education courses at the University of South Alabama. Every week the Eastern Shore Art Association sponsors spend-the-day-painting sessions and the county writers' club holds regular meeting. Swimming is popular most of the year, and golf and tennis are perennial pursuits. You can gig flounders by torchlight, cast a net for mullet, fish for trout, ling, croakers, and reds any day in the year, and catch abundant tasty crabs off the municipally owned 1,000-foot fishing pier.

Fairhope's semi-tropical winter climate rivals that of the famed French Riviera in spring. Temperatures reach freezing only a few times each year and canny retired schoolteachers come here in numbers to spend the winter at a third the price they'd pay in nearby South Florida. Being a summer resort, Fairhope's rates drop sharply in winter. From October to April housekeeping cottages go for $85-$120 a month, hotels charge $54-$63 weekly with meals, and small furnished homes (rather short) rent for about $100 a month. Housekeeping costs are extremely reasonable. You'll love those big platters of giant boiled fantail Gulf shrimps you buy almost at wholesale. Oysters sell at $2.50 a bushel, crabs are 75¢ a dozen (or free off the pier), and fryers 33¢ a pound.

For a longer stay or permanent retirement, you'll find modern two-bedroom apartments at $135 a month unfurnished. Older one and two bedroom homes sell from $9-20,000, new two-bedroom homes $11-22,000. All costs are low; a maid runs only $20 a week, a gardener $1.25 an hour; and for $9 a day, two meals included, you could spend the winter at the unpretentious Colonial Inn.

Alabama's Bargain Winter Riviera.
Throughout the balmy winter, when all rates are rock-bottom, Alabama's tiny coastal communities become true bargain paradises. For a really delightful winter sojourn or for permanent retirement, consider Magnolia Springs, a once famous spa nestled under shady oaks on the banks of the winding Magnolia River. Enjoying the soft lazy air and tranquility of this delightful old river town are some 300 permanent residents, many retired. Their homes line the river bank for miles, their mailboxes poking out over the water . . . for here your letters are delivered by a waterborne mailman. Fishing is naturally excellent and there are scenic drives to nearby Creole fishing villages like Bon Secour and to the bright lights of Mobile, 45 miles away.

Also in this same area is the quaint restful community of Marlow; and also Orange Beach. Then across Mobile Bay, near famed Bellingrath Gardens, is that quaint and picturesque fishing village, Bayon La Battre—a favorite with Alabama's painters and photographers. Beyond Bayou La Battre, you come to historic Dauphin Island, former capital of Louisiana and today a sparkling resort of wide, white beaches, a casino and golf club. At all of these places, apartments and cottages are available in winter for $85-$125 a month and all real estate is priced right for truly inexpensive retirement. As a livelier retirement site, Dauphin Island offers a golf and country club type of life at comparatively low cost. Beautiful waterfront and tree-shaded lots sell from $1,550-$5,000, with two-bedroom homes from $8,500.

Most unusual feature of this unusual town is the Single Tax Corporation, which owns 25% of all the land and rents it out on 99-year leases. In return, the corporation pays your poll and auto taxes plus your property tax *regardless* of the *value* of the *house you build*. Incidentally, the annual property tax recently on a $20,000 home was only $90.

Almost as charming is the smaller commuity of Daphne five miles north. Here people with creative minds retire in dignified older homes of an earlier era. Along the bluff-lined shore, clear streams wind through forests of moss draped trees and everywhere you feel the pervading sense of history. Don't look for the low prices of beehive type retirement villags. But like Fairhope, Daphne also has large beautiful wooded building sites at relatively inexpensive prices and building costs are well below the national averages.

More information: Eastern Shore CoC, Box 507, Fairhope, Ala. 36532.

GULF BEACH STATE PARK, ALABAMA. For a cut-rate winter sunshine vacation on one of the finest beaches this side of Mexico, sample this history-soaked Alabama beach park. For 27 miles the park flanks the Gulf's singing surf, and within its sun-kissed 4,807 acres are three clear-fresh-water lakes, a superb 2¼-mile beach of bone white sand, and a historic fort which served under seven flags. From April 1 through Labor Day, Gulf Beach is Alabama's most popular park. But the rest of the year, though it's almost deserted, the weather stays sunny and mild and park authorites confidently state, "the climate justifies year around vacations." For this reason, accommodations are kept open all winter and $30 a week gets you a pleasant lakeside cabin big enough for four; monthly rates are just $75. Larger cottages for 8 cost $40 a week or $115 a month and a duplex apartment $50 or $135, utilities included. Summer rates are 50%-100% more.

You'll find swimming invigorating and even in January, you can quickly tan. Surf or boat fishing is excellent and deep sea charter boat rates are exceptionally low. And, of course, you'll explore hoary old Fort Morgan 22 miles west, oldest fort in North America, where the first European landed on Unitel States soil, with an exciting history of seven bloody battles. Nine miles in the opposite direction is Gulf Gate Lodge—a fisherman's Utopia—where $60 a month gets you a comfortable housekeeping cottage for the entire winter season. Gulf Beach State Park also has a 1,000' long fishing pier.

More information: The Manager, Gulf State Park, Gulf Shores, Ala. 36542.

TRUTH OR CONSEQUENCES, NEW MEXICO. For a winter resort with a high, dry, zestful and invigorating climate, head for this peaceful old fashioned spa, which lies beside U.S. 85 on the Rio Grande about ninety miles north of El Paso Texas. In all directions the seemingly limitless horizon is etched with mountain ranges and the wide blue sky is bare of clouds on 318 days each year. In fact, T or C enjoys 85% of possible sunshine—more than almost anywhere else in the country—and rainfall totals an insignificant seven inches annually. The relative humidity seldom exceeds 15% and though winter nights can be snappy, daytime temperatures often reach 70° in the intense January sun.

Every winter, hundreds of health seekers from Kansas and Minnesota flock to T or C, seeking relief from their arthritis in the revitalizing sunshine and healthgiving mineral waters. Built over Palomas Springs, where mineral-rich waters gush forth at 110°, T or C has 22 bath houses complete with every type of spa bath (50¢-$1.25) and massages ($2-$3). Scores of residents originally came here as bedridden arthritics and the town is a perennial haven for victims of emphysema, rheumatism, asthma and respiratory ailments.

Originally called Hot Springs but renamed Truth or Consequences in 1950 for the Ralph Edwards radio program, the serene little community remains one of the most inexpensive and overlooked winter sunshine resorts in America. At an altitude of 4,240' and with a population of only 7,500, unfashionable T or C enjoys a leisurely atmosphere with crystal clear skies and the purest of air. You can play golf all year on the 9-hole course and hundreds of miles of riding and hiking trails lead through the splendidly scenic hills to ghost towns and abandoned mines rich in agate, jasper, fossils and petrified wood. Just north of town, mighty Elephant Butte towers like a sentinel over a vast lake stocked with oversized catfish while trout are also plentiful in the Rio Grande. Every evening the local recreation center hums with card parties or dances and there's a well stocked small library.

As America's least known winter desert resort, T or C is thankfully free of gilded luxury motels, pseudo-French restaurants and touristy gift shops. Instead, comfortable older hotels and apartments provide very adequate accommodation at down-to-earth prices. Hotels charge $25 a week while small furnished apartments are available at $50-$80 a month and cottages from $75. But to secure these inexpensive rentals, you must arrive early, well ahead of the midwinter season. For $14-$25 a month, you can park your trailer on a shady riverside lot.

Grateful to T or C for restoring their health, hundreds of former visitors have settled here permanently. Cozy two bedroom homes sell from $9,000 and for $13,500 you can buy a brand new two bedroom home with a two car garage poised on a hill above the Rio Grande (with taxes of $250 annually). Low cost evaporative coolers air condition homes during the warm summer days but nights are always crisp. The people are friendly and warm . . . and T or C remains one of America's top buys for retirement or sparkling, golden winter sunshine.

More information: CoC, Box 31.

BILOXI, MISSISSIPPI. To some people Biloxi's buzzing bars, neon signs, and night clubs are the serpents in an Eden. To others, who recognize them as an expression of the city's Gallic *joie de vivre*, Biloxi is an historic, exotic, and languorous resort, and among Gulf Coast cities, a genuine Utopia. Frequently called "The Poor Man's Riviera" nothing is really expensive and from September till February, most prices are downright cheap.

One of America's most colorful small cities, Biloxi is famed for old gardens, oysters and shrimp. As the world's largest shrimp port, its cannery-lined Back Bay is home port for 900 shrimp trawlers manned by brawny cosmopolitan French and Dalmatian fishermen. The raucous cannery whistles that echo a cacaphony from time to time are a signal that the shrimp fleet is in, and down at the Old World docks, you can hear the fishermen's French patois drifting across hundreds of odorous seafood barrels and miles of drying nets. Such a wealth of seafood means low prices and you can anticipate an epicurean vacation. For less than $2 you can dine on an amazing variety of bouillons, bisques, and gumbos plus shrimp in every conceivable form—stuffed, boiled, broiled, and creole. Some enterprising places even serve shrimp-burgers and shrimp spaghetti.

But away from the canneries along 27 miles of gleaming white beach is Biloxi's other side, a world of ante-bellum homes under patriarchal, moss-bewhiskered oaks. You'll discover this charming Old Southern side is amiable, restful, and relaxing, more attuned to the mood of tangy salt winds, moonlight, magnolias, and mocking birds.

Biloxi, oldest French city in America, crowds a tiny, sun-kissed peninsula between the green-blue Gulf and the busy waters of Back Bay, which, fortunately, insulate the city from cold northern winds so that winters are the mildest on this coast. Winter visitors claim it is cheaper to live in Biloxi than to fire furnaces at home. Which may be true when you consider most rates are reduced from September 15 through January 30. Room and board can then be found for as low as $90 a month, motel housekeeping units range from $25-$40 a week, deluxe cottages run about $45, and there are hotels for as little as $90 double by the month. For a full off-season sojourn you can find furnished apartments at $75-$90 and furnished homes from $85-$100 a month, maids will work for $20-$22 a week, and seafood and vegetables sell at rock bottom prices.

Activities are legion: you can catch delicious crabs off bridges and piers, spear flounders, cast a net for mullet, or enjoy first rate deep sea fishing for a fare of $6 a day. There is plenty of sightseeing, daily boat cruises to offshore islands, beer and boiled shrimp suppers are standard social fare, and Biloxi's live and let live attitude frowns on neither cockfights nor gambling.

Scores of ex-military and business couples are enjoying retirement in Biloxi. Many hail from the Midwest, particularly from Illinois. An added draw for ex-servicemen is the large U.S. Veterans Hospital plus a PX and depot facilities. Lots tend to be small on this crowded penisula, but you'll find some attractive older 2-bedroom homes selling for $8-9,000 and many new ones for $10-11,500.

Much the same thing can be found in the neighboring beach resorts of Gulfport and Pass Christian. But do not attempt to vacation here between May and Labor Day, when vacationing hordes overrun the beaches, prices soar and Biloxi becomes another Atlantic City.

More information: CoC's at Biloxi, Gulfport and Pass Christian.

GRAND ISLE, LOUISIANA. Pirate Jean Lafitte displayed questionable taste in his choice of occupation but his taste in resorts was impeccable. At Grande Isle, he and his swashbuckling crew relaxed between forays until after the War of 1812, when Lafitte left behind a handful of reformed raiders and an aura of glamour which still clings to the island. Today, you can drive to Grand Isle down a dead-end road that parallels atmospheric Bayou La Fourche for 66 watery miles. And apart from a superficial veneer of modern day America, you'll find Grand Isle much as he left it.

QUAINT OLD SOUTH: PAWLEYS ISLAND

If you're seeking a low cost sea, sun and sand vacation in a quaint old Southern setting, sample Pawleys Island in the Carolina Low Country. Ringed by historic plantations, this small 4 x $1/_4$ mile island was the favorite summer retreat of Carolina rice planters throughout the 18th and 19th centuries. And today the island is dotted with picturesque old houses having gabled roofs, around-the-house porches, and board walks to the sea—all in a restful setting of high sand dunes and dense scrub oak. Between October and April, costs are rockbottom at the island's inns and apartments and though Pawleys is practically deserted, the cultural attractions of Charleston are within a comfortable 90 minutes drive. Nearby Bulls Island is another flavorful retreat. More information: Pawleys Island Realty Co., Pawleys Island, S. C.

Flanking an 8-mile beach and only 1 to 6 city blocks in width, Grand Isle retains much of the flavor of wilder days. Shady, white shell lanes tunnel through oleander, elder, and chinaberry where the island's lusty ancestors once lived. Stocky and dark, the islanders betray their Mediterranean ancestry, speak a mixed French patois, and still remain rather shy and impassive. At least, they do on weekdays. But on Saturday night the islands goes gay and many a grandmother kicks off her shoes to lilting oldtime dances in the two dance halls. Over beer with jambalaya or crayfish bisque the islanders soon become expansive and not a few are mildly proud of their buccaneer heritage. Adding to the island's color are the families of oilmen who work on the rigs that stud the waters offshore. These rigs lure so many fish that Grand Isle is considered one of America's top fishing centers.

Rich soil brought down and deposited by the Mississippi formed Grand Isle and gave rise to the verdant background of leaning palms, windblown oaks, Spanish dagger, and subtropical flowers. In winter, when rates are down to half summer prices, it's rather chilly for swimming but you can loll on the beach and only during a few chilly midwinter days need you wear a jacket at all.

Endless logs line the beach and among them is strewn an abundance of grotesque driftwood and shells. Treasure hunting is a popular pastime, and many an islander believes Lafitte's hoard lies buried near one of many neighboring Indian shell mounds. With a rented pirogue or skiff you can explore a jig-saw maze of meandering waterways, pick enough crabs and oysters in an hour to supply your table for a week, and after dark you can gig giant flounder by the light of a flare. All island waters teem with every kind of fish from fighting wahoo and cobia to trout, blues, redfish, and pompano. You can linger for hours in the fascinating harbor among tanned nets and an armada of white hulled oyster dredges, shrimpers, and luggers, and for sightseeing there's a pirate graveyard and old Fort Livingston a mile across Barataria Sound on Grand Terre Island. Thousands of migrating birds also find Grand Isle an ideal winter resort and if you enjoy bird watching, this place is a Mecca. It's also a Mecca for devotees of the local, highly seasoned French seafoods. For night life, Grand Isle boasts one movie, two dance halls and a variety of cocktail lounges.

From November through April—Grand Isle's "off-season"—you'll find plenty of hotel rooms at $35 a week and fully furnished apartments at $40-$60 a week (with rates proportionately lower by the month). All accommodations are newly built since Hurricane Betsy devastated Grand Isle in 1965. Also new are the big oil company heliports, housing installations and offshore drilling supply depots. But relatively few tourists visit Grand Isle between October and April and the island continues to offer a bargain priced winter fishing holiday in the sun.

More information: Rotary Club, Grand Isle, La.

TYBEE ISLAND, GEORGIA. Eighteen miles from Savannah over a drive lined with palms and oleander, is one of Georgia's six Golden

Semitropical Hideaway: Bull's Island, South Carolina

Anyone seeking the ultimate in an unspoiled semitropical island teeming with wildlife can do no better than to turn off U.S. 17 twenty miles north of Charleston, South Carolina, and follow the Wildlife Service markers for five miles to the isolated boat landing which serves Bull's Island. A further five-miles trip by boat through a maze of tidal marshes and winding creeks brings you to Bull's Island, showpiece of Cape Romain National Wildlife Refuge.

Within its compact 6 by 2 mile area, this low, little known island packs a superb six-mile stretch of beach and a surprising variety of wilderness scenes. Over 12 miles of sandy trail, winding through silent pine forests and moss-bearded oaks matted with jungle creeper, you'll see shiny stands of tropical bamboo, grotesque dead trees, huge sand dunes, shipwrecks, a ruined fort of pirate days, and delightful pools blanketed by water lilies. Deer, wild turkey and raccoon are everywhere and the shores are alive with egrets, ibis, wading birds and sea fowl. Huge turtles and porpoise splash about in the creeks and alligators up to fourteen feet long often lie sunning on the shores. If you like studying or just plain enjoying our wildlife heritage far from highways and bustle, Bull's Island could be a real discovery.

Best time for a visit is November until May. During summer, bugs can be a problem whenever the sea breeze drops. But in the sunny winter months, you can stay at the amospheric Dominick House (Bull's Island, Awendaw, S.C.) for $10-$12 daily per person with meals. Reservations are needed at both lodge and boat landing (boat fare $4 r.t.)

More information: Cape Romain National Wildlife Refuge, Headquarters, McClellanville, S.C. 29458.

Isles—Tybee, with its miles of firm white beach, gently rolling surf, and summer cottages built on stilts where Savannah's elite spend the social summer season. But soon after Labor Day the crowds depart, some businesses close up altogether, and those which stay open slash rates a full 75%. The result: if you don't care to swim, you can enjoy the same warm, sunny weather as at many resorts farther south—at bargain prices.

"Winter guests find Savannah Beach (Tybee) a delightful and inexpensive place to visit," says the Chamber of Commerce. From November 1 till April 1, a score of resorts offer a completely furnished modern housekeeping apartment one block from the ocean with all utilities, automatic heat, TV and daily maid service for four people at around $30 a week, and motel efficiencies are often only $22-$25 weekly. For a lengthy stay, there are nicely furnished homes at $75-$100 a month.

Tybee, where General Oglethorpe first set foot on United States soil, and one of Georgia's oldest resorts, makes a fine center for visiting old Fort Pulaski and Savannah's historic shrines. There are miles of winding inlets where the big ones bite all winter, you can catch crabs by the dozen right off the boat docks, and on all but a few chilly days you'll enjoy lounging on the peaceful sands or beachcombing beside the blue Atlantic surf. Savannah Beach also has excellent surfing facilities and charter boats for deep sea fishing.

In neighboring Savannah, a picturesque old Southern city of restful, tree-shaded squares, historic town houses can be picked up very inexpensively and are easily refurbished by the handyman.

More information: Savannah Beach CoC, PO Box 223, Savannah Beach, Ga. 31328.

CHAPTER 5

Paradise Isles of the Summer Seas

Here they are for your summer vacation . . . America's most beautiful island paradises . . . unspoiled, untourited and as unknown as their names. There are Gabriola, Galiano, Orcas and Campobello; Savary with its tall ferns; the idyllic Sucias, and Lummi, Lopez, Grand Manan and countless more. The sea winds sing their place names . . . Friday Harbor, Departure Bay, Dark Harbor and Windigo Inn.

These are the islands of the northern seas and lakes, intricately carved by winter storms into thousands of flawless escapist spots in the most tantalizing settings. Among them you'll find the lowest prices in all of North America.

GRAND MANAN ISLAND, NEW BRUNSWICK. Twice each day, a small car ferry slips unobtrusively out of Blacks Harbor, New Brunswick, bound across Fundy's gray-green waters for the sea-girt bastion of Grand Manan Island. Newcomers among the handful of escapists always on board gasp incredulously as the island's great craggy cliffs and surfpounded headlands loom dramatically above the broad sweep of sea. "Why didn't someone tell me before there was such beauty as this?" is the first-time visitor's stock exclamation. The answer is simple. For years the ethereal beauty of Grand Manan has been kept a jealously guarded secret by a handful of discriminating people who wished to spend their summers undisturbed in this idyllic island paradise.

The two-hour voyage still discourages curiosity-seeking tourists. Neither commercialism nor crowds have tainted Grand Manan to date.

Grand Manan—16 miles long and 6 miles wide—is an irresistible island world of unique customs, hospitable fisherfolk, striking scenery, and rich seafood. Scenery is on a colossal scale. Along the brooding western coast, gaunt cliffs and majestic headlands tower hundreds of feet above the turbulent Atlantic. The east coast is softer, dotted with snug ports and harbors where gaily painted fishermen's cottages, strung with lobster pots, nestle cozily among windswept trees. Hundreds of shrieking gulls perpetually dip and soar above the tiny harbors and over every picture-postcard village hangs the rich aroma of hickory smoke from the herring houses.

Herring is king on Grand Manan and life is governed by Fundy's huge 38-foot tides. Over 100 circular herring weirs supply the islanders' livelihood, and any fisherman will take you out to watch the silvery catch being scooped into nets. The weirs, which cost

$10,000 apiece, bear colorful names like Bear's Den, Bread and Butter, Gold Seeker, Bonanza, and Last Ditch. In the islanders' soft speech they roll from the tongue as easily as Grand Manan's intriguing place names: Swallow Tail Light, Whale Cove, Little Dark Harbour, and Seal Cove. Breathtakingly beautiful silver beaches and coves rim the island's 55 square miles of deep, rolling woodlands and sunny fields.

Grand Manan was an early rendezvous for pirates and buccaneers, and Captain Kidd buried a cool two hogsheads of doubloons at Money Cove. But the island wasn't permanently settled until after the Revolution, when fleeing Loyalists settled there to produce the hardy Scotch- and English-descended fisherfolk you meet today. Their long isolation has produced some curious customs. For example, kids prefer to chew seaweed instead of candy. At Seal Cove, a community of fish-stands built on stilts, boats sail right up the watery main street. Two mounted policemen keep law and order in the island's nine hamlets, there is no jail, and no one ever locks doors. Seagulls—as individualistic as the island's humans—nest in trees. Liquor can be purchased only at a government liquor store, there are no honky tonks or dance halls, no night clubs or bars, and no tourist prices. Unspoiled Grand Manan is guaranteed to satisfy the soul of the most discerning island hunter at prices anyone can afford.

The flavor of the sea penetrates every corner of this realm of rock and spray. Over winding island roads you can bicycle in solitude for miles, the silence broken only by the rustle of the wind in the pines and the haunting cry of seabirds above the booming surf. Artists and writers return for the summer year after year and Willa Cather wrote most of her books at Whale Cove. And so delicious is island seafood that Grand Manan has published its own cook book. Lobsters are second to none and your days here will be a round of never-to-be-forgotten delicacies like fish chowder, steamed clams, corned pollack, cod fish tongues, periwinkles, smoked herring, gulls egg meringues, and the universally toasted seaweed called dulse. A box of smoked herrings that'll last you a year costs only $2.50.

There are absolutely no organized tourist activities, but you'll find plenty to do. Bathing is a trifle chilly in the salt water lagoons, but there are splendid beaches for sunbathing. Hiking trails wind for miles over breath-stopping clifftop scenery. You can explore caves, take an all-day boat trip round the island for $3 with a piping hot fish chowder lunch thrown in, and there are endless points of interest like the Southern Cross and amazing geological wonders such as the Seven Days Work. At low tide, you can explore miles of uncovered ocean floor, dig clams and scallops, and join in frequent beach lobster picnics —a long-standing island institution. Friendly lighthouse keepers welcome visitors and islanders can be counted on to regale you at any time with exciting stories of heroism and shipwrecks. Island lakes are stocked with trout and bass and Grand Manan, home of 275 different birds, is an ornithologist's Utopia. At the bird colony on Machias Islands, you'll see curious puffins and terns, guillemots, sea parrots and sea pigeons, as well as porpoises, seals, and perhaps a whale en route. After dark, there are movies, impromptu fishermen's square dances, and cheery evenings around blazing log fires. If you like, you can shop for fine English bone china at well below United States prices, while the islanders make and sell all kinds of knitted wear, rugs, mats, cork and glass floats, and handcarved seagulls at extremely reasonable prices.

Weather is ideal from June to October and rates are reduced in June and after Labor Day. Grand Manan is completely free from pollen and you can expect invigorating cool days and nights throughout spring, summer, and fall. But the best news of all is the inexpensive rates at the island's inns and comfortable boarding houses. Don't expect a private bath, but $45 a week buys full room and board and many places will serve lobster as often as you wish. Most charming place is the Anchorage, midway between the quaint villages of Seal Cove and Grand Harbour, a 250-acre seashore estate with rates of $92 a week per person with meals. At North Head, one of the most picturesque villages, is the Marathon Hotel, charging $65-$85 a week with meals, Shore Crest Lodge charging $10 a day with meals and Whale Cove Cottages (each with a large fireplace) charging $9 a day for full board. Then at Seal Cove, you'll find Birdy's Shore Cabins, where a housekeeping cottage for four is only $42 a week, and the Double D Cabins and Tree Point Cottages with slightly higher rates. More accommodations are needed on Grand Manan and opportunities are good for would-be island hoteliers and moteliers.

Housekeeping cottages rent for $55 a week and food is inexpensive: all fish is low priced and lobsters retail at $1 or so per pound. Crabs, periwinkles, herring, clams, and pollack are free for the taking. And a haircut can still be had for $1.25.

To reach Grand Manan, take the auto ferry from Blacks Harbour, N. B. Fares are inexpensive. Motoring is attractive on island roads. Check with the address below for latest sailing information.

More information: Board of Trade, Grand Manan, N.B., Canada.

CAMPOBELLO AND DEER ISLANDS, NEW BRUNSWICK. A bare couple of miles off Maine's northeastern tip and accessible in a few minutes by ferry from U.S. 1 are a pair of untouristed Canadian islands, which, together with larger Grand Manan, form that magnificently beautiful trio known as the Fundy Isles.

Deer Island, only a mile out across the sunlit waters of Passamaquoddy Bay from Eastport, Maine, is a smaller facsimile of Grand Manan. Smallest of the three, and perhaps the most delightful, its hills and dales have long earned for Deer Island the title "Little Scotland of the Maritimes." Bold seascapes shelter picturesque fishing harbors like Chocolate, Lords, and Cummings Coves, where fishermen toil to fill the largest lobster pounds on earth. Offshore, enormous tides cause the phenomenal Great Whirlpools which have made Deer Island famous for deep sea fishing.

Twenty miles of road, 8 of which are paved, wind over the hills, with superb sea views, to sunny beaches and picnic spots like that on the island's tip overlooking Old Sow, a whirlpool second in size only to Norway's Maelstrom. Deer Island measures 7½ miles long by 3 miles wide and snug harbors and beaches alternate along its 17 miles of rugged coast.

Campobello Island, two miles away, was chosen by the late President Franklin Roosevelt as site of his summer home. Scenery is less rugged, but you'll discover flawless beaches with names like Herring Cove, Mallock, and Bull Dog Beach, and pollack swarm in island waters. Several wealthy American families maintain summer homes here. But despite a new bridge linking Campobello to Lubec, Maine, both islands are completely unspoiled, the hardy fisherfolk inhabitants hospitable and warmly sincere. In every other way, the islands resemble Grand Manan.

Picturesque spots like beautiful East Quoddy Light, and great rocks like the Sugar Loaves and Bording Stones, abound on diminutive 9 x 3 mile Campobello Island. There's a lot of history too: besides the Roosevelt home built by James Roosevelt in 1880 and usually open to summer visitors, you can see the remains of Benedict Arnold's house at Snug Cove and various places associated with the Acadian expulsion and English loyalist settlement.

Places to stay? On Campobello Island, Gen's Tourist Home, Sol Aqua Motel, the Ponderosa Motel and Head Harbour Haven provide comfortable accommodations at prices ranging from $40-$70 a week for two, meals extra. On Deer Island, the Private Home at Lord's Cove charges $7 a day for two while the Forty-fifth Parallel Motel at Fairhaven charges slightly more. Elsewhere, housewives on both islands provide inexpensive room and board and Deer Island has a restaurant; huge New England style shore dinners cost about $2.25. If you arrive early in the season, you can probably rent one of a handful of modern housekeeping cabins for around $40 a week, or an older one for $30; substantial discounts apply by the month. For a longer stay you may be able to rent a house, or even buy one outright at a reasonably low price. Several Americans have discovered ideal retirement living on the islands at moderately low cost. But don't go at *any* time of year without prearranged accommodations. Deer Island has a beautiful campground.

You reach Campobello Island by the 900-yard bridge from Lubec, Me. while Deer Island is served by a toll ferry from Eastport, Me. The islands are also served by ferries from the New Brunswick shore.

More information: Board of Trade, Campobello Island, N.B.; Deer Island Development Association. Cummings Cove, Deer Island, N.B., Canada.

SAN JUAN ISLANDS, WASHINGTON.

SAN JUAN ISLANDS, WASHINGTON. Ninety miles north of Seattle, America's loveliest island archipelago floats in a cool green sea between the snow-capped Cascades and the rugged Olympic Mountains. The 475 isles range from tiny Robinson Crusoe dots to wooded, mountainous islands webbed by waterways and cut by crooked inlets alive with salmon. Over 170 of the velvet green islands bear names. Some have fiords that rival Norway's and most have driftwood-cluttered beaches dense with clams and scuttling crabs. From the islands' ragged edges countless inlets wind back to inviting beaches and half-hidden harbors and there are thousands of sheltered coves and quiet bays green the year around with twisted madronas, windswept junipers, and huge Douglas firs.

Although there's a boom in retirement and summer homes, outside the summer tourist season, the islands haven't changed too much since the British flag last waved over American soil here in 1872. Spanish explorer Francisco Elisa discovered the islands in the late 1700's and gave them their Spanish names: Orcas, Lopez, San Juan, and Guemes. Then both the British and Americans laid claim until 1872 when the German Emperor, acting as arbitrator, turned them over to Washington State. Today, old fashioned general stores selling everything from wood stoves to skin diving equipment still do business in every settlement, and you'll meet many an old pioneer ready to spin yarns of the islands' earlier days. Except in July and August, the islands are still thankfully free of the noise, crowds and turmoil of the mainland.

Social life centers around beach clam fries and salmon barbecues, favorite summer night pastime. Only on Saturday nights when everyone gets together for a traditional island square dance, does life depart from its usual leisurely tempo. Peace and seclusion in this enchanting setting are valued more than money. Although a short season and extra freight rates tend to raise costs, no prices are really high. Every resort gives one day's stay free each week.

Housekeeping cabins, averaging $75-$95 a week for four, let you live close to nature and you can take woodland walks, camera-hunt deer and seals, visit Indian reservations, and comb unlimited miles of shore for bright shells and driftwood, big glass fish floats, purple starfish, and sparkling agates. At low tide, vast uncovered expanses of kelp bed and reefs reveal such curious undersea creatures as red sea cucumbers and sea plumes, green chitons, jellyfish, and spiny sea urchins. You can dig big butter clams for frying or chowder and squirting clams for steaming or catch delicious crabs. Apples, strawberries, and blackberries abound all over the islands. Approximately 100 miles of scenic drives honeycomb each of the three larger islands and with your car you can view spectacular seascapes and visit fascinating historical spots.

But the big draw is fishing. Salmon, cod, red snapper, sea bass, and halibut are here in abundance. A $4 license lets you troll for the big fighting kings and silver salmon and to jig for cod and ling over the deep kelp beds. Outboard powered boats rent quite inexpensively. And with a boat you can also explore scores of uninhabited islands such as the idyllic Sucias only two miles off larger Orcas Island. Skin diving in the clear island waters, mountain climbing on the larger islands, studying the 170 species of birds, and shopping for island handicrafts are other pastimes. General stores sell Indian moccasins, baskets, Indian rugs, ceramics, ivory jewelry, fish spoons, and knit sweaters, all made by local Lummi Indians or island craftsmen, and economically priced.

Large auto-carrying ferries serve the principal islands and if you come by car, you can choose from half a dozen. Aboard the mailboat MV *Bristol* you'll call at several smaller islands in addition. Each island has its own special flavor, scenery, and charm. So to help you pick your own special island, here is a brief report on each.

Lopez Island (29.45 square miles). This is a smaller off-beat island with gently sloping beaches and a spectacular shore line of rocky crags indented with picturesque bays. Flatter than most of the islands, Lopez nonetheless offers incomparable views of the majestic Olympic Range. Fertile valleys inland support dairy and chicken farms; the air-clear waters are superb for skin diving and the island has a nine hole golf course. Lopez has no towns but color-packed Mackay Harbor is home port for the island's fishing fleet. You'll find camp sites at Odlin Park.

Principal resort here is Pantley's, with accommodations ranging from a housekeeping unit for two at $91 a week to more expensive deluxe units. There are good opportunites for other, less expensive housekeeping cottages. Washington State Ferries serve Lopez from Anacortes, Washington, at $3.80 r.t. for car and driver, $1.70 per passenger. More information: Lopez Island Commercial Club, Lopez, Wash. 98261.

Orcas Island (56.92 square miles). The largest island with over one dozen resorts, Orcas is a picturesque horseshoe of wild, rugged beauty cut by a deep, ten-mile bay. Scenic roads traverse its valley forests to the Turtle Back Mountains and to scores of cozy bays and beaches of sand and pebble. Another road winds through the 6,000 primitive acres of Moran State Park to the 2,400-foot crest of Mount Constitution, claimed to have the second finest maritime panorama on earth. Five deep lakes are kept stocked with cutthroats and rainbows, and you can camp overnight at Cascade Lake, Mount Lake, or Doe Bay. Tiny communities like Deer Harbor, Olga, and Eastsound are popular for retirement and the island has a museum and 9-hole golf course. Orcas also has a movie house but on Saturday nights everyone heads for the Rosario Resort to dance in a one time millionaire's mansion.

With its art school and gallery and summer visitor trade, Orcas offers more accommodations, some with lower rates. Among places that are attractively priced are the Orcas Hotel and Outlook Inn, Glenwood Inn's housekeeping cottages and Beach Haven's housekeeping cottages on the rustic northwest shore, which are typically priced at $50-$70 a week. Other rates are similar and some places charge less. Washington State Ferries serve Orcas from Anacortes, Washington, at $5 r.t. for car and driver, $2.20 per passenger. The same ferries also operate from Sidney, British Columbia. More information: Orcas Island Chamber of Commerce, Eastsound, Wash. 98245.

San Juan Island (55.39 square miles). Site of Friday Harbor, the county seat, San Juan is an island of green, wooded hills and low mountains surrounded by a rugged cove-indented shore and deep blue water. Fragrant columbines, coralbells and blue camas lilies border 150 miles of highway leading past striking marine views to historic points like Deadman's Bay, Smallpox Point, and the old English blockhouse. Scores of fishing boats jostle in the busy port at Friday Harbor, which, with 800 people, is the largest town in the island group. Here are the only jail, sheriff, dentist, and hospital in the islands—but there's no traffic to bother you. Here, too, you can view a large collection of sea life in the University of Washington's Oceanography Laboratories.

All resorts are small, far removed from competitive city confusion, offer views of snow-capped mountains, and most are inexpensively priced. Washington State Ferries serve Friday Harbor from Anacortes at $6.80 r.t. for car and driver, $2.40 per passenger. Similar service operates from Sidney, British Columbia, and there is air service from Bellingham. More information: San Juan Island CoC, Friday Harbor, Wash.

Few people know it but the San Juans enjoy excellent weather from May until October. Smack in the middle of a rain shadow created by Mount Olympus, the islands receive less rainfall than New York City and more sunshine and less fog than almost any other part of the Pacific Nortwest coast. The Japanese Current keeps summers 10° cooler and winters 10° warmer than the neighboring mainland and the grass is green and flowers in bloom throughout the winter. Thus vacationing is attractive before June 1 and after Labor Day when all resorts cut rates by 10%-35%. During these months housekeeping cottages rent for as little as $100 a month and hotel rates come down to $80 double monthly per room. For still lower priced accommodation in private homes at any time of year, you should inquire at general stores.

Housekeeping isn't remarkably cheap but grade A eggs, apples and seafood are often quite attractively priced. Outside Friday Harbor, only beer and wine are sold, so it's best to bring your own bottle. Most larger islands now have golf clubs and riding stables.

The San Juans are noted for the longevity of their residents and are ideal for mildly active, invigorating retirement. A few older homes sell from $9-11,000, but most newcomers must build. Inland, tracts sell from $500-$1,500 an acre, waterfront lots from $3,000 up. Many retired educators and architects have chosen Lopez Island, where beach privileges are available to inland dwellers (not always the case elsewhere). Construction and grocery costs are slightly above those on the mainland but property taxes, auto insurance, clothing and electricity costs are low and gardens, orchards and fishing can substantially cut food bills. Too, many retirees find part-time work. Property in the interior of islands is still inexpensive and realtors list scores of farms, resorts, lots and acreage. By contrast, a modern two-bedroom home on beachfront will run $15,000 or more. With its growing summer visitor trade, the San Juan Islands need more fishing lodges, resorts and trailer parks—all ideal business opportunities for retirees. A splendid medical-dental center on Friday Harbor has made older citizens less dependent on mainland medical facilities.

A word of caution: the islands have become extremely popular in July and August. For a quiet. inexpensive vacation, we recommend visiting the San Juans only between Labor Day and June 15.

PRINCE EDWARD ISLAND, CANADA. Canada's smallest province is an incredible island crescent of gently sloping beaches with some of the warmest sea bathing this side of Florida, and prices so low that a family of four can spend a week in a farm guest home for as little as $120.

Reaching the island is easy. You simply drive aboard the big, luxurious ferry *Abegweit* at Cape Tormentine, New Brunswick. Half an hour later, out in the sparkling blue waters of Northumberland Straits, you thrill to the sight of the brilliant colors of Canada's Garden Isle. The shore is a solid band of sea-sculptured red: rugged windswept red cliffs and headlands shelter irregular bays and beaches. And topping the red as far as the eye can see stretches a multicolored patchwork quilt of waving green fields, white birches, fresh red earth, and tidy farms, all blending into an unforgettable landscape of sylvan perfection.

From the ferry you drive into a different world of tree-shaded highways meandering through a serene land of rural charm. The quiet Old World villages of neat homes and well-kept flower gardens remind you of England. Mile upon mile of wide sandy beaches backed by dunes are broken only by craggy headlands, guarded by pencil-thin lighthouses.

Jacques Cartier discovered the island for France in 1534. Two hundred years later the British deported the Acadians and in 1722, two thousand stocky Highlanders landed at Charlottetown, the capital, to colonize the island under Scottish lairds and chieftains. Even today you can find memorial cairns and all over the island, valleys and villages are named for places in Perthshire and Dumfries, Skye and the Hebrides. About 60% of the islanders are Scottish, the rest—mostly fishermen—are descendants of the French Acadians, and scattered here and there is a handful of surviving Mic-Mac Indians. Life by the sea in this pastoral paradise has created a unique and embarrassingly honest people. You'll find every islander gentle and open-hearted, without a trace of tension, and with the leisure to talk across the fence or to invite you out fishing.

Though Prince Edward Island measures only 140 miles long by 3 to 35 miles wide, and is Canada's most densely populated province, its low rolling landscapes are hardly overcrowded. Even the more frequented beaches, where lifeguards teach swimming, are never packed. But along Prince Edward Island's 1,100-mile sweep of gleaming shore are miles of magnificent undeveloped beaches so deserted you can claim them as your own "private" property for weeks on end. You'll find shells and driftwood in abundance and after a storm, you can gather armfuls of Irish moss.

It sounds unbelievable but off the island's shallow beaches, the sun-warmed surf averages 70° throughout the summer. Deep sea fishing is superb almost everywhere and most fishermen will take you out just for the asking. Picturesque paved roads and byways invite days of leisurely motor exploring to numerous points of historical interest and to a national park rich in associations with Green Gables farmhouse, immortalized by island authoress Lucy Maude Montgomery in her *Anne* of *Green Gables*. Roaming the quiet, peaceful squares of Charlottetown, you'll visit beautiful Victoria Park, the stately-spired St. Dunstan's Basilica, and the fine old colonial Government House.

Sea trout and rainbows swarm in island ponds and you can golf beside the sea on one of Canada's finest courses. Green fees total exactly $25 a week. Summer is the time for Highland Games and country fairs, while Old Home Week in Charlottetown means a round of horse and sulky racing with parimutuel betting. Not to be missed are Charlottetown's dignified Old Country shops. Local craftsmen turn out magnificent hooked rugs at $20-$30 and beautifully designed handmade quilts at $15-$20. At equally low prices you'll find Hudson Bay point blankets, oil paintings, wood carvings, and fine Spode, Wedgewood, and Royal Doulton English china. And for cultural entertainment, Charlottetown's Center Theater features a summer season of drama, ballet, opera and other toprung entertainment.

All accommodations are bargain priced. First class, though not deluxe, hotels at Brackley, Cavendish, Keppoch, and Stanhope beaches charge only $9-$16 daily single with meals. Elsewhere you stay in housekeeping cabins or cottages averaging $50-$75 per week. Or at still less cost you can stay in comfortable farm tourists homes serving typical island seafood and delicious home cooked meals, all for as little as $42-$49 weekly per person with meals. Not all these places have television, private baths, flushing toilets, and continuous hot water. But what they lack in modern gadgets is more than made up by the warm island hospitality and kingsized meals. Rates drop 10%-15% before June 1 and after Labor Day, when weather still is good. Summers are like New England's but cooler and less humid. You'll need blankets every night. Rain is slight, hayfever practically unknown, and the sun shines on every summer day.

Housekeeping costs are surprisingly low. Garden fresh vegetables are available all over the island and tasty strawberries and cream can be very inexpensive, especially at roadside garden centers. You'll find splendid campgrounds everywhere.

Prince Edward Island is a big hunk of sea-surrounded paradise dotted with a wide variety of tiny Edens. Choose the north coast if you like smooth sand beaches with dunes. Here you'll find the national park, its front a solid unbroken 25 miles of superb white sands. Famous beaches like Brackley, Cavendish, Dalvay, and Stanhope rank with the best on the entire Atlantic coast. For more rugged scenery you'll prefer the south coast. Here, too, are splendid beaches; Keppoch's is outstanding. To help you select a vacation paradise, here is our run down of Prince Edward Island's most alluring low-priced beauty spots.

Baltic is a small north shore community on Baltic River bordering Malpeque Bay. Capes shelter the sandy beaches and local tables groan under piles of oysters, home-made ice cream, home-baked cookies, rolls, pies, and dessert. The Cosy Corner Tourist Home on a large shady lawn near quiet beaches charges $49 a week per person including all meals.

Bedeque is a picturesque and hospitable rural community of fine farm homes near Summerside. Both the Tourist Home and Hav-a-Rest Tourist Home offer delightfully peaceful vacationing for just a few dollars a day.

Brackley Beach lies in the national park on one of the north shore's most attractive dune-backed beaches. Bathing is the warmest on P.E.I., and you can play golf and tennis or fish for trout. Full board at Brackley Beach Lodge, Edgewood Farm Tourist Home, and The Point Tourist Home runs approximately $35 a week.

Cascumpeque is a quiet rural spot on the North Shore, convenient to a broad strand fringing a sheltered bay. You can stay at Mrs. Jennie Thomas' Old Farm Home. However, no lunches are served.

Cavendish is one of the north shore's largest resorts with excellent beaches, tennis, and fishing. Here are Green Gables farmhouse and the storybook Green Gables golf course. Larger hotels charge from $70 weekly with board but the same thing at the McCoubrey Farm is only $45 a week.

Fortune, one of the island's real beauty spots, overlooks the ocean and beach. Summer homes here were for years the hideout of famous stage stars. You stay at a lodge that does you well for $7 a day including meals (or $42 a week).

Georgetown is a fishing village on a splendid natural harbor, famed for fishing, hunting, and swimming. For a magnificent view, from your window, of Brudenell Island, ancient burial place of Scottish settlers, rent a cottage at Island View Cottages at about $50 per week.

Kensington, strategically located near bathing, tennis and trout fishing, is site of several budget priced tourist homes which will "do you proud" for $98 weekly per couple, including all meals.

Keppoch, beautifully located on one of the south shore's finest terra cotta beaches, is home of the nicely appointed Keppoch Beach Hotel charging $100 a week for a 3-4 bedroom housekeeping cottage with fireplace (that's $16.50 a week apiece when shared among six people).

Little Sands looks out across lovely Northumberland Straits. Back of the beach is a sylvan land of rural simplicity. Best bet here is Glover's Tourist Home.

Margate, near Cavendish Beach, is known for its picturesque beauty. Several comfortable tourist homes charge $30 a week per couple or around $80 with meals.

Montague is an attractive town beside a sandy beach with tennis, boating, and unusually good trout fishing. A selection of tourist homes provides overnight accommodation or full board at rockbottom rates.

Murray Harbor, on the island's southeast corner, is the colorful home port for Prince Edward Island's fleet of graceful sailing schooners. There are good beaches and lots of seafood. Best bet here is a housekeeping unit cottage at $60 a week.

Murray River is one of Prince Edward Island's most flavorful villages. Local fishermen make a specialty of taking visitors out in their boats. A large two-bedroom cottage can be rented for only $50-$65 a week.

New Glasgow, noted for its tranquil charm, is one of Prince Edward Island's most celebrated beauty spots. The north shore beaches are just a short drive. A delightful spot to stay is the MacEdward Manor, on a hilltop overlooking a river, at $42 weekly with meals; several tourists homes charge less.

New London is known for its fine estuary views and proximity to the National Park and North Shore beaches. The New London Tourist Home, with trout fishing on the premises, charges $12-$14 daily for two with all meals and free picnic lunches and free horseback riding.

Rustico (North), also near the national park and uncrowded north shore beaches, is a quaint Acadian fishing village that delights painters. Hillside Lodge charges only $6 a day, including all meals, while several other tourist homes charge $5 a night per couple.

Sea View on the north shore, is widely known for splendid bathing and sea fishing. McKay's Farm (shady lawns, free boat) is a good buy.

Souris, a larger village with good fishing, faces one of the island's finest beaches. The Sea View Hotel, near the beach, is inexpensive and there are several tourist homes.

Stanhope, a larger resort bordering the National Park, has golf, tennis, fishing and good bathing. Kiloran Lodge provides splendid full board for $60 a week.

St. Peter's Bay, a delightful village amid beautiful scenery, with fishing and swimming nearby. For a restful week on a typical island farm, try Kendoral Farm, which charges $6 daily for two.

Summerside, with 9,700 people, is the western capital of Prince Edward Island, a busy shopping center and home of the silver fox fur industry. An ancient Scottish kirk looks out over beautiful Bedeque Bay and there are golf, tennis, bowling, dancing, and sailing. Hillcrest Lodge, near the beach, charges $24 weekly per couple and also takes trailers. Other guest homes, several located in the island's finest old homes—near beaches surrounded by tree-shaded lawns and often furnished with antiques—charge about $7 a day all inclusive.

Tignish, home of friendly French Acadian and Scottish lobstermen, is a picturesque village on Prince Edward Island's northern tip. There's a good beach two miles away and Gaudet's Lodge, famed for home cooking and seafood, charges very reasonable rates.

Tea Hill, with a sweeping view of Northumberland Strait and near a splendid South Shore beach, also lies conveniently near Charlottetown. There are tourist homes in the area.

Tyne Valley is a beautiful village touched by an arm of the sea from Malpeque Bay.

Victoria is a restful, unspoiled village with rich red beaches, green coves, and big trees looking out across blue Northumberland Straits. Local hostelries are famous for lobsters and seafood. Tourist homes like Dunrovin charge around $40 a week or $125 a month with meals. In June and September, rates are only $80 a month with meals, October to June as low as $60 a month. Housekeeping cottages are $50 a week up in season.

For a longer stay on Prince Edward Island, you can, with some persistence, often turn up a small furnished home for $125 a month or even buy a retirement home for $4-7,000. Some, which can easily be renovated, sell for as little as $2,500. Land taxes are very small and if you want to live in style, you can hire a housemaid for $18-$21 a week.

Prince Edward Island, North America's largest and cheapest island paradise, is easily reached by car. Frequent ferries cross from Cape Tormentine, New Brunswick, to Port Borden, and from Caribou, Nova Scotia, to Wood Island (fare $3.00 round trip). Bus tickets can be bought straight through to Summerside or Charlottetown. By train, ask for a ticket through to Prince Edward Island via the Canadian National Railway. Or by air, you make connection with island planes at Moncton, New Brunswick or at Halifax, Nova Scotia.

More information: Prince Edward Island Travel Bureau, Charlottetown, P.E.I., Canada.

MANITOULIN ISLAND, ONTARIO. Well known to sports fishermen but almost entirely overlooked by the average vacationing family, this world's largest fresh-water island on Lake Huron's rugged north shore, offers a wonderful back-to-nature family vacation at fishing camp prices.

Manitoulin, which means "Home of the Great Spirit" in Indian, is more often called "Island of a Hundred Lakes." Within its 100 x 40 mile confines are scores of cold, clear streams and spring-fed lakes. Towering white cliffs and pineclad headlands are the only breaks in miles of hardpacked white beach. Offshore, a galaxy of balsam-scented islands invites the picnicker and camper.

Manitoulin is definitely Northwoods. Rural villages nestle among groves of cedar and white birch and scenic mountain roads wind past Indian reservations, burial grounds, and Indian schools and churches. Picturesque Indian customs handed down for centuries still persist and islanders, who have never regarded fishermen as tourists and regard all tourists as fishermen, always have time to sit down and talk.

Fishing, of course, tops all pastimes. Probably nowhere else in America can you find a greater population of tackle-smashing black bass, pike, lake and speckled trout, or walleyes than in the island's well stocked lakes and bays. But you can use the same fishermens' boats, which rent for $2-$2.50 a day with oars or $6-$7.50 a day with motors, for family fun and picnics. Saddle horses can also be rented and in the towns of Gore Bay and Little Current, stores carry imported English china and woolens along with fishing tackle and mackinaws.

News is something that comes over the radio from mainland centers. Nothing of headline importance has happened on Manitoulin since 1952, when archeologists found the island to be the site of one of North America's oldest Indian civilizations. In some respects, Manitoulin has a look of New England, albeit on a more rugged scale. Fishing villages, sandy beaches, lighthouses, ancient clapboard churches and hidden coves such as might be seen in Cape Cod or Maine are all part of the Manitoulin scene.

Whether you want to write a book or take the whole family for a secluded vacation among magnificent scenery, Manitoulin's water-edge housekeeping cottages are ideal. You'll find scores accommodating four persons at $40-$65 a week, often with a boat included. Some rent for $35. And there are plenty of fishing camps with many of the features of resort hotels, where room and stupendous meals are yours for $8-$10 per person per day or $50-$65 a week. You can also camp at Indian Point Park on Bayfield Sound.

A novel place to stay is on Treasure Island—an island within an island—in Manitoulin's Lake Mindemoya. Weekly rate for a fireplace cottage with all meals is $80.

Manitoulin's balmiest summer weather comes from June 15 to September 15. Hayfever is unknown and the unfailing lake breezes keep black flies and mosquitoes down to almost zero.

By car you can reach Manitoulin Island via the auto ferry from Tobermory or from Canadian Highway 17 on Lake Huron's north shore. There is also direct air service to Gore Bay and train service to Little Current.

More information: Ontario Department of Tourism & Information, 185 Bloor Street East, Toronto, Ont.; also Manitoulin-Espanola Regional Tourist Council, Box 429, Little Current, Ont.

GULF ISLANDS, BRITISH COLUMBIA. In case you've never heard of British Columbia's enchanting Gulf Islands, you'll find them on your atlas clustered in Georgia Strait between Vancouver and Victoria. Dozens of islands compose this forested archipelago—actually an English-flavored extension of our own San Juan Islands. There are scores of tiny islands entirely uninhabited and a round dozen larger, timbered islands where blue wood smoke rising from small seaside settlements is often the only visible evidence of human habitation. Yet tucked away in virgin woodlands beside long silvery beaches are lone guest houses and lodges where you can find peaceful seclusion at surprisingly low cost.

The Gulf Islands are very, very English. Long associated with British Navy men, the island's place names—Trincomalee, Ganges, Thetis, and Hornby—were taken from ships, stations, and admirals, of Her Majesty's Navy. Salty retired captains and commanders run island farms and guest houses and while avid tea drinkers, they're equally partial to a tot of grog. Whether you like tranquil seclusion or prefer to mingle with gay little groups of vacationing doctors and professors, the Gulf Islands are large and varied enough for you to do both, or anything in between. And at all times you'll be surrounded by myriad bays and coves, and a panorama of ships passing through rippling green waters below a backdrop of Vancouver Island's majestic peaks.

Bring your strongest fishing gear. From June until October island waters swarm with big spring, blueback, and cohoe salmon lusting for battle. Cod, sole, and flounder are found inshore, and inland are mountain lakes crammed with record sized cutthroats and small-mouth bass. Surprisingly, too, most of the larger islands have tricky 9-hole golf courses and tennis is universally played. Scores of woodland trails wind for miles to mountaintops and shorewards, to secluded bays and driftwood-scattered beaches, where big clams squirt jets of water in defiance at your approach.

Overtones of English social life don't mean you'll need a letter of introduction to be accepted. On these small islands, which accommodate only a few dozen visitors at most, you are automatically invited to Old World garden parties and to the more familiar wiener roasts and beach barbecues which are standard fare. Shops on the larger islands, and even general stores on the smallest island, carry fine English bone china and a choice of island pottery, handmade handkerchiefs, moccasins, handwoven scarves, and jewelry at prices lower than any you'll find at home.

If anything the climate here is superior to Victoria's much lauded weather. The Gulf Islands are so sunny, Canadians call them "The Poor Man's Caribbean." Off the beaches, water temperatures range in summer from 70°-80°. Otherwise the climate is similar to that of Vancouver Island, but the Gulf Islands are milder in winter and off-season rates are lower. Pollen and mosquitoes are not unknown but are seldom bothersome.

Accommodations range from modern deluxe lodges and cabins to rustic farm cottages with outside plumbing and wood-burning cook-stoves. But one and all share magnificent views, and many professional couples who return to the islands summer after summer prefer the more rustic accommodations. Island cooks are famous for their home-cooked bread, rolls, hot muffins, oysters, clams, and rich cream and you'll eat as well in farmhouses as in the plusher lodges. Despite haulage costs, groceries aren't really high while lamb and poultry are often quite inexpensive.

Each of these "Islands of the Pacfic" has its own individual character and its differently assorted accommodations. Here are the highlights of each.

Bowen Island lies off the Canadian Coast an easy 25 minutes by car and ferry from Vancouver. Though Bowen is more frequented, it remains unspoiled. Here are waterfront subdivisions like Snug Point with attractive cottage homes from $4-10,000. The Evergreen Park Resort has cottages from $60 a week or from $500 for the entire summer.

Denman Island is a heavily forested isle with fine shell beaches and winding rustic trails. It's a mile off Vancouver Island with spectacular moutain views. Two hundred people, including many retirees, live here and there's a well-stocked general store. At Hadley's Beach Cabins on Metcalfe Bay, large rustic log housekeeping cabins are $30 a week.

Gabriola Island opposite Nanaimo on Vancouver Island, is a sylvan isle of rural charm. Rates at the rustic Surf Lodge are $126-$138 weekly per couple, including all meals; Taylor Bay Lodge is modern and charges $117-$138 weekly for two, all meals included.

Galiano Island is a paradisaical spot famed for its shallow sandy beaches, surf boarding, sweeping vistas, warm tidal pools, salmon fishing and golf. You can enjoy a week at Galiano Lodge, which charges $175 weekly for two, including excellent meals and a free rowboat. Each of the modern motel type units has a private bath and a picture window with a view of Active Pass.

Hornby Island is 24 square miles of silent beauty. Mountainous bluffs fall away through a carpet of evergreens, orchards, and berry patches to broad silvery beaches lined with weird sandstone formations, caves, and Sphinx-like rocks. One beach is rich in fossils, and pine-carpeted trails lead to Indian heiroglyphics and to brooding glens where timid deer hide. Thirty families live on Hornby, which has two stores and a cafe. You'll find pleasant semi-rustic cottage accommodations at Sea Breeze for only $120 a week for two with all meals. Or for $50-$65 a week, you can rent a well equipped housekeeping cottage at Shingle Spit Resort, Cottage Tribune, or Whaling Station Bay Resort.

Mayne Island is location of beautiful Bennett Beach and two resorts with average rates.

The Pender Islands, exceptionally restful, have alluring beaches and a store. The Maples guest house beside the beach charges only $42 single or $75 double weekly including meals.

Salt Spring Island, the largest, is dominated by Mount Maxwell Provincial Park. Magnificent seascapes are seen from its 2,000-foot high peak, accessible over part of the island's 100-mile highway network. Eleven beautiful lakes include 600-acre Lake Mary, one of British Columbia's best fishing spots. At Ganges, the principal town, are shops, a beer parlor, a community hall holding weekend dances, golf, and a yacht marina with swimming pool.

Accommodations are varied. Informal Harbour House on Ganges Harbour charges $135-$150 weekly for two with all meals. Booth Bay Resort near Ganges offers nicely equipped housekeeping cottages for two at $70 a week. Smaller housekeeping cabins are available at St. Mary's Lake Resort at $65 a week, larger ones up to $95 a week, with a 33% reduction in the off-season. Arbutus Court is another resort with housekeeping units at $70 a week, less off-season. Then there's Vesuvius Lodge, with rates as low as $5 a day. Other inexpensive places to stay include the tiny Ship's Anchor overlooking Ganges Harbour, Rainbow Beach Resort on Booth Bay, and the Cottage Resort and Blue Gables Resort at St. Mary Lake.

Savary Island bears an undeniable resemblance to Hawaii. Long reefs with breakers shelter blue lagoons and tall lacy ferns crowd the miles of dazzling beach completely encircling the island. Though this is the most northerly of the archipelago, the water is amazingly warm. And stimulated by the presence of the lively Royal Savary Hotel, the island is a gay little paradise. There are clambakes most evenings and dancing follows. Part of the hotel's 1,000 acres includes a beach golf course with long fairways for which guests pay no green fees—golf clubs and golf lessons are free, too. All this is yours for a weekly rate of about $115 per person with meals. You can drive to Savary Island. From Vancouver, take the hourly Horseshoe Bay-Langdale ferry and follow the dramatically scenic highway via Jervis Inlet and Powell River to Lund, where you park your car and transfer to a launch. Alternatively, take the ferry which sails from Comox, Vancouver Island, across the Strait of Georgia.

The Gulf Islands draw as many retirees as Washington's San Juans. Modern permanent retirement homes are springing up all over the islands, especially on Salt Spring. All have impressive sea views and on Salt Spring at least, all city amenities, including a good hospital, doctors, a dental clinic, churches of all denominations, and good schools. Milk, eggs, butter, meats and fresh vegetables are produced on all the islands; other costs are about the same as, or slightly lower than, on Vancouver Island. But even the remotest island is served by frequent and inexpensive ferries with connections to the mainland in under two hours.

Car-carrying ferries from Swartz Bay and Crofton, Vancouver Island, provide a 30-minute link with Salt Spring, Mayne, Pender and Galiano Islands, and similar ferries operate from Nanaimo, Vancouver Island, to Gabriola Island. Denman Island is served by ferry from Buckley Bay, Vancouver Island, and Hornby Island is reached by an onward ferry from Denman. Fares average $6 r.t. and about $10 r.t. for your car.

More information: for Salt Spring, write Salt Spring CoC, Ganges, B.C.; for other islands, address the accommodations mentioned, followed by name of island, British Columbia, Canada.

VANCOUVER ISLAND, BRITISH COLUMBIA. Up in the Pacific Northwest where majestic scenery is routine, Vancouver Island ranks with the outstanding—an entire continent in miniature and one of the most fabulous islands in the whole of North America. Within its 282 x 55 mile expanse, you'll discover long, sinuous fiords, at least one thousand coves and as many miles of sandy beaches, deep cool forests and placid lakes, snow-capped mountains and an incredible pink snowfield, dashing waterfalls and high alpine meadows, primitive Indian villages and roaring logging camps, and in the south a pastoral countryside reminiscent of Devonshire with a sedate, unhurried capital city straight out of Sussex.

Everywhere there's an ageless charm. From the long Pacific rollers bursting in white plumes of spray against the rugged west coast, to the long graceful sweep of the placid east coast beaches, nature's artistry has carved an island of matchless scenery enhanced by far-reaching views of Mount Baker and the snow peaked Olympics. So varied, so spacious is Vancouver Island, that inevitably, somewhere along its timbered shores or in its miniature glaciated Rockies, you can find a Utopia exactly tailored to your dreams. Your choice can run the whole gamut from the big, beautiful city of Victoria to rustic housekeeping cabins out of sight and sound of civilization. And though there are deluxe hotels, you'll also find comfortable housekeeping cottages for $50 a week and cozy inns with cheerful log fires and unlimited food for $50 and up weekly all inclusive.

Nowhere are you more than yards from water. And you can bet that water is teeming with fish. All summer, salmon up to 70 pounds swarm along the coasts, and inland the mountain-girded lakes are crammed with lusty rainbows and fighting cutthroats. Fishing is free in salt water; a freshwater license costs $10. Wherever you stay on the shore, you can rake tasty clams, swim in cool but not cold waters, and for something unusual, beachcomb the sands on bicycles. Up-Island, that is outside Victoria, horses rent for $2 an hour and you can golf on a choice of the greenest courses on this continent. Day-long sea cruises operate out of most places, taking you through a maze of clustered islets and long, winding fiords. A thousand miles of breathtakingly beautiful highway take you to historic totem poles, weird petroglyphics, and world famous flower gardens. And with a few dollars left over, you can explore Victoria's old fashioned Fort Street shops for buys in British woolens, tweeds, plaids, and tartans; Indian-made or cashmere sweaters; and totem poles, jewelry, English china, and leather at prices far below those you'd pay at home.

Surprisingly, while most of Vancouver Island lies north of the United States, its winters are milder than in all but our southernmost states. Victoria on the dry eastern shore, receives barely two thirds of New York's rainfall. Actual temperatures average 41° in January and 63° in August. Thus on the drier eastern shore you can enjoy a pleasant, uncrowded vacation in the weeks preceding June 1 or after Labor Day when most places reduce rates 10% or more. Victoria—where roses bloom in January—boasts six hours of sunshine every day in the year and though mornings are misty, you can soak up a good tan by noon.

Accommodations range from beach resorts to lakeshore lodges and from gleaming motels to informal cabin camps ideal for relaxing. You won't encounter crowds but some places have only a handful of rooms or cabins, so be sure to reserve well ahead in July and August. For camping, there are improved camp-sites at many favorite beauty spots and in provincial parks at Elk Falls on Campbell River, at Miracle Beach looking out over the Gulf Islands, and at Englishman River Falls. Park sites are $1 per night during the summer months.

It would take an entire book to catalog all the islands' potential Edens but to help you choose, here are a few places combining unparalled beauty with inexpensive costs. Most places give substantial weekly and monthly reductions.

Upper and Lower Campbell Lakes, on the east shore Up-Island, offer an unspoiled mountain and lake wilderness. If you can possibly afford it, stay at Forbes Lodge, which charges $21.50 daily or $140 double weekly with meals. Housekeeping cottages are $7.50 a day.

Campbell River is 21 miles east. Sturdy seiners and trollers dot the harbor against a spellbinding background of densely forested mountains. Mackinawed loggers stroll the village streets and nearby is excellent stream and river fishing. Just offshore at Quathiasca Cove on Quadra Island you'll find April Point Resort with a lodge, apartments, and housekeeping cabins from $34 daily for two, all meals included; elsewhere, housekeeping cottages can be had for $40 a week.

Comox, also on the eastern shore, flanks a flawless sweep of safe, clean beach in a thriving logging region. There's excellent salmon fishing all summer, boating and golf, and it's just a short drive to the fantastic mountain and lake scenery of Forbidden Plateau. At Radfords on the Sea you can rent a spacious beach housekeeping cottage for $63 a week, a cottage for four at $77.

Cowichan Bay is noted for the charming Old Country atmosphere of Cowichan Bay Inn. Rates: $8 for two overnight.

Ladysmith, on the east shore, among poetic coves and white shell beaches, is famed for succulent oysters. One hundred dollars a week covers all expenses for two at Manana Seaside Lodge on an inlet 3 miles north, and $144 weekly is enough for two at Yellow Point Lodge, a delightful country home in a 200-acre seashore park. (For private baths you'll pay $166.) The tiny Driftwood Motel, overlooking the sea and Gulf Islands, gives good value at only $6 double per night.

Isle of Clayoquot: Pacific Coast Eden

Halfway up the wild west coast of Vancouver Island, lost in an incredible jigsaw of lochs, fiords, channels and hidden lakes, is a 140 acre chunk of Pacific Coast Eden. Only a few score people have ever landed on the Isle of Clayoquot. And no wonder! To get there at all, you must take the bus to Alberni on Vancouver Island, go by motor launch through the beautiful Alberni Canal to Ucluelet, taxi the length of 18-mile Long Beach to Tofino and then phone the Clayoquot Hotel to come and get you—a mile long crossing in the island boat. By car, you can drive as far as Tofino which is also served by air.

Whichever way you go, you'll never regret it. Clayoquot is an island for connoisseurs. An outpost of the British Commonwealth on the edge of the vastness of the real Pacific, Clayoquot has perfect ocean-laved sandy beaches, great surf washed rocks, and caves, coves, grassy banks and lovely trees. Snow clad mountains reach along the adjacent shore and each evening, the snow capped tops of Forbidden Plateau loom in the sunset-painted distance. Both Captain Cook and the early Spaniards considered Clayoquot the most enchanting of their discoveries and the Indians of last century chose the island to trade their sealskins to Hudson Bay Adventurers. As many as 100 war canoes lined the shore and you can still see the doors of the jail that took care of the miscreants of those early days.

You make your own amusements here, such as landing a ten pound salmon before breakfast—an everyday occurrence. Salmon fishing is superb and with a rented boat you can explore the nearby islands, lochs and fiords day after day. A delightful old country store serves the simple requirements of outdoor life.

But Clayoquot's biggest surprise is the modern little ten room hotel and several housekeeping cottages complete with lighting plant and efficient plumbing. All foodstuffs are fresh from the island's own farm and the home cooking is really delicious. Rates are $252 weekly for two with meals—a bit steep but worth it. Housekeeping cottages run $92 up weekly. For more information about Clayoquot (pronounced Clack-wuot) and how to get there, write: Mr. Robertson, Clayoquot Lodge, Tofino, B.C., Canada.

Long Beach, on the irregular west shore, possesses 12 miles of hard-packed sands 300 yards wide, all backed by lonely sand dunes and forests. Hiking trails meander to unsuspected bays, and you can dig razor clams, pan for gold, fish for trout, and hunt up Indian relics. Long Beach is reached via a wonderfully scenic 4½-hour cruise through Alberni and Barkley Sounds on the M.V. *Uchuck* from Port Alberni, fare $9 r.t. Singing Sands Camp offers six inexpensive cottages at $25 a week or $75 a month while Ucluelet Lodge charges only $5 a night per couple and housekeeping cabins for 2-4 people at Surfview Cabins are only $35-$40.

Qualicum Beach, a larger resort on the east shore, offers a long, gracefully curving beach with inspiring views of the tumbled mainland mountains. Inexpensive rooms are available at the Qualicum Arms Inn, which has beautiful views and its own beach, and also at Fishermen's Cove Lodge, Buena Vista, Rosewell Court, St. Andrews Lodge and Riverside Motel. For inexpensive housekeeping cabins, try Miles Haven, Oceanside, Seaview Auto Camp and Sherwood Camp.

Parksville, on the east shore, is famed for its long sweeping beach, warm bathing, sparkling mountain vistas, and tidal pools. Several hostelries rent housekeeping cottages at attractive prices.

Victoria, with a population of 250,000, is a bustling seaport surrounded by some of the most leisurely and exquisite suburbs on this planet. An alluring resort itself, the city slopes down to beaches on the south and east and dips into storybook countryside on the north and west. There are endless green lawns and flower beds ablaze with color and Old World baskets of gay annuals hang from every lamp post. Butchart Gardens, the largest, simply bankrupts the vocabularly. If you prefer an urban setting, you can live a unique chapter of your life in this most English of North American cities. Despite its high rise motor hotels, Victoria is so English, in parts it's downright stuffy. For a sample, take afternoon tea and crumpets with the city's straight laced *dames* in the ornate dignity of the ivied Empress Hotel. But elsewhere you'll find the Victorian flavor tempered by a reserved and tea-drinking but more cordial people who, though sporting tweeds and tartans themselves, shun the more stuffy of English mores.

In Victoria you can swim, play golf all year on half a dozen challenging courses, sail, fish, ride, play tennis, or watch cricket. There are summer concerts in Beacon Park and music and dramatics at Butchart Gardens. By far the most atmospheric place to stay in town is Old England Inn, 429 Lampson St., a traditional antique-furnished Tudor inn charging $25 double daily with meals; guest houses charge less. Alternatively, you could live 40 minutes outside at a choice hostelry overlooking a sea inlet, where $100 weekly covers full room and board for two.

Vancouver Island, where an agreeable climate, floral beauty, and a scenic wonderland overlap, was made for retirement. Three-room unfurnished city apartments rent at $100-$135 a month. You can buy an older 2-bedroom home for $10-14,000. And Up-Island, $20,000 will get you a spacious 3-bedroom home on two acres of beautiful lawn with sweeping views of ocean and mountain. Other living costs ,are about the same as in the United States.

Reaching Vanouver Island involves a short sea voyage from either Seattle, Bellingham, Anacortes or Port Angeles in Washington, or from points north and south of Vancouver, British Columbia.

More information: Victoria Visitors Bureau, 786 Government St., Victoria, B.C.

ISLE ROYALE NATIONAL PARK, MICHIGAN. Every year some 140,000,000 people throng our National Parks, jamming facilities and camp grounds. Yet there's one park where you can still spend an enjoyable summer vacation far from the madding crowd. For Isle Royale National Park, a unique untouched wilderness island far out in Lake Superior, cannot be reached by car. There are no automobiles, no roads, no phones, and the only transportation is by boat. "The quiet solitude of wilderness trails, bracing air, and scenic vistas of wave-swept shores are soul-satisfying and will long be remembered," is how park authorities aptly describe it.

Isle Royale, actually an archipelago including 200 smaller islands, is a beautiful primitive North Woods wilderness isolated from the mainland by 15 miles of deep, blue Lake Superior waters. The isolation created by these waters is evident in every corner of the island and in its landscapes. Remains of prehistoric mining and varied wildlife and rare wild flowers make it utterly unlike any National Park you may have visited before. The fortress-like Rock of Ages lighthouse and others stand sentinel over its stark rocks and reefs and moose wander through the moss-carpeted forest.

Bring a boat if you have one. There are over 200 smaller islands to explore or you can troll for giant lake trout over reefs seldom fished. You can hold a family fish fry amid the complete privacy of enchanting tree-fringed bays just minutes from park headquarters. Easy trails lead to old Indian mining pits, where you can observe primeval hammer-stones, and to inland lakes, geological landmarks, delightfully remote harbors, and woodland dells verdant with lichens, moss, rare flowers, and the island's 36 varieties of orchids. No license is needed to fish for the pike, perch, walleye, trout or 40 other species of fish which swarm in island waters. More rugged hiking trails take you far into the interior, to strange lava and basalt ridges, and to the heights of Ishpeming Point 775 feet above the lake. There are also sightseeing boat cruises, conducted nature walks, and illustrated evening lectures at Rock Harbor Lodge and Windigo Inn.

Summer temperatures rarely go above 80° and nights are refreshingly cool. You'll need a light raincoat for occasional showers and mosquito repellent for walks in the woods. Throughout the park season, early May through October, Isle Royale is a haven from hayfever.

Camping is the best and cheapest way to enjoy this untrammelled beauty spot. Twenty-two improved campgrounds dot the island and most have three-sided, screened sleeping shelters. But it's still advisable to bring a tent. An abundance of fish and wild berries is there for the taking but, otherwise, only staples are sold and if you're preparing your own meals, you should bring foodstuffs with you. Modern housekeeping units at Rock Harbor Lodge, overlooking Rock Harbor, cost $105 a week for two. The lodge also provides plush accommodation and all meals at $32 daily for two (but only $27 if you stay at the plainer guest house). At Windigo Inn on the southwest coast, the same thing costs $26-$28 a day. Advance reservations are required.

Three boat services link Isle Royale with the mainland. Thrice weekly the 165' motor vessel *Ranger III* sails from Houghton, Mich., for the 5-hour voyage; fare is $15.00 r.t., and small boats are carried at extra charge. The 60' *Isle Royal Queen II* sails daily from Copper Harbor, Mich., making a round trip; fare is $14 r.t. per passenger and $10 r.t. for boats. Or you can go via a daily 64' launch from Grand Portage, Minn., to Windigo Inn. Another boat, the *Voyageur*, leaves twice weekly to circle the island. Cars can be left at any of these departure points and mail is delivered on the island thrice weekly. Houghton, Michigan, is the most convenient departure point if coming by public transportation. Seaplane service is also available.

More information (including ferry schedules): The Superintendent, Isle Royale National Park, 87 North Ripley St., Houghton, Mich. 49931.

HECLA ISLAND, MANITOBA.

HECLA ISLAND, MANITOBA. When Iceland's Mount Hecla erupted in 1873, a flood of lava and drift ashes buried miles of the finest pasture. The remaining land could not support the population. Some of the people had to leave.

The first emigrants settled in Ontario but in 1875, they pushed west seeking a country more like their own. And on Lake Winnipeg's western shore they found it. At Willow Point, in a broad bay rimmed by white sand beaches, they established their colony and called it Gimli (Paradise). Today, the town of Gimli is center of the world's largest Icelandic settlement outside Iceland and 60 miles to the north is Hecla Island, commemorating in name the disaster of 1873.

Hecla projects like a thin finger of rock, 15 miles long and 3 miles wide, into the vast expanse of Lake Winnipeg. The southern tip flanks the west shore near the town of Riverton, 100 miles north of Winnipeg. The northern extremity at Gull Harbor, a quaint fishing village, parallels the south shore of Black Island. Together they form a barrier between the south and north arms of Lake Winnipeg.

Hecla Island is thickly studded with pine, spruce and balsam with here and there some vagrant stands of birch and poplar. Sandy beaches, broad and white, sweep inland to the tree line. In summer, lazy waves wash in. But in early spring and fall, giant rollers assault the limestone cliffs. Bays, inlets and shallows, rimmed with wild rice and marsh grass, punctuate the shoreline and here, mallards, canvas-backs, Canada geese, and a score of varieties of waterfowl nest and feed.

Through the middle of the island winds a motor road. Thus it is now possible to travel from your own home anywhere in North America, right to the doorstep of Gull Harbor Lodge at Hecla's northern tip. Here, Helgi Jones (short for Jonasson) jolly proprietor of the only visitor's lodge on the island, meets you with the traditional Icelandic greeting, "Velkomin"—Welcome and dwell happily among us.

Sports fishing in Hecla waters is good. There are quiet bays on either shoreline which afford excellent wind cover, and in which dwell over-sized northern pike, walleyes, goldeyes, mooneyes, saugers and perch and where even an occasional whitefish will rise to a plug or bait.

You'll find a variety of outdoor activities available at Gull Harbor Lodge. Swimming, boating, picknicking, motor boat excursions, sun-bathing and hiking are favored pursuits and there are frequent island-style dances at Hecla village five miles south. Gull Harbor Lodge provides all the comforts of home. Housekeeping cabins run $35 a week for two or $45 for four people with children accommodated free. Each cabin has electric light, stove, refrigerator and wood. Alternatively, you can camp at the Government operated campground.

You can drive to Gull Harbor over hard surfaced highway No. 8 north from Winnipeg as far as Arnes. The remaining twenty-five miles to the ferry landing are on all-weather provincial roads No. 234 and No. 233.

More information: Tourist Branch, Department of Tourism & Recreation, 408 Norqua Bldg., Winnipeg 1, Manitoba, Canada.

BONAVENTURE ISLAND,QUEBEC. Just $2\frac{1}{2}$ miles from the silver sands of Percé off the very tip of Gaspé's rugged sea-carved peninsula, is an island eternally crowned with a white mantle of seabirds. Literally millions of gannets, puffins, auks and guillemots cloud the peaks and are forever circling the ledges of Bonaventure Island.

Today, the island is a paradise for birdwatchers and photographers. But centuries ago, swashbuckling French privateer Pierre Duval made Bonaventure home base for raids on passing French ships, and the first mission church was built here in the early 1600s. Meandering footpaths still lead to historic farms and scattered ancient buildings; others wind along clifftops carpeted with wild flowers to secluded beaches with magnificent bathing. You can ramble right around the island's 12 mile circumference and no two views are exactly alike. Apart from a few farmers and a handful of summer residents, the whole island belongs to the birds and the fortunate guests of the Hotel Ile Bonaventure.

The hotel—a Utopia *par excellence*—certainly lives up to its slogan: "We believe in the wisdom of nature's design." From the dining room high above the water, captivating seascapes reach in every direction: to Gaspé's green mountains, red-roofed Percé village, and the huge bulk of Pierced Rock. You can choose between double rooms without bath at $8 a day, a private cottage for two at $12, or a larger room for five people, furnished with antiques and overlooking the sea, at $18. Meals are priced from $1.50-$4. Mother does the cooking and seafood delicacies—fresh salmon, lobster, and Grand Banks cod—are standard daily treats. Every bit of the hotel's rustic furniture was handmade on the island and each evening a cheery log fire blazes in the huge lounge. Boating, fishing and hiking trips are planned each day for guests. You can also view the birds on daily carriage rides or ride around the island in an old fashioned horsedrawn straw cart.

To reach the island, simply drive to Percé, leave your car at the Robin, Jones and Whitman service station, and board a launch which regularly ferries passengers across in a ten-minute ride. The hotel, sole island accommodation, is open from June 1-September 30.

More information: Hotel Ile Bonaventure, Bonaventure Island, Gaspé, Quebec, Canada.

APOSTLE ISLANDS, WISCONSIN. Clustered in southern Lake Superior are the 22 historic Apostle Islands ... the enchanting isles of Ketchi Gamme. Ranging in size from a few acres to the 14 x 3 mile expanse of Madeline Island, the Apostles are rimmed by driftwood littered beaches and studded with ruined lighthouses and ancient Indian cemeteries. In tiny island fishing villages that remind you of Nova Scotia, you'll discover a complete sense of detachment from everyday life.

From time immemorial, the islands were the cradle of the Ojibway Indians. Then in the early days, French explorers who spotted only a dozen of the group, gave them their name. French missionaries followed and the islands became fortified strongholds for the expanding fur trade. Eventually, the Apostles passed from French to British and American hands and in 1819 served as headquarters for the Astor fur empire. Next came the Lakes shipping boom and British and Scandinavian captains settled in the islands. Not until half a century ago did the Apostles first attract visitors, a colony of Nebraskans whose dignifed mansions still stand on Madeline Island's Nebraska Row. Today's islanders, a mixture of all these, are still largely Indian, French and English—an embarrassingly honest people always ready to stop and pass the time of day.

Nowadays, Madeline holds immense appeal for individual artists and camera enthusiasts. Organized painting classes are also sponsored by an amateur group which returns to the island each summer for an idyllic two-week work session.

No art colony has ever spoiled its environment and the Apostle art group is no exception. Commercialism has yet to intrude and Madeline, the only island with roads, is still pleasingly free of traffic or noise. Three jolly little night-time gathering spots exist but neon-lit niteries are noticeably absent. In fact, only 150 people live in La Pointe, Madeline Island's only village, and other islands are inhabited only by scattered fishing camps and roving bears.

Best way to know the Apostles is to take the daily excursion boat during summer or fall out of Bayfield, on the mainland opposite La Pointe. For a fare of about $3.00, stops are made at several fishing camps among the islands; coffee and sandwiches are available at the Rocky Island Fishing Camp. Only in this way can you begin to appreciate the islands' wild and primitive beauty, their varied rocky shorelines, the miles of beautiful sand beach, and the flavor of the past that lingers everywhere. Over 1,200 deer roam on Madeline and other islands are the haunts of bear and smaller game.

Things to do on Madeline? You can comb the beaches for decorative driftwood, hike or ride horseback over forest trails, play golf or tennis, explore sandstone caves, and hunt for easily-discovered arrowheads and French and Indian relics. Utterly unique are the Ojibway cemeteries, each grave protected by a wooden roof and picket fence. The Museum and Craftshop are always worth seeing and you can bring your car and tour uncrowded roads.

All this can be yours at a flat weekly rate of $100-$135 in July and August or just $100 in June and after Labor Day. Those are the rates at the Chateau Madeline, a fine old mansion with individual cottages open to the public but with a semi-club atmosphere. In addition to feeding you three huge meals daily—featuring the island's specialties of trout, whitefish and berries—the chateau has its own free court, boats and motors, and a cruiser for island exploration; frequent beach picnics and similar affairs are organized. Everything but riding and golf is included in your rate. Lower cost housekeeping accommodation is available at Leo Kron's Cottages; Emil and Leona's Bar; and Moore's Beach Cottages.

Madeline Island is easily reached by frequent competing ferryboats —a three-mile, 15-minute ride from Bayfield, Wisc., at $1.75 car and driver.

Excepting Madeline, the other Apostle Islands are slated as a National Seashore. Most can be reached via the daily excursion boat and all offer unsurpassed primitive camping. You may also camp at Madeline Island State Park. Yet another resort in the islands is Laurie Nourse's Resort at Rocky Island. While the Apostles are locally popular and Madeline Island boasts a Chamber of Commerce and a marina, library, museum and airstrip, the islands are far from spoiled.

More information: Chateau Madeline, La Pointe, Wis. (mid October-June 19, Mrs. Thomas Vennum, 4209 Country Club Road, Minneapolis 24, Minn.).

MICHIGAN'S FRIENDLY ISLES. Every day between April and October, a colorful procession of Great Lakes steamboats and foreign freighters glides through sinuous blue channels that often take them within a stone's throw of the pinewoods and white beaches of the St. Mary's River Islands. "Ship watching", in fact, is a popular diversion of those few hundred fortunate Americans who every year vacation on these cool river islands. For cabins and cottages dot the shores and you can swim, fish and watch ships go by right from your front door.

The islands are clustered just below Saulte Sainte Marie, site of the Saulte Locks, which annually handle more shipping than does the Panama Canal. Day and night the freighters endlessly pass, high and empty in the upbound channel, laden down to their marks on the downbound side. Sugar, Neebish and Drummond Island are American; St. Joseph Island lies on the Canadian side of the river. Car carrying ferries serve the islands and on each, gravel roads take you deep into the restful seclusion of the primeval forest.

Drummond Island is 136 square miles of cool pine and balsam forest studded with more than forty lakes and rivers. Age old trails lead to ruined British forts, parade grounds and graveyards and for variety, there's golf, tennis and restaurants. Like the other islands, Drummond is free of hayfever or asthma-producing pollens. You get here by a twenty minute ferry ride from De Tour, Mich. More information: CoC, Drummond Island, Mich.

Neebish Island boasts unsurpassed fishing for great northern pike, walleyes, perch, bass and muskies and cool forests full of deer, wild orchids and mushrooms. This is a particularly good island for ship watching. For information write to Mr. J. J. Driver or to Mr. J. M. Cummings at Neebish Island, Barbeau P.O., Mich.

Sugar Island, reached from Saulte Sainte Marie by a short ferry trip, has a cove-lined shore famed for boat fishing. For information, write Smiths Cottages, Rogers Cabins or Gil Nelson's Resort at Sugar Island, Saulte Sainte Marie, Mich.

St. Joseph Island is 99,000 acres of virgin woods and its miles of cove-lined shore offer privacy enough for anyone. Visitors always enjoy exploring old Fort St. Joseph, now a bird sanctuary, and for evening entertainment, you'll find gay, small dance halls. You get here by driving Canada's Highway 17 to Wilson's Landing and taking the free ferry *St. Joseph Islander* across to Ontario's "Garden of Algoma." More information: CoC, St. Joseph Island, Ont., Canada.

On all four islands, tucked away in the woods beside trout streams or along the shore, are comfortable housekeeping cottages and cabins which rent for an average $50-$70 a week.

Not far away (25 miles west of DeTour on Michigan's Highway 134) are the friendly little communities of Cedarville and Hessel, jumping off points for the 35 wooded Les Cheneaux Islands. Famed for their big trout and perch and their vivid displays of spring wildflowers, Les Cheneaux Islands offer a choice of moderately priced cottages scenically set amid the beauties of lake and bay. More information: CoC, Hessel or Cedarville, Mich.

Moving southwest across the big Mackinac Bridge and down the east shore of Lake Michigan to Leland, near Sleeping Bear Point, yet another Michigan island beckons. South Manitou Island, seven miles offshore, is uninhabited most of the year but in July and August a ferry calls there from Leland and you'll find a warm welcome at the rustic cottages of Manitou Haven Resort. A lighthouse built in 1839 dominates the island's primitive 5,260 acres and along the west shore, sand dunes tower 400 feet high. Exploring this virgin island is fun. There are miles of quiet, beautiful beach for rockhunting and bathing, and inland you'll discover such relics as an old one-room schoolhouse and handsome stands of ancient white cedar. More information: Manitou Haven Resort, 2910 Westmont Ave., Lansing, Mich. 48906.

Adding spice to an island vacation on Lake Michigan is the presence of large schools of coho salmon. Averaging two feet in length and 15 pounds in weight, these sporty Pacific Coast fish have been successfully introduced into Lake Michigan to replace indigenous species wiped out by lamprey eels.

CHAPTER 6

Unspoiled Seashore and Fishing Villages

There's something about a fishing village—the tanned nets, the tangy smell of seaweed, the salt-stained cottages, and the restless sea—which has lured people for generations. In fact, so popular have some villages become that during summer, fishing takes second place to netting tourist dollars. The "discovered" fishing village with its plush inns and gift shops sandwiched between cottages is a poor substitute for the real thing.

The fishing villages and other seashore communities in this chapter are not self-consciously quaint. For the most part they live by the sea and any visitor who happens along is welcomed as much for his presence as for his extra dollars. All the villages here offer inexpensive vacations.

CEDAR KEYS, FLORIDA. For a really different Florida vacation, sample Cedar Keys, a remote unspoiled island ghost town full of twisting creeks, houseboats, fish nets, winding lanes, and tiny beaches. An aura of the past hangs over every corner of this haphazard fishing village. Immediately you drive across the three bridges linking Cedar Keys to the mainland, you step out of booming Florida into a turn-of-the-century atmosphere where possession of $100 constitutes prosperity.

Cedar Keys is a jumbled village of old frame houses occupying one of a group of low islands in the Gulf of Mexico. Battered buildings and vacant lots tell of hurricane after hurricane which took their toll in years gone by. Villagers still measure time by the memory of these storms. "The depression, why that was between the blows of '29 and '34," our fishing guide remarked.

More than twelve bridges span canals winding through the village, their banks lined by fish houses and picturesque boats. Some 850 villagers, Old Southern whites of Tennessee hill-folk extraction, and Negroes who greet you politely, lead simple lives and harvest an abundance of seafood from the Gulf. Nobody has much money, few cars are less than ten years old, and the bank is probably the smallest in Florida. At the hillside cemetery, quaint shell borders mark fishermen's graves. Despite its ramshackle appearance, the many peach trees, fishing boats, and nets lend watery Cedar Keys a charm all its own. If you're looking for a place with character, an island fishing community where unpainted weathered doors creak idly in the breeze, and where tourist hordes are as rare as neon signs, this dilapidated village will not disappoint you.

A small group of discriminating people *has* discovered this forgotten village and Mine Hostess of the hundred-year-old Island Hotel, Mrs. Gibbs, caters to their palates with some of the most superb seafood served anywhere in Florida. The Island Hotel, with its old fashioned verandahs and high ceilings, its bits of decorative seaweed and driftwood, is a flavorful place to stay. Rates are $10 per night per couple in some of the typical island style rooms while for those desiring modern luxury there are amazing underground apartments built in old cisterns and used from time to time as a hideout by some of the South's most influential political figures. Crab, turtle steak, scallop and broiled pompano appear on the hotel's menu daily. Housekeeping motel units run about $50-$60 a week and if you arrive early enough (say, in November) you can often rent a modest furnished apartment or cottage for the benign winter season at $100-$125 per month.

A good fish dinner for which you'd pay $3-$4 in Miami can be had for $2 here. Other prices are reasonable. We paid $20 a day for a skiff with motor and fishing guide. You can rent small boats for $3 a day and catch bucketfuls of trout, reds, snapper, and mackerel. And you can explore the neighboring keys, one a wildlife preserve, and visit the lighthouse on lonely Seahorse Key. The cocktail hour is always gay at the Island Hotel's congenial bar, frequented by locals with a raft of queer yarns. Traffic is so light you can ride around on a bicycle. There are fishpacking plants and crab canneries to visit and a museum depicting the history of the Keys. Painters and photographers go into ecstacies. Cedar Keys has no jail and is so remote that radio programs are sometimes hard to pick up.

Because rates do not rise in winter and temperatures average only 5° cooler than in St. Petersburg, you can winter here in a mild sunny climate for a third of the cost at resorts farther south. In summer, breeze-fanned Cedar Keys shares the same climate as summer resorts along the Gulf where rates are twice as high. It's a fine spot for off-beat retirement. Waterfront sites are still available, occasionally with an older home with a sweeping bay view.

To reach Cedar Keys, turn off U.S. 19 at Otter Creek, Florida, and drive 22 miles down dead end State 24. By public transportation, head for Gainesville and continue by bus. Because the island is locally popular with weekending vacationers from nearby Gainesville, it's best to arrive on a weekday, especially on a Monday.

More information: CoC, Cedar Keys, Fla.

NEWFOUNDLAND, CANADA. Anyone for a vacation in an undiscovered fishing village? A village where tiers of painted cottages cling miraculously to the side of a steep stone cliff. A village of sturdy fishermen, generous, sincere, and unspoiled, whose dialect betrays the speech of Devon, Dundee, and Dublin. A village where spinning wheels stand in cottage doorways and housewives bake taste-tempting salmon, cod tongues, and three-inch-thick blueberry pies. Ah, you say, if such a dream village could really exist!

You need look no farther than Newfoundland. Around its 6,000 miles of fiord-slashed coast, you will find not less than 100 fishing villages answering this description exactly. There are tourist homes and cottages in or near many of the most picturesque hamlets. And if you pick your spot, $40 a week covers full board and room, homespun but often including a rich round of seafood and home-baked bread and country butter.

Newfoundland, Canada's newest province and the world's tenth largest island, has yet to be discovered by American tourists. From the jumbled interior—a mass of rocky "tolts," bleak barrens, thick fir forests, tundra, and marshes—salmon-filled rivers pour down to long arms of the sea that knife inland. Almost all Newfoundland's settlements line its innumerable bays. Many are without roads, their sole link with the outside world the weekly boat. Despite new road construction, the sea is still the island's highway.

The villages are like this. Over every outport hangs the smell of drying cod. Along the water's edge, thousands of cod dry on rows of multi-imposed flakes (stages). Overhead, gulls maintain their lonely vigil, wheeling about the masts of fishing schooners in which sturdy Newfoundlers daily challenge the turbulent Atlantic. Not infrequently you'll see icebergs drifting past your cottage window.

Most of the people are English or Irish and entire villages are usually of a single religion: Catholic, United Church, or Anglican. Although Newfoundland was settled before the Pilgrims reached America, its people still retain many of the customs and habits of the land of their forebears. The odious term "tourist" is seldom heard. A word of greeting to a villager may even be returned by a cordial invitation to come in for tea.

What else would you expect of a country with place names like Heart's Delight, Pushthrough, and Spaniard's Bay? Geographers say no other part of the world bears such a variety of unusual names. Within a few miles of Trinity are Sker-Wink, The Naked Man and the Naked Woman, The Nuddick, Maggoty Cave, and Hog's Nose—all local names of formidable rocks and headlands.

Finding things to do is hardly a problem. It's not too cold to swim from the island's sandy coves and, in summer, seldom too rough to borrow a dory and jig for cod or squid just offshore. Fishermen welcome visitors along on their trips for the fresh conversation. Crabs, mussels and seafood are plentiful and there are acres of wild blueberries for the picking. And with a $35-a-day license and a guide you can bag your limit of supercharged Atlantic salmon. Every corner of Newfoundland is a photographer's Mecca. There are literally thousands of scenes to paint; few have ever appeared on canvas before.

Pleasant picnic spots abound, some with tables. If you possibly can, attend one of the village dances, usually reels to fiddle and violin. Frequently there are soccer matches. In larger centers you can shop for handsome hooked rugs; knitted socks and sweaters; sleek jackets, gloves, and slippers of seal skin; Eskimo carvings of whale and walrus tusks; and earrings of labradorite from Labrador.

Your Northland fishing village vacation will be cool but never cold. Few people realize it, but even in winter zero temperatures are rare in Newfoundland. Thus you can often spend pleasant days vacationing before June 15 and after September 15 when rates drop 10%-20%. It can rain at any time but fog is less common than on the Canadian mainland and a 90° temperature is almost unheard of. Newfoundland is entirely free of hayfever but come prepared with insect repellent.

Be sure to reserve accommodations well ahead. Vacationing New-foundlers enjoy these calendar-picture villages too. In most places you can stay at lodges, inns, guest houses, and private homes for $5-$6 a day with meals. You probably won't get a private bath but the scenery and food are ample compensation. You can rent rustic but otherwise comfortable housekeeping cottages while campsites for motorists are increasing rapidly. Living costs can be kept quite low if you purchase seafood and local farm produce. Fresh salmon and lobster and that rare Newfoundland delicacy, cod's tongues, are very inexpensive. Groceries cost about the same as at home but you can get a haircut or hire a maid at refreshingly soothing costs.

By making arrangements with local housewives you can find board and lodging in private homes almost anywhere. As a matter of fact, it's not unheard of to arrange with a lighthouse keeper and his wife to live in the lighthouse with them. But here, by way of suggestion, are a few beauty spots where you can count on arranging accommodations ahead by correspondence.

Grand Bank and Fortune, at the toe of Burin peninsula, are the historic, schooner-packed headquarters for Grand Banks fishing fleets. You'll find several hospitable tourist homes charging $7-$9 a day with all meals.

St. Lawrence also occupies an extremely picturesque section of the Burin peninsula. Mr. F. Alyard's Laurentian Cabins at $10 double daily are extremely comfortable. Or you can stay at Giovannini's Hotel or the Tourist Home for $6-$7 with meals.

Holyrood, on Conception Bay, lies on the Avalon Peninsula, a his-tory-steeped section that was once colonized by Lord Baltimore. There are squid jigging grounds off the beaches and beautiful coastal drives through scores of fishing villages, no two ever alike. Nearby, at Chapel Arm, you may see whale boats driving pot head whales up on the beach. The Beach Cottage Hotel supplies full board at $7 a day.

Makinson's, also on Conception Bay in a similar setting to Holy-rood, is site of Makinson's Ltd. cottages which rent at $60 per week.

Trinity is an historic town on Bonavista Peninsula. Rusting cannons solemnly dominate its magnificent harbor. Its square, solid houses clustered round the bay are reminiscent of a village in the Scottish

Lowlands. You can drive the Cabot Highway the entire length of the Bonavista Peninsula, to the red and white striped lighthouse at its tip, where Cabot made his landing. At Trinity Cabins, a mile from town, you will find comfortable housekeeping cabins among the pines on an arm of the harbor, at $42 a week, double. Rates at guest houses are $80 a week, double with meals, and at the Lock Leven Hotel $112 weekly for two, including all meals.

Heart's Content, home of a trans-atlantic cable station, lies on the eastern shore of Trinity Bay and makes an excellent base for exploring the picturesque fishing villages of the Avalon Peninsula. In this area, tourist homes and guest houses charge $6-$8 daily with meals.

Bonne Bay, over on the scenic west coast, lies among steep cliff-lined inlets in a setting of unparalleled beauty. Moose abound, salmon and trout swarm in rivers, and there are beaches galore. Local tourist homes supply board very inexpensively and there are housekeeping cabins.

Bell Island, in Conception Bay and served by ferry from Portugal Cove, is site of Basha's Hotel: $9 a day with meals.

You can reach Newfoundland by sea, air, rail, or car. From New York City the air fare is $71 o.w., $142 r.t. By combination rail and ferry from Sydney, Nova Scotia, the fare to St. John's, the capital, with overnight steamer berth is around $60 r.t.; costs are lower for points west of St. John's. For details on taking your car by ferry via Sydney, Nova Scotia, and driving island roads, write the office named below. They will also supply information on sea travel and on accommodations other than those we have mentioned. There are many good campsites.

More information: Newfoundland & Labrador Tourist Development Office, Confederation Bldg., St. John's, Newfoundland, Canada.

NORTHERN MAINE. Along the rugged, rocky coast north of Portland are some of Maine's prettiest coastal towns and scores of unchanged fishing villages rich in Down East flavor. Farthest removed from the noise and confusion of big city life is huge Washington County on the Canadian border. Here you'll discover more Down East atmosphere than anywhere else in Maine. Larger than either Connecticut or Rhode Island, Washington County covers 2,500 square miles yet has a population of only 32,000. Its 700 miles of wildly scenic coast reach from just north of Bar Harbor to the New Brunswick line. The only two towns of note are Calais (population 4,500) and Eastport (2,500). This is one place in America where you can still walk for miles beside the sea without meeting anyone or hearing any disturbing sound . . . just the echo of the surf, the song of a bird, or the rustle of the wind in the pines.

Amusements are self-made in Maine's tiny coastal towns but no mention of things to do would omit the amazing Firemen's Benefits and Church Suppers at which, for about $1.50, you can sample unlimited quantities of such Down East specialties as rolls jammed with huge chunks of boiled lobster, barbecued Maine chicken, sweet-tasting clams, homemade Anadama bread still warm from the oven, and blueberry pie. These fund-raising events are held without fanfare in almost every Maine town or village throughout the year, the only announcement being a handwritten sign in a local shop. Yet they're eagerly patronized by everyone from fishermen and lobstermen to world famous writers, artists, poets and composers.

According to a recent article in the *New York Times*, more musicians, actors, writers, poets, craftsmen and artisans are actively at work in Maine today, in ratio to the population than in any other state. Many of these creative people have purchased cottages in tiny communities along Maine's northern coast, where they can find the serenity and privacy they seek. As a result, summer theaters and concerts are popular and dozens of art exhibits are held every summer, almost all of which are small, informal and intensely personal. Dozens of retirees and others make homemade pottery, silverwork, hooked rugs, weaving, bird carvings, Maine dolls and ceramics for sale to summer tourists.

Best time to explore the Maine coast is from Labor Day until October 31 or in late spring. During these off-seasons, rates are among the most reasonable in the East while roads and beaches are uncrowded and untrammelled. Because of the ameliorating influence of the sea, Maine's coast has relatively mild winters, and scores of eminent and wealthy people who could afford to winter in the Caribbean enjoy living here throughout the year. Although high interest rates can produce a scarcity of housing here just as anywhere else, Maine has traditionally had a large number of older homes, both for sale and rent, ideally suited for retirement with extra rooms easily converted into hobby rooms or a painter's studio. Costs are usually quite attractive.

In places like Bar Harbor you'll find miles of beautiful shore and mountain walks with views of rugged surf-pounded islands offshore. There are picturesque fishing villages galore, some with odd names like Bailey's Mistake. The rivers are filled with salmon. Within easy reach are Baxter State Park, famed for mountain hiking, and Moosehorn National Wildlife Refuge, near Calais, home of bear, moose, beaver and seal. During August, hundreds of local people earn extra income by picking blueberries in Washington County's vast barrens. And if you enjoy home decorating, you'll eagerly attend the local auctions, where you can pick up such long-forgotten items as antique milk stools or ice cutting tools for the proverbial song. Rounding out the attractions of living on the coast are the brilliant wildflowers of spring and the flaming russet and gold colors of fall.

Here, the length of the coast, are some of our favorite small towns and fishing villages.

Boothbay Harbor, a picturesque peninsula fishing village in an alluring setting on a landlocked harbor, has a busy boat-thronged waterfront and an art colony with craft shops.

Camden, with its mountain backdrop, flower-trimmed lamp posts, and schooner-packed harbor, is easily the "prettiest" coastal town. A music, literary, and arts and crafts center, Camden features a summer harp colony and a summer theater with Shakespearian Festival. At the height of summer, you can camp inexpensively two miles out at Camden Hills State Park. The village is a choice retirement spot.

Friendship, a lobster fishing village, lies amid beautiful coastal scenery on island-dotted Muscongus Bay. You'll find plenty of color and an abundance of scenes to paint.

Mount Desert Island, site of Acadia National Park, is Maine's rock-bound coast at its dramatic best. From the peaks of Mount Cadillac through dense pine and spruce forests to great cliffs and headlands like Schoodic Point and America's only Atlantic fiord—Somes Sound —Mount Desert's scenery will keep you fascinated. Bar Harbor, the famous summer resort, lies in a setting of supreme scenic beauty; Northeast Harbor is at the entrance to Somes Sound; and Winter Harbor—a real little gem is a delightful shore fishing village. During the more expensive summer season, you can camp in Acadia National Park.

Pemaquid Neck, a showpiece of tortured coastline and magnificent seascapes, terminates in one of America's most spectacular headlands. Along its length, the several Pemaquid villages nestle among spruce and balsam forests, their harbors filled with mackerel boats and schooners, and their shores ringed by beaches and miles of rounded rocks. Enticing forest trails wind high above the sea. All the villages are delightful little Edens, as is neighboring New Harbor, Maine's most picturesque harbor village. Among the most picturesque villages, we like Bristol, South Bristol, New Harbor, Round Pond, Medomak and Bremen.

Rockport, a busy lobster fishing village on a deep blue landscaped harbor, is a summer center for artists, writers, musicians and craftsmen.

Wiscasset. Arches of giant elms shade this quaint New England seaport. Abandoned schooners and historic shipowners' mansions complete the air of old seafaring times.

More information: Department of Economic Development, State House, Augusta, Me. 04330.

NOVA SCOTIA, CANADA. An easy 250 miles by car from Calais, Maine, is a lobster-shaped peninsula rimmed by 5,000 ragged miles of the wildest coast in eastern North America. Nova Scotia's coastline totals three times the length of the entire United States Pacific seaboard and every mile is an enthralling marine masterpiece. Between green-clad capes and bold forested headlands are more beaches than anyone could count. In fact, beaches are so numerous and tourists so few that on an August afternoon you can find a dozen empty beaches within as many miles. There are countless unruffled inlets where the haunting stillness of the forest overlaps the sea. And everywhere are changeless, church-spired villages lined by rustic flakes of drying cod, piles of gaudy marker buoys and lobster pots, and weatherbeaten old salts mending long tanned nets.

You will relive the Evangeline story in Acadian villages where oxen still occasionally draw plows. And you will find complete peace and relaxation in hundreds of beauty spots where prices are similar to ours back in the depression. In country stores, like that at Petite Riviere, the owner still gives a creditable haircut for $1. Almost anywhere, giant cooked lobsters, smoked herrings, kippers, and cods' tongues and cheeks—a real delicacy—can be had at down-to-earth prices.

Jutting far out into the Atlantic, Nova Scotia almost touches the Gulf Stream. Sea water temperatures are higher than in most of New England, and bathing is surprisingly pleasant. Although many commercial fishermen have changed to sports fishing, you may still find old style fishermen who will invite you out for the day to watch them haul their curious set nets and bowl traps and, for a dollar or so towards the gas, they'll also let you fish for pollack. Indian hiking trails abound in the woods, you can canoe in quiet waters, and attend garden parties and country style square dances. Mealtimes mean delicious country cooking and prime Nova Scotia seafood—lobster, scallops, herring, swordfish, flounder, and salmon—and home-made bread and pastries are regular fare.

In Nova Scotia you can count on brow-cooling breezes (and even occasional sea mists) when New York and Chicago are sweltering in humid heat. While the weeks between June 15 and September 15 are undeniably best, proximity to the Gulf Stream also means mild weather in late September and October, when rates drop by 15%-25%.

Deluxe hotels are few in unspoiled Nova Scotia, but you will find a greater satisfaction among a choice of immaculate cottages, guest homes, and farms, which take guests by the day or week. Don't look for a private bath but most have hot and cold running water in rooms and often showers. Too, housekeeping cottages are widely available. And if you take advantage of fresh farm produce and the abundant seafood, eating costs will be less than at home. A whole large codfish sells for 75¢ and all the crabs, clams, oysters, blueberries, and cranberries you can possibly need are free for the taking.

As a matter of fact, you can easily arrange inexpensive room and board in any of Nova Scotia's sea-stained fishing villages. But in summer, at least, it's wisest to have confirmed reservations before you go. Described below are the bargain paradises of mainland Nova Scotia:

those villages offering the utmost in serene beauty, color, charm, and atmosphere at lowest cost. You can camp at almost all.

Atlantic Shore

Blandford, an unpretentious village among the misty coves of Mahone Bay, retains much of the flavor of its Hanover-German inhabitants. Rail fences network the countryside, flower beds surround cottages, oxen toil in the fields, and families bear quaint Hanoverian names like Rafuse and Publicover. Local housewives take guests or you could stay at nearby Chester described below.

Chester, one of Canada's most scenic small resorts, bears all the flavor of an English village. Spellbinding is the combination when Chester's mellow chimes echo back from its magnificent harbor studded with 365 gemlike islands. There is a Red Cross-supervised beach, tennis, golf, and a sizeable art colony. Craftsmen work in wrought iron and there is much handlooming and painting. Guest homes like Casa Blanca charge $76-$96 a week for two people, including all meals, and rooms in private homes run $5 double a day. Retirement homes sell for $8-11,000.

Dublin Shore is a pretty, small fishing village of well-kept homes at the mouth of the La Have River. The villagers, of German ancestry, display extreme hospitality. No one is regarded as a tourist. Artists come to paint the picturesque fishing boats and wharves; there are many enjoyable leafy walks and good bathing beaches. Private homes and small guest houses at nearby Petite Riviere offer full board with delightful home cooked meals for about $60 single per week.

East Dover, near famed Peggy's Cove and in some ways offering greater variety, is a quaint fishing village on a cove dotted with net-laden dories. Firred headlands provide magnificent panoramas. There is a sandy beach littered with staghorn-shaped driftwood and there are trout and sea fishing. At present, the nearest accommodations are at Indian Harbour, below.

Hubbards is a confirmed beauty spot and the home of French and German families. You'll find bathing on safe, sand beaches and boating, dancing and fishing. The Anchorage Hotel charges $74 weekly for two, including all meals and a free boat.

Indian Harbour, an unspoiled gem among gripping seascapes, clusters around four coves at the east entrance to St. Margarets Bay. Close offshore rises the immense rock mass of Shut-In Island. Peggy's Cove is just three miles. You can stay at Harbour View Cottages, a fine old fashioned tourist home with superb food, for $45 a week per person with meals.

Lockport, a fishing village almost on an island, abounds with tantalizing seascapes and possesses its own special quality. No commercial buildings mar the beauty of its magnificent sweeping beach. Friendly villagers are quick to accept strangers and the atmosphere is entirely relaxed and leisurely. The single juke box does little to ruin this seashore Eden. Full room board for two at MacMillan Manor runs $150 a week. Beach housekeeping cottages at Seaside Cabins are $35-$56 a week.

Lunenburg: if you like a larger village, Lunenburg with a population of 3,000, is home port of the largest deep sea fishing fleet on Canada's Atlantic coast. From the forest of masts lining the wharves of front harbor, the brooding fishing port atmosphere extends throughout its broad, old fashioned streets and hills. You'll discover historic churches and famous shipyards which still build wooden ships in traditional style. Beaches and coves reach away in rugged grandeur, to the unbelievably perfect fishing village of Blue Rocks and to the serrated rock ledges of The Ovens Park. Older tourist homes and hotels charge very reasonable rates.

Mahone Bay, a traditional shipbuilding village, overlooks a panorama of countless islands and coves. Captain Kidd is reputed to have buried treasure on Oak Island and it has been a mecca for treasure hunters for over a century. You can reach it by boat. There's good bathing, boating and fishing. Lockies Cottages has cottages available at $65 a week.

Marie Joseph is another flawless fishing village on a wide arc of bay and harbor. There are scores of fine bathing beaches and sheltered coves for lobster boils. Rates at the superior Hotel Harbour View are $60 a week single with meals. This is a real bargain, for every meal is a culinary masterpiece and the cooking has won the praise of countless food authorities.

Peggys Cove is a classic among fishing villages, so well known that hundreds of artists come to paint it each summer. Yet despite the visitors, Peggys Cove deserves mention: for its superb location on vast, rounded bare rocks yellowed with seaweed; for its tiny coves surrounded by colorful fishing shacks; for its white lighthouse on a massive boulder; and for its lively Saturday night square dance to real old time music. Best place to stay is at nearby Indian Harbour.

Petite Riviere, a village dating from 1632, occupies an enchanting setting in a peaceful valley beside a river and the turbulent Atlantic. It abounds in sandy beaches and informal country living. Housekeeping cabins at MacLeod's Cottages are $30-$40 a week while full board at Arenburg House runs $45 a week.

Queensland possesses a really magnificent beach on the incredibly blue waters of lovely St. Margarets Bay. Rates at Seabreeze Hotel range from $5.50 to $8 per couple per night.

Bay of Fundy Shore

Bear River rises in tiers from the riverbank to terraces lining deep ravines in the green encircling hills. Clams and cherries are free for the picking, and each July 20 sees a color-packed cherry carnival. Off-beat Bear River, up a side road, is seldom visited by tourists. At River View Lodge room and full board runs $60 a week.

Clam Harbour, an off-beat village down another side road, is famed for its long beach of hard, white sand, and fine surf bathing. Clams abound. At the present time, accommodations are available only at private homes.

Digby, a larger village, occupies a uniquely beautiful site above broad Annapolis Basin and dramatic Digby Gut. Colorful scallop boats polka-dot the harbor. There are golf, dancing pavilions, large scale clam bakes, canoeing, and riding. St. Mary's Bay Hotel, Salvia House, New Scotia Hotel and The Corner House are all priced right.

Freeport lies at the west end of spindly Long Island, reached by ferry from Digby Neck. Fishing, boating and swimming are good in this peaceful spot and you can stay inexpensively at Churchill House.

Little River lies far out on the long, rocky peninsula of Digby Neck. Fishing and bathing are good and there are interesting rocks for collectors. Inexpensive accommodations are available in the area.

Parrsboro is the place if you enjoy beachcombing for amethysts, agates, and rare trap minerals. Fundy's phenomenally high tides also leave behind large deposits of edible dulse seaweed. You can visit Partridge Island, a mile offshore, and have a wonderfully quiet vacation bathing, fishing, or playing tennis or golf. Hotels and tourist homes at Parrsboro charge $5-$8 double without meals. Alternatively, you can stay at restful Five Islands nearby; Island View Cottages rent at $50 a week for four.

Sandy Cove is one of the most picturesque villages in the Maritimes, a fine spot to fish for cod, haddock, and pollack and with many alluring seashore walks. It's near Digby and interesting Brier Island. Weekly rates with meals at Orchard's House are $56 per person.

Victoria Beach, far out at sea on a peninsula, is an ideally scenic and restful off-beat hideaway. Fundy View House provides full board at $60 a week, with even more attractive family rates.

Westport, a real Down East fishing village, lies on beautiful Brier Island. Not far away on the island's south shore, a fantasy of gigantic columns rears precipitously from the sea. You can stay at the Bailey Tourist Home for $10 a day, all meals included.

Good paved highways lead north to all parts of Nova Scotia or you can go direct by frequent steamer service from Bar Harbor, Maine, to Yarmouth at its southern tip. Rates are only $7.20 per person, cars $21.10, cabins $4.40-$5.50 extra if desired.

More information: Nova Scotia Travel Bureau, Provincial Bldg., Halifax, N.S., Canada.

DESTIN, FLORIDA. Whether you want to sample some stupendous fishing or just get away from it all in a mild winter climate, you can do so at bargain prices in this quaint fishing resort village on northwest Florida's snow-white sands. Better bring your sun glasses, even in January, for Destin is dazzling. To appreciate it best you must stand high atop Destin's sandy bluffs overlooking shimmering East Pass and the landlocked harbor crammed with jostling fishing boats. Under the strong Florida sun, every hue of blue, green, and white meets your eyes as it roams the ultramarine shoal waters, the indigo blue of the ocean, and the labyrinth of soft green bayous filtering back from enormous Choctawhatchee Bay. The high, steep bluffs along the shore remind you of New England and the Down East setting is heightened by the peaked roof houses that surround the harbor, by the net spools and docks along the beach, and by the white church steeple in the distance. Destin, on its narrow sand spit, is almost entirely surrounded by water, and that makes its winters milder than anywhere else in this part of Florida.

After the big annual Fishing Rodeo in October, Destin's modern accommodations go empty till the following April and throughout the winter you'll find a wide choice of motel housekeeping units at around $50 a week or $100 a month—50%-70% under summer rates. For an entire winter, you can usually rent a small apartment at $75-$95 a month or a small furnished house at $90-$120. You won't need much in the way of heat, for the mercury dips below freezing only half a dozen times each winter and the few cold spells stabbing south from Canada are usually felt simultaneously in St. Petersburg.

Fishing is so colossal that some tourists have paid for their entire vacation by selling their catch (including cost of a commercial fishing license). Every day in winter, at least one party boat departs for the two hour run to the red snapper banks where for $8.00 fare you can battle all day with giant snapper and grouper. You'll need a big game rod and reel, for it's nothing unusual to hook a 400-pound Warsaw grouper (fishing boats have rods for rent). For more relaxing sport you can cast for pompano off the beaches or pier and for evening entertainment, enjoy the typical Southern hospitality of the villagers at Destin's lively Community Center.

Retired southern executives and military officers have found Destin a haven for the Golden Years. You'll see their airy retirement homes crowding bluffs above the beach and along the restful bay shore and bayous flanking Choctawhatchee Bay. Older homes are scarce but there are plenty of new two-bedroom places to choose from at $8,500 up and taxes are low.

More information: CoC, Box 8, Destin, Fla. 32541.

SOUTHERN OREGON'S COAST. For 400 miles north of the California line, the coast is a sea-carved medley of titanic rocks, wild seascapes, snug coves with wide sandy beaches, and phenomenal drifting dunes. The northern half lacks nothing in scenery. But the southern half, out of reach of Portland's weekenders and 350 miles from San Francisco, more closely approaches the peaceful quietude of a Utopia. In tiny, uncrowded resorts such as Bandon, you can live in a setting of wild rhododendrons hundreds of feet above piling breakers.

Nature dealt lavishly with Oregon's shore. Superb stretches of sandy beach fit snugly between rugged headlands guarded by outlying rocks awash in the thundering surf. From the 800-foot heights of Cape Perpetua or from the basalt cliffs of Otter Crest you'll view the most spectacular seacoast in the entire United States. So rugged is this Oregon Coast that the single mile of U.S. 101 through Devil's Elbow south of Sealion Point cost more to build than any other mile of federal highway. From craggy cliffs you can watch whales play and sealions sport on rocky ledges; there are deep troughs and sea caves where the tides eternally churn in and out; the beaches are dotted with agates and semi-precious stones; and among evergreen hills rising abruptly from the shore, you'll find the only myrtlewood groves outside the Holy Land.

There's a perpetual freshness about this invigorating coast. Wild flowers grow in profusion—purple foxglove, goldenrod, and azaleas—and miles of wind-tossed rhododendrons and huckleberry carpet the dunes. Sometimes sea fogs drift in with the warm Japanese current. But summer days are invariably cool, dry and comfortable, and even in August log fires blaze at night in the lounges of coastal lodges. Winter means rains and storms. But there are people, and you may be one, for whom winter possesses a magnetic attraction. Imagine sitting in a cozy lounge high above the fury of the storm watching mountainous waves pile over savage rocks . . . a thrilling stimulation you can enjoy when rates are 25% lower than in summer. And those same mammoth winter seas deposit the agates you'll find during August and create the ever changing marine gardens exposed at low tide.

Grab yourself a clam gun (coast parlance for spade) and you can shovel out huge blue neck clams, so large a single one makes a full meal. Scattered along the shore with these giants are delicious quahogs, razor clams, butter clams, bay clams, and cockles—all yours free for the picking. Striped bass 20-50 pounds lurk in the bays; rivermouths and inlets teem with chinook and silver side salmon as well as bottomfish and crab; and in fall, steelhead abound everywhere.

This is a beachcomber's paradise! The sands are littered with agates, gem stones, seashells, delicate driftwood, and the big green and violet glass floats of Japanese fishermen. Starfish, sea urchins and sea anemones can be gathered off the rocks at low tide and within easy reach are fascinating tidal pools and beautiful marine gardens. You can dip smelt in season. And you can do practically anything else from riding or bicycling on the beaches to having a field day with brush or camera. All but 23 miles of Oregon's coast is public land, there are scores of seaside state parks with picnic tables perched high above the surf, and sightseeing trips galore.

Sheer distance from large cities keeps this coastal wonderland uncrowded and prices reasonable. For a bargain vacation you can camp in a host of beautiful state parks and forest camp-grounds at $1-$1.50 per night. From 35 dollars a week will secure a housekeeping cottage though without reservations you'd better count on paying $40-$60), while rates at coastal lodges start at $40 a week for two, meals additional. From October 1 until May 15 rates tumble one fourth: for an off-season bargain stay, you'll often find surprisingly mild weather as late as November and again in late April and early May.

Beauty spots! The coast is bulging with them. Write to the Oregon Coast Association for their Oregon Coast Travel Guide. Here, in brief, are a few you'll like.

Bandon has an out-of-this-world beach and some of the most breathtaking scenery on the Oregon Coast. It's a gem hunter's Mecca and a great cranberry center.

Brookings, overlooking the sea in a delightful coastal setting, is surrounded by acres of scented Croft lilies and azaleas, and is famed for its birdlife. Nearby are giant myrtlewood trees and a magnificent Redwood Park. Brookings is ideal for retirement.

Florence, on the Siuslaw River, lies ringed by rivers, lakes, and sand dunes carpeted with dense rhododendron.

Gold Beach gets its name from the sparkling gems in its sands. It's a sports fishing center at the mouth of fabulous Rogue River and among its southern coves are the finest rock oyster in Oregon.

Port Orford, most westerly incorporated city in the United States, occupies a magnificent setting among the wildest seascapes on the entire Pacific Coast. North and south from this little logging and fishing village, there are striking marine views: scenes of perpetual animation as huge knife-edged combers beat continually upon long rows of jagged rock outcrops.

Waldport, as far north as you should go to avoid crowds, has 18 miles of agate-dotted beaches and abundant bay and razor clams.

Yachats (pronounced Yahots) lies near Cape Perpetua and the phenomenal Devil's Churn. From the mouth of Yachats River, miles of tortured rock and sandy dune-backed beaches line the restless surf. You'll find excellent surf fishing and surf bathing, good stream fishing, and plenty of agates. Smelt run here in spring and summer.

If a few damp winter months don't mar your retirement plans, the Oregon shore scenically outranks every other coastal retirement spot in the nation. You could live in small resorts at the quieter southern end or at slightly larger, busier places like Gearhart and Seaside closer to Portland. You'll find thousands of ideal homesites with building costs running $14 a square foot. Older homes start at $8-9,000 and year around rentals average about $85 a month for small unfurnished apartments and $100 for two bedroom unfurnished homes.

More information: Oregon Coast Association, Newport, Ore.

YANKEETOWN, FLORIDA. When you turn off U.S. 19 at Inglis, Florida, and drive down dead end State 40, you leave the motels and neon sign behind for a charming corner of unspoiled "Old Florida." At the road's end lies Yankeetown, a neat, clean, little fishing community of trim white homes nestled drowsily under moss-hung oaks

---

Eden on the Riffles: Agness, Oregon

If you're willing to brave 40 miles of slow, winding road frequented by mammoth logging trucks, you can drive your car to Agness. But the U.S. Post Office prefers to send in mail by river boat. For all practical purposes, Agness is sealed off from the outer world by Oregon's primitive Siskiyou Mountains. Its sole links are the jet powered mail and passenger boats which make their daily 32-mile dash up the beautiful Riffles of the Rogues River from Gold Beach on the coast.

The mailboat ride ($4 r.t.) is a classic among American river trips. All morning the boat forges through foaming water between towering hills and through majestic Copper Canyon, where inquisitive deer and bear fearlessly look on. Then at noon you reach Agness, a tiny post office and a huddle of cottages, tucked away in a virgin paradise of superb mountain scenery and deep, shadowy canyons. Here you can rent a housekeeping cottage at Singing Springs Ranch for $14 a day double; or stay at Lucas Lodge for $12.50 daily per person with meals. Alternately, camp on the riverbank for free. The Rogue's salmon and steelhead fishing is world famed and you can yarn with trappers and settlers or explore old Indian villages and battlegrounds.

Reserve ahead on the mailboat by writing the Rogue River Boat Service, Wedderburn, Ore., and also Singing Springs Ranch, or Lucas Lodge, Agness, Ore.

beside the jungly Withlacoochee River. But it's the river itself which catches your eye. Clear and clean, its bass-filled waters swirl lazily seawards between dense walls of century-old cypresses and curving palms, untouched and unspoiled. Here is tropical Florida in the raw, the Florida you see in pictures, as primitive as when Seminole canoes plied up and down. Here, just 3 miles from busy U.S. 19, surrounded by jungle and luxuriant hammocks teeming with wildlife, is another world of peace and quiet and rest.

Yankeetown has no cocktail bars, theaters, rows of ranch houses, or pseudo-Spanish mansions. But you'll live comfortably and well. Rates are stable throughout the year and it's a delightful spot in any season. Constant shade and Gulf breezes make summers pleasant and there are few mosquitoes. Winters are only 4° cooler than in St. Petersburg and you can winter in the sun here for half of what you'd pay in resorts farther south. Pleasant housekeeping cabins on green lawns overlooking the river are just $35-$55 a week or $125-$150 a month for three people. Or you could enjoy the Old World hospitality at Izaak Walton Lodge, where guests are called to meals with a cowhorn; rates are $70 weekly and $280 monthly single or $125 weekly and $450 monthly double, including all meals and unlimited helpings. There's also a trailer park charging $20 a month and a few furnished apartments can be found at $70-$95 monthly.

Fishing is so fabulous, it's spoken of in whispers. With a rented boat you can fish in tranquil solitude among endless creeks for giant bass, bream, and channel cat and just a few minutes down river is the biggest trout flat on the Gulf of Mexico. In season, tarpon, redfish, grouper, and kings provide magnificent sport and you can bag your limit of quail, duck, deer, and wild turkey in the great Gulf Hammock just a few steps from Yankeetown. Oysters and shellfish are yours for the picking, and you'll find a whole archipelago of subtropical islands to explore, some with Indian shell mounds. The river is fine for swimming all year and, as a visitor, you're automatically invited to community fish fries, cards, and homey entertainments with the gracious, unhurried, friendly folk who have discovered their Utopia on the wooded banks of this delightful river.

If suburban retirement isn't for you, yet you prefer such conveniences as street lighting, paved streets, garbage collection, and fire protection, Yankeetown is an ideal haven for living in the later years. Living costs are low and gardening lucrative. Drawbacks: there is no doctor or hospital here and sandflies are bothersome at times. Occasional older 2-bedroom homes sell for $6,000-$7,500 and new 2-bedroom frame homes from $8,700 (or $12,700-$14,700 beside the river). Riverside trailer park sites start at $20 a month. Yankeetown also has a beach.

More information: Knotts and Lynch, Yankeetown, Fla., 32698.

CHAPTER 7

Escapist Isles of Tropic Seas

F ew people are aware of it but the stars and stripes wave over a surprisingly variety of languorous tropical isles. Without leaving United States soil you can vacation on alluring tropical islands with a choice of Spanish, Polynesian, Japanese, Danish and calypso backgrounds or an Old Florida setting of early pirate lore. Without even leaving a United States highway you can drive your car onto coral islands and by short ferry trips you can drive onto tropical cays similar to those in the Bahamas. Air fares—tax free and lower than those charged on other international routes—bring the Caribbean and Pacific islands within range of the average vacationer.

Here are the best of these exotic isles, together with complete reports on the hideaways beyond their hotel skylines. All the islands are American.

SANIBEL AND CAPTIVA ISLANDS, FLORIDA. Twenty miles over a toll causeway from bustling Fort Myers are the most sinfully lazy, beautiful, serene, and secluded pair of tropical islands in the continental United States. Sanibel Island is carpeted by rakish coconut palms and fringed by the world's most famous shelling beaches. The whole place looks like a page out of Maugham. There are village stores, quaint balconied frame hotels, a single road with sandy trails leading off to palm-dotted hideaways, and a genuine South Seas atmosphere enhanced by miles of secret bayous, impenetrable mangroves, and uncrowded beaches where your only companion are the rare roseate spoonbills, darting sandpipers, and spindly-legged egrets, white ibis, and herons.

Centuries ago, these twin tranquil islands echoed to the seaboots of José Gaspar's buccaneers. The larger island Gaspar called Santa Isabel after the queen of Spain. Time has shortened the name to Sanibel. On the smaller island the pirate kept his captive damsels—hence the name of Captiva.

Captiva, linked to Sanibel by a concrete viaduct spanning jungly Blind Pass, is straight out of New England. Tucked deeply away in groves of murmuring Australian pine, Old World cottages look out through arches of seagrape to the sweeping crescent of Captiva's shell-encrusted-beach.

Merely to step ashore on these lush isles is to experience a feeling of escape from the world. And the island's relaxing atmosphere completes the feeling. Time is meaningless on Sanibel, where hurry, worry, schedules, and high pressure are unknown. Because they offer such relief from harrying city cares the islands have their own following of cultured, educated people able to find contentment through their own inner resources. You'll discover solitude, privacy, and a lazy carefree existence unduplicated elsewhere in Florida.

About 300 congenial escapists live year around on the islands. Best place to get acquainted is Harbor House on Sanibel. Here you will be able to meet all the habituees who drop in daily for a beer. No door is ever locked on Sanibel, and newcomers desirous of practicing the art of relaxation are genuinely welcomed. In this unhurried island society, simplicity and privacy are valued more than money. Most islanders are discriminating people who came to get way from maindland Florida's gaudy hoopla and ballyhoo. Alexandra Tolstoy, Anne Lindbergh, and Wilbur Daniel Steele are among those who have sampled Sanibel's peaceful balm. And today's islanders want Sanibel to stay secluded and unchanged. Despite the causeway linking Sanibel to the mainland, the $3 toll scares off most tourists.

Don't come without a huge sack for the rare and beautiful shells you will pick up on Sanibel's powdery beach. You may not have given a hoot about shells before, but once on the island *everybody* becomes an ardent conchologist. High tides and winds pile shells 3 and 4 feet deep. You'll discover sculptured beauties in all sizes and colors—delicate angel wings, rose cockles, rare calico shells, pink hued conches, and hundreds more.

Along with the shells you can pick up delicious clams, oysters, and scallops or with equal ease secure bucketfuls of tasty stone or blue crabs. Coconuts and key limes are free for the picking. And the sky blue waters teem with so many fish that anglers speak of the islands with wonder. In summer, big tarpon run thicker in Blind Pass than probably anywhere else in Florida, and throughout the year, snook, trout, snapper, jewfish, blues and others swarm in the warm Gulf waters.

Other folk enjoy Sanibel's abundant wildlife. Both islands are a Federal Wildlife Preserve and from the observation tower you can watch hundreds of rare tropical birds and timid raccoons. A rundown of other activities includes superb swimming, painting, boating, hunting for decorative driftwood, and exploring Indian mounds on neighboring cays. Organized entertainment simply does not exist and the only movies are those shown in winter at community houses and hotels.

Drawbacks in paradise? There are minor ones. Island water is so brackish you must drink bottled water in many areas. There is no regular doctor: a retired Florida physician deals with emergencies in return for gifts. And modern phones weren't installed till 1962. But Sanibel's former scourge—the ever present mosquito hordes—are now controlled by drainage projects and regular fogging operations.

On these isles of perpetual summer, the mercury is only a few degrees higher in June than in January. But from December 1 to April 30, rates are double those charged the rest of the year. So if you want to go native at a price you can afford, plan to sample the islands' comfortable isolation in the cheaper spring, summer, and fall. Other than brief afternoon thundershowers, summer rain is rare.

You'll stay at comfortable motels or in housekeping cottages near the beach. From May till June 15 and from Labor Day till December 15, housekeeping cottages or efficiency apartments average $85 a week. But efficiency units at By-The-Sea Motel were recently only $68 a week and at Blind Pass Cottages, a studio apartment cost only $36. There are several restaurants and trailer parks. Winter rates are more than twice as high.

If you'd like to retire on Sanibel or Captiva, you'll want to know that land is still cheaper than at other Florida beaches. Building lots with beach access privileges start at $2,750 and you can build a nice home for around $14 a square foot. The island's rental shortage also means there are still opportunities to invest in income-producing cottage colonies and beach motels. Many small business needs are still unserved and in winter there are part-time jobs at hotels. Groceries aren't exactly cheap but inexpensive seafood evens up living costs: for instance, scallops and oysters free for the taking.

The islands have several general stores, various small shops, several churches, a grade school, and daily mail service. Gardens and tropical fruits flourish.

From Fort Myers, Florida, you can reach Sanibel by driving down State 867 to Punta Rassa and crossing the toll causeway to the island. Charter plane service is also available at $12 for two persons.

More information: write the accommodations mentioned or the CoC, Sanibel Island, Fla. 33957.

ST. JOHN, U.S. VIRGIN ISLANDS. After World War II, novelist Richard Ellington and his wife set out for Tobago, the most beautiful island he had ever seen. En route, the Ellingtons stopped in the Virgin Islands and visited St. John. They have yet to reach Tobago. "I wouldn't have believed it possible if I hadn't seen it but this island is more beautiful than Tobago," Ellington says. "Besides, it's American."

St. John lives up to every expectation of a tropical island paradise. Emerald green mountains rise abruptly from crescents of snow white beach and the sapphire seas are dotted with green cays and bleached coral reefs. In the island's rugged 20 square miles, oranges, limes, and tobacco grow wild and any moment you expect to see a Tarzan swinging from the trailing vines which sway from lush bay trees. Cinnamon, tamarind, cashews, soursops, mangoes, and all the fruits of the tropics grow in wild confusion while rakish coconut palms line miles of empty, languorous beaches on the island's north shore. On the irregular south shore, multi-colored rock headlands thrust out into the Caribbean, and, inland, ruined sugar mills polkadot the roadless, up-and-down landscape. On this forgotten paradise, the common cold is unknown.

"Hi, Mon" is how the island's 900 colored natives greet the white continentals who have discovered their own paradise here. Rich cotton and indigo plantations once thrived in St. John, but nowadays the natives lead a relaxed existence, either working on Government-sponsored projects or guiding tourists around their lush habitat. Racial problems have yet to appear, and there is virtually no crime. Jeeps are the preferred vehicles for traversing the rough-hewn dirt roads and steep donkey trails. Now that most of St. John has become a national park, the island's primitive beauty seems destined to remain unchanged. Never will crass commercialism ruin St. John as it has St. Thomas, the big resort island of the Virgin Islands three miles west.

On December 1, 1956, some 9,500 of St. John's 12,000 acres were dedicated as the nation's 29th national park. Natives will continue to hold their land for the tenure of their lives, after which it will become public property. Camping is permitted in some idyllic spots. Mosquitoes are few, sandflies the only bothersome insects. You can obtain information about the park by writing the Superintendent, V.I. National Park, P.O. Box 1707, St. Thomas, V.I.

Cactus thriving on St. John testifies to the island's dry, salubrious climate. Temperatures are only mildly tropical, humidity extremely low. The 50 inches of annual rain fall mostly at night in spring and fall; throughout the year, caressing trade winds bring cool comfort around the clock. This isle of perpetual summer knows neither heat waves nor cold spells.

St. John is an island for individualists, where you can find contentment in your own resources. Loneliness is impossible; no one remains a stranger long. "Continentals"—visitors from the U.S.—get together at fish fries, seining parties, and beach picnics, where you'll be served island delicacies like conch chowder, fish and fungi, tania roots, turtle steak and spiny lobster, all washed down by sizzling punches made of duty-free liquor, which sells as cheaply as on St. Croix. The powdery beaches are your playground: snorkeling, swimming, sailing, skin diving, fishing, and underwater photography are the favorite pursuits. Too, you can explore the age-old North Trail which winds as it did in plantation days between Cruz Bay and Coral Bay, the island's main hamlets.

Cruz Bay on the northwest tip, with a population of 800, is the tiny island capital. Colored wooden houses cluster around a historic Danish fort. Nearby are the Post Office and an excellent clinic. Nowadays, St. John has 24-hour electricity and there are three well stocked stores and a commissary. Eight miles over the jeep trail at the island's eastern end is Coral Bay, the other village.

As at St. Croix, most rates go up from December 1 to the end of April, so that economical vacationing, or a longer stay, is possible only during the other months. During summer, comfortable housekeeping cottages for two rent at $110 a week at Gallow's Point, Holiday Homes and Lille Maho. But for a short summer vacation, Lille Maho and Meade's Inn offer fairly reasonable rates. Alternatively, there are improved campgrounds in exotic settings in the National Park. Camping is free and is particularly enjoyable at the lovely campground at Cinnamon Bay (tents rent here at $25 a week for two or you can rent a starkly simple cottage for $10 a day). Reservations well in advance are required.

For retirement, St. John is a more primitive version of St. Croix and so healthful that it boasts the lowest death rate of any civilized community in the world: six per 1,000 annually. Building lots are hard to find and expensive but with persistence you can find one for $12-15,000 and you can build a home for about $25,000 more. Although few homes have window glass, costs are increased because you must build your own rainwater cistern. St. John has no water supply. Taxes are low by stateside standards. Telephone, TV, radio and telegraph provide communication to St. Thomas.

To reach St. John you must first fly to St. Thomas and then take the hourly scheduled ferry out across choppy two-mile-wide Pillsbury Sound to Cruz Bay, fare $1. But air fares are cheaper than to other Caribbean islands. From New York to St. Thomas the fare is $70 o.w., $140 r.t.—a 4-hour flight; and from Miami $63 o.w., $126 r.t.—a 4½-hour flight. Both journeys are tax free.

More information: Visitors Bureau, Department of Commerce, Box 1692, St. Thomas, Virgin Islands 00801.

THE HAWAIIAN ISLANDS. Two thousand miles southwest of California, in the Hawaii that lies beyond Waikiki, you can still lead a lazy vagabond existence in a beachcomber's South Seas paradise. On islands like Maui, Kauai, Hawaii, and Molokai, there are unspoiled corners of Old Hawaii where dreamy legend-steeped villages nestle among coconut groves on curving tropical beaches sheltered by surf-pounded coral reefs.

Anywhere off the usual tourist circuits, you'll be welcomed by

---

FLORIDA TOWN OFFERS TRANQUILITY

The natives are afraid that Steinhatchee, a little-known fishing hamlet at the bend of the Florida Gulf Coast, is getting too big. The population has shot up from 700 to 1,000 in the last few years. To the visitor, though, the danger is not so apparent. Though there are several housing developments, the building seems to be proceeding at a leisurely pace. The whole settlement has a quaint and relaxed flavor—undoubtedly because it is off the beaten path and reflects a timeless quality. To reach it, you turn west off US19 some 30 miles south of Perry. A bridge takes you over to the village, stretching out along the west bank of the Steinhatchee River. Stately cedars and wide-branched oaks line the river bank.

In all, Steinhatchee has four fish houses, four stores, a number of motels, docks and quite a few houses. But the town has never been officially incorporated. There are no town officials, no police department or firemen and only an occasional constable.

The people prefer it that way. They make their living by fishing and their fortunes rise and fall with the market for fish. An independent lot, they feel that theirs is the best of all possible lives. Where else could one live in a ruggedly beautiful place with a winding river running through their homesteads down to the sea? There are good motels, fishing lodges and rental cottages and five excellent seafood restaurants. All costs are inexpensive and Steinhatchee offers excellent opportunities for low cost retirement off the beaten path.

friendly brown islanders and invited to luaus and kukilaus (feasts and fishing festivals) that tourists never see. During our first three days on Hawaii's south Kona Coast, for example, we were invited out for deep sea fishing in outrigger canoes, taken all over the island in an ancient station wagon, and outfitted with goggles and rakes for an underwater sea urchin hunt which was followed by a family pig-and-poi luau on the lawn of our fisherman host.

Our Polynesian friends taught us Hawaiian words like *limu* for sea-weed and *moku* for island and *haole,*which we discovered meant us. Within a week we became completely absorbed in the life of the village. We knew everyone's first name and everyone knew us. We helped haul fishing nets on the beach, loafed and sunned by the surf, attended the weekly church luau and Saturday night dance, became experts at spearing papio under water, and even helped weave pandanus into lauhala gifts for sale to tourists. The small hotel where we stayed at $10 a day with meals has closed. But nearby you can rent a housekeeping resort apartment for $70 a week and, allowing $30 for groceries, two can still vacation here for $50 a week apiece—actually, less than it cost some years ago. At most Hawaiian resorts, comfortable apartments rent for $12-$16 a day for two, or about $75 a week, and by preparing your own meals, a couple can vacation almost anywhere on about $8 a day apiece for room and meals. At still less cost, you can camp. You'll find scores of superb beach and mountain parks where you can camp out in insect-free comfort.

Hawaii's climate is so near-perfect, the Hawaiian language contains no word for weather. Average temperatures range from 72° in January to 78° in August with constant trade winds fanning the languid, balmy air. Rain varies from nightly showers on eastern coasts to almost nil on the island's western lee shores. Only during a brief kona period in winter are skies cloudy. Throughout the year huge plumerias, poinsettias, jacaranda, hibiscus, oleander, jasmine, and bougainvillea are in continuous bloom.

Chinese, Japanese and Philippine immigrants have brought overtones of the Orient to these island homes of Polynesian kings. You will see Buddhist temples and Japanese sampans and in summer, hundreds of colorful kimono-clad girls dancing to weird Oriental music at Bon Dances. Sometimes you will have difficulty in realizing you are not in a foreign land but still under the Stars and Stripes. Off-beat Hawaii is about as different and unusual as any place you can vacation on American soil.

Where will you find these bits of paradise? As far as possible from Honolulu. Although you can find a stretch of Old Hawaii along the Wainae Coast on Oahu (the principal island, where Honolulu is located), it's best to catch the first plane out of this urban island for one of the others. Here, to help you choose, is a run down on typical off-beat beauty spots where you can camp or find lower cost accommodations on the outlying islands.

Hawaii, the Orchid Island, is the largest island in the group. Dominated by the cloud-hung peaks of Mauna Loa and Mauna Kea, dormant volcanoes over 13,000 feet high, Hawaii falls away through luxuriant rain forests and dense fern jungles to coffee groves and sugar plantations lining its rocky, lava shores where most beaches are black.

If you like a resort area, stay on the Kona Coast. At the seashore town of Kailua, you can stay fairly reasonably at Kalanikai Apartment Hotel or at the Kona Dolphin Hotel, Leialoha Hotel or the Kona Hukilau Hotel. Then for the atmosphere of a Hawaiian coffee country hotel, try the Hotel Manago at Captain Cook, 16 miles south of Kailua, surrounded by tropical fruit groves and with stunning views. Another inexpensive Kona Coast hostelry is Teshima's Inn at Kealakekua. Or if you prefer to camp, try Hoonanea Beach Park where you can camp among fragrant foliage close to lovely Sapoopoo village and its underwater coral gardens; an ancient city of refuge is nearby.

To come closest to finding the heart of Old Hawaii, sample the Hamakua Coast on the northeast shore, scenically the most spectacular on the island. Here you'll find small villages color-dotted with flowers, rich tropical verdure and pencil-slim waterfalls. A short distance inland you can camp in an ethereal gorge beside the idyllic Akaka Falls. Or farther west, within easy reach of an ancient Shangri-La of Hawaiian kings, Waipio Valley, you can stay very inexpensively at the modest Hotel Honokaa Club overlooking the beach in the town of Honokaa or at the equally modest but inexpensive Andrades Honokaa Hotel (also called Chris' Cafe). These are hardly the most stylish hotels on the island but you'll find more true Hawaiian hospitality here than in the glittering resort areas with their ersatz flaming torches and overdone sundown ceremonies. Honokaa is a true western style town of about 1,100 Hawaiians who work in the sugar and macadamia nut plantations. Waipio Valley, enclosed on three sides by perpendicular 2,500-foot mountain walls, is ribboned with slender waterfalls and opens out to a palm-laced beach pounded by Pacific surf. You'll see women fishing in its still lagoon.

Along the southeastern Puna shore there is excellent camping in MacKenzie and Isaac Hale Beach Parks. You will camp under Australian pines near the abandoned village of Pohoiki, where mangoes and guavas grow wild and footpaths lead off to cool springs and pools deep in fernwalled caverns. Not far away at Kalapana village close to a ruined temple, an historic church, a Hawaiian queen's private bathing pool, and a cave of refuge, is Kalapana Beach Park, where camp-ground tables have been hewn from virgin lava. Within minutes, are the fabulous black sands, raging surf, and swaying coconut groves of Kaimu Beach.

For a longer stay or permanent retirement, consider Hilo, the flavorful island capital, which usually offers a choice of inexpensive rentals and homes. Although it's rainier here, Hilo is relatively inexpensive. Such hostelries as Kaleimomo Apartments (on hilltop with view), Crescent Manor or Lehua Apartments Hotel all offer very reasonably priced apartments while the traditional old Palm Terrace Hotel also has inexpensive rates. More information: Hawaii Island CoC, 180 Kinoole St., Room 203, Hilo, Hawaii 96720.

Kauai, the Garden Island, greenest and most beautiful of all the Hawaiian Islands, is a scenic jumble of travel-folder mountains and waterfalls, limpid pools, deep canyons, golden beaches, and winding rivers. Its Na Pali Coast, damp and cool green, rises abruptly from the sea in misty headlands 2-3,000 heet high. There are deep fern grottoes, enchanting valleys, caves, spouting water horns, and scores of tiny villages whose residents still doggedly believe in *menehune*—the little men. Numerous beach parks and the Kokee State Forest provide delightful campgrounds.

One of the best is Anini Bay Park, where at night the flickering torches of fishermen twinkle on distant reefs. Then on the edge of the heavenly Na Pali Coast, there's fine camping at Haena Park with topflight swimming nearby at Ke'e Beach. Another delightful low cost spot is Kokee State Park, 4,000' up in the mountains near picturesque Waimea Canyon where fully furnished state park cabins are only $55 a week for two.

Lydgate Park on Wailua Bay is another of Kauai's picture-postcard east coast camp-grounds. Nearby are fern grottoes and a ruined temple and city of refuge. At Kukuiula Bay, picturesque fishing sampans ride in the harbor and not far away is Poipiu Beach Park, a camp-ground with excellent swimming. Here, too, are Poipu Shores Apartments, offering quiet housekeeping efficiencies at around $16 daily per couple. The white sand beach here is protected by barrier reefs and nearby you can watch a natural spouting sea horn.

Another good camp-ground is Niumalu Beach Park on Nawiliwili Harbor, a typical Pacific island port. A mile away in Lihue, the island capital which has a shopping center and surprisingly lively night life, are such inexpensive hostelries as Ahana Apartments, Hale Ka Lani, and Motel Hi-Way, most with inexpensive housekeeping apartments. Also in Lihue are pleasant small inns like the Hale Pumehana or Hale Lihue, both very reasonable. Richer in island flavor, however, is the traditional Palm Haven Hotel in Lihue, in an old island house. Another lovely spot is the Tropical Inn, a traditional island plantation house in a beauty spot on the Wailua River. But perhaps the best buy in Kauai is the Hotel Coral Reef at Kapaa on the east coast just above Wailua, a modern hostelry conveniently near to splendid swimming.

More information: Kauai CoC, PO Box 69, Lihue Kauai, Hawaii 96766.

Maui, the Valley Isle, consists of two mountain masses joined by a low isthmus. Within its beach-rimmed shores, Maui packs everything you'd expect of a tropical Pacific Isle: waterfalls, placid inland pools and clear streams, luxuriant valleys and mountains, lava tubes and vivid flowers. Looming over everything is the mighty crater of Haleakala, a 10,000-foot dormant volcano. A second Waikiki style resort complex is rising along Kaanapali's 3-mile beach. But elsewhere, life goes on much as it did in the days of the kings. At Hana, you'd swear you were back in the days of long ago. Like Kauai, Maui has excellent beach campgrounds, especially in the Mahena section. You can camp among groves of bamboo, kukui and kamani and you can pick wild guavas and mangoes while seafood is always abundant.

There are two towns worthy of consideration. Wailuku, an attractive little city of shady narrow streets on the slopes of West Maui Mountain, is the least expensive place to stay and the best base for touring the island. Inexpensive apartments are available at Hale Nani Apartment Hotel and Puuone Gardens Apartment Hotel while Kodani Lodge is also inexpensive.

Lahaina, the other town, lies on the sunset side of Maui, as dreamy and picturesque a small Hawaiian town as you will find in the islands. An enormous banyan tree shades its main square, and every garden overflows with radiant flowers. Down on the sea wall, ancient cannons point out over a harbor dotted with Japanese sampans. Old Hawaiian burial grounds and tropical gardens complete the feeling of tropical languor. Unspoiled Lahaina is also close to a small village where the people are more pure Hawaiian than almost anywhere else. There are frequent luaus and hulas, sometimes at the Holy Innocent Church, famed for its painting of an Hawaiian madonna. Best place to stay is the atmospheric and reasonably priced Pioneer Inn on the waterfront. Or for about $13 a day, you can rent an apartment at the Nagamine Apartment Hotel.

Immediately north of Lahaina is the Kaanapali Beach resort area and here, beside the plush hotels, are such less expensive hostelries as Pohailani Apartments on Kahana Beach, the Mahinahina Kai Motel and Nalani Apartments, all offering efficiency apartments at $70-$100 a week. Another spot you'll like is Kihei, an unfashionable beach resort near Kahului on the southwest coast. Reasonably priced accommodation is available.

But for real Polynesian atmosphere, you must go to Hana, a wildly scenic drive of some 50 miles at the eastern tip of the island. Here, for about $10 a day, you can live in modern comfort at the apartments of Kauakea Cottages or the Motel Heavenly Hana.

Plan to spend a few days hiking across Maui. Available to hikers are several cabins high up on the crater rim in Haleakala National Park and in four days you can make an exhilarating walking tour clear across the island, staying overnight in the cabins. Alternatively, another low cost spot in the mountains is Paia, where the Nalu Kai Lodge charges only $45 a week for two. Equally cool and refreshing is Iao Valley, a rich tropical glen surrounding a needle-like pinnacle 2,200' high. Here you can stay at the Hotel Iao Needle. Both settings offer cool mountain living and you could easily drive back and forth to the beach.

Molokai, the Friendly Isle, and probably the least visited, is a tranquil piece of Old Hawaii with a Western flavor heightened by its cattle ranches and pineapple plantations. There are tall green mountains in the eastern part, and the colossal cliffs of its northern Pali Coast are as grand as any in the islands. Sheer 2,000-foot precipices seal its leper colony of Kalaupapa from the outer world. You'll discover splendid bathing beaches of sand and coral along the southern and western shores with clamming and fishing off rocks and piers.

At Kaunakakai, the busy little port, you can stay on the beach at the Seaside Inn with an alluring view of Lanai Island. The cocktail bar is on a patio below a huge banyan tree and rates are $10 a day for two. Less expensive is camping at Palaau Park where you can enjoy a botanical garden and stroll clifftop paths for scenic views over the leper colony.

Lanai Island, owned by the Dole Pineapple Company and seldom visited by tourists, nonetheless has a beach studded with wrecks from whaling days and a prehistoric village called Kaunola. Lanai City, the company town, lies in the shade of giant Norfolk pines and boasts a sporty 9-hole golf course. You can camp under the kiawe trees at Manele Beach—a tiny community with a made-to-order vagabond flavor—or for $28 a day, meals included, two can stay at Lanai Inn, a charming beach hideaway in an old plantation house.

Adding to costs in Hawaii is the necessity for a rented car (Budget Rent A Cars has VWs at $6 a day and 6¢ a mile) but you can sometimes save money by renting a scooter or even bicycles. An unusually good buy, however, are the campers, available on most islands at $150 per 8 days, which provide both accommodation and transportation in a single package. Hawaii, Kauai and escpecially Mauri are ideal for retirement but inexpensive homes and rentals are scarce. In most areas, however, lots sell from $3-5,000 and you can build a 2-bedroom home for $14,000. In Maui's large Kahalui housing development, 2- and 3-bedroom homes often sell from $11-13,000 with liberal financing. With your home paid for and by utilizing fresh island foodstuffs and the wealth of tropical fruits, two can enjoy a lazy island retirement on $5,000 a year, probably less in rural regions.

Getting there? From any West Coast city, you can fly to Hawaii for $85-$100 and for only $5 extra per island, you can visit each of the Neighbor Islands.

More information: write the Hawaii Board of Agriculture and Forestry, King and Keeamoku Streets, Honolulu, for information on parks and camping (they also have a few mountain cabins available). For general information, write the Hawaii Visitors Bureau, 2051 Kalakaua Ave., Honolulu, Hawaii 96815. There are also branches on the major islands and in New York, Chicago, Los Angeles and San Francisco.

ST. CROIX, U.S. VIRGIN ISLANDS. In 3½ hours you can fly from New York City to a rugged, tropical Caribbean island and step out into an unbelievable 17th century town with peaked red roofs and ancient cannons on every corner. St. Croix is so foreign it's hard to

realize you are still on United States soil. Streets in Christiansted, the
capital, bear Danish names like Kongensgade and Kirkegade, and under
weathered brick arcades and graceful arches, Old World shops burst
with Scotch at $3 a fifth and United States cigarettes at $1.80 a carton.
Automobiles observe the left hand driving rule and the courteous
colored natives speak a delightful, sing-song calypso English.

St. Croix, once owned by the Knights of Malta and then a Danish
colony, was purchased by the United States in 1917. Scattered across
this mountainous island, crumbling plantation houses and vine-covered
windmills with names like Envy, Jealousy, Whim, and Blessing tell the
story of once fabulous wealth when sugar made St. Croix one of the
richest islands in the Caribees. Today, the planters and their slaves are
gone. Under the impetus of a mushrooming tourist trade, an aluminum
plant, a jet airport and a championship golf course, among other
things, St. Croix's slow rhythm has speeded up. Yet by comparison
to most other places, the island is still a relatively relaxed and carefree
haven.

St. Croix, 22 miles long and seven miles wide, is rimmed by cobalt
beaches and surrounded by translucent, aquamarine seas. For a truly
moving experience, you must don goggles and float out off the beaches.
Crystalline clear, the sea is a pageant of moving color. Blue parrotfish,
rainbow triggerfish, and swarms of half blue-half yellow coralfish drift
idly in and out among antlers of living coral. Deeper down, waving sea
fans of purple and lavender shade giant conches and speckled lobsters.
Overhead wheel man o' war birds, and inland, rain forests cloak the
heights of Mount Eagle and Blue Mountain.

For the more wary, there are trips in island sailing boats to view the
reefs and for $14 you can take an all-day cruise on an island schooner
to lovely Buck Island (lunch and drinks are extra). There are movies,
tennis, horseback riding, Sunday cockfights, and art clubs. But most
days are like this: mornings you swim or fish from a choice of scores
of beaches (most are privately owned but nobody minds); afternoons
you take a siesta; and by then it's time for cocktails, which means
lounging in a planter's chair sipping island rum (which costs $1.25 a
fifth). Dinner usually includes typical West Indian Creole dishes, and
later, you can dance at small night clubs or a bar. The Virgin Islands
observe no fewer than 22 annual public holidays, and they celebrate
each one with dances, donkey races, fancy dress parades, and calypso
singing. Between holidays, you can rent a car or scooter and explore
Centerline Road, which winds 17 lush tropical miles between the two
chief towns. Either town, Christiansted or Frederiksted, could rank as
an Eden, and you won't go far wrong whichever you stay at.

So picturesque is Christiansted, its oldest buildings are preserved as
a National Historic Site. Island schooners moored in the harbor add
to the air of bygone days which the Danes left behind. Stores sell
delicious Danish cheese, sausages in great variety, and prime ham. A
17th century fort looks down over arcaded sidewalks and houses
painted in bright pinks and blues and yellows.

A similar fort guards Frederiksted's wide, blue anchorage. Color-filled Victorian houses with lacy galleries line the streets of this other sleepy town.

Cheap luxuries allow continentals—island name for Americans from the mainland—to lead a lazy rich man's life. Because the Virgin Islands are a free port, a case of 120-proof rum costs only $15, Champagne is $3.75 a bottle, Spanish brandies $1.75, and Johnny Walker $2.90, other Scotches as low as $2.50 a bottle. Imported Jensen silver, Wedge-wood china, Swiss watches, Guatemalan leather, and the best of other foreign products sell in island shops at 25%-50% below United States prices. But other things aren't so cheap. In fact, from December 1 till April 30, when sun-seeking winter tourists throng here, rates soar.

For this reason, we strongly urge you to visit St. Croix only between May 1 and November 31, when rates are more reasonable. Summers are only 6° warmer than winters and the mercury never goes above 91°. In fact, residents say April to July is their favorite time of year. Only September and October are likely to be muggy.

During these breeze-fanned summer months, you can stay at small efficiency apartments at $115-$135 a week, which, with groceries, works out to only about $13 a day for two people. Or you can stay at less expensive hostelries like Coff's Guest House (P.O. Box 723, Christiansted) or the Haanchen Hus (10 ABC Queen St., Christiansted) neither of which is listed on the island's hotel rate sheets, or the Caravelle, Duke's Manor, Living End, or Richmond House. For house-keeping, try Pink Fancy Apartments or Sunset Beach Cottages.

Although groceries cost 15% more than at home, you can actually shade housekeeping costs below United States prices by concentrating on local foods. A sign of the times are supermarkets, which are bringing food prices down. Other signs of the times are St. Croix's flourishing tourist industry, championship golf courses, jet airports and humming industrial plants. Nowadays, most of the accessible beaches near Christiansted are privately owned (but you can swim free at Altona Beach and elsewhere). Yet St. Croix remains almost as relaxed as before. However, the new prosperity has created job opportunities for continentals. The Virgin Islands Employment Security Office on St. Croix recently reported work opportunities in hotels, stores, banks and factories and in the service industries. Most continentals with a skill could have recently found work. But things *could* change. So check with the employment office before you come to the island to seek work.

Has the industrial boom changed the character of St. Croix? Unfortunately, yes. Some would-be visitors have already gone elsewhere. But these are modern times. Nothing stands still. By comparison to most Florida resorts, St. Croix is still dedicated to relaxation. During summer, you can have a delightfully tranquil island holiday at (for the West Indies) fairly reasonable cost *if* you patronize a less expensive hotel or apartment. Be sure to send for the island's *Summer Hotel and Guest House* rate sheet and select a place to stay *by price*. Otherwise, you'll encounter some of the world's most scalping prices.

Heating costs are nil in this summery island, where few windows have glass and clothing demands little beyond shorts and beachwear. Taxes are low and with your own home paid for, two could retire in St. Croix on anything from $400 a month up. On an average lot, a two-bedroom home would run about $32,500. Both Christiansted and Frederiksted have modern hospitals, public libraries, piped water, and electricity.

Taxwise, retirement in St. Croix may cost you less. There are no appreciable import, excise, or transportation taxes, and property taxes are limited to 1¼% of assessed valuation. There is no duplication of any federal taxation as on the mainland and estimates say that overall, taxes in the islands run barely one seventh those levied on the mainland. Then, too, if you want to start a business with a capital investment of $15,000 or more, an industrial subsidy pays 75% of your income taxes during the first ten years and you are also exempt during this period from paying real estate taxes, trade taxes, and licensing fees. For hotels to qualify, however your capital investment must be $100,000. You'll find many income opportunities by providing tourist accommodations and cottages.

Best way to reach St. Croix is by air. From New York the minimum fare is $88 o.w., $175 r.t.—a 4-4½ hour flight. From Miami, it costs $62 o.w., $124 r.t. and takes 2½-3½ hours. Both flights are tax free.

More information: Virgin Islands Department of Commerce, St. Croix, Virgin Islands 00820.

GASPARILLA ISLAND, FLORIDA. Every winter morning for 48 years, Seaboard's southbound express pulled out of Penn Station with a dozen Pullman cars, each bound for a different resort on Florida's West Coast. All but one car terminated its run at a brassy Florida resort. The exception was a single inconspicuous car bound for a quiet and luxuriant tropical isle. At noon next day, that car clattered out over a long trestle bridge, across a mile of blue-green water, to West Coast Florida's little known Gasparilla Island. From the hectic tempo of big northern cities, passengers stepped out into one of the vacationer's last frontiers, a remote and intriguing one time pirate haunt.

But Gasparilla's remoteness ended abruptly in 1958 when a new causeway was built to replace the ancient automobile ferry and passenger train service was suspended. Strangely, however, few motorists seemed to discover the causeway and Gasparilla continues to remain the same quiet haven that it has always been. Perhaps its aura of wealth discourages tourists. For few people are aware that for most of the year, from late-spring until mid-December, you can enjoy this quiet and lovely island at comparatively inexpensive rates.

On traffic-free roads you can bicycle the island's 7-mile length: through the Bahama-like resort village of Boca Grande, and down to the tarpon-jammed waters of fabulous Boca Grande Pass at the island's southern tip. You'll be impressed by the touch of foreign color at the nitrate docks, where freighters flying the flags of Norway, Greece, and Panama load nitrates for ports around the globe. And nowhere will you be far from Gasparilla's nine miles of flawless half-moon beach.

Gasparilla's fine deep-water harbor was first discovered by swash-buckling José Gaspar, who gave the island his own nickname. Nowadays a steady flow of nitrates from Central Florida rolls across the trestle bridge and into an elevator for loading into ships bound for ports across the globe. On watery Gasparilla, there's even a floating library which calls regularly at a score of smaller escapist cays close by. But most unexpected of all is Gasparilla's remarkable Johann Fust Library, laid out round an oriental courtyard and fountain. You enter through a pair of doors from an Indian temple to find yourself in a library stocked with such rare works as a leaf from the Gutenberg bible, a Cretan writing tablet, and some original works of Omar Khayyam. Soft classical music floats through the balmy air and an exotic orchild house adjoins the library.

It is the proud boast of Gasparilla's 500 permanent escapists that no one on the island ever hurries and that there are absolutely no planned activities. This is true with one exception. From mid-April to mid-July, Boca Grande Pass is a hectic battleground of sweating fishermen, frantic leaping tarpon, and broken rods and tackle. Record-breaking tarpon swarm in the pass throughout the warmer months and thirty other edible species can be taken at any time of year. The beach is a shell collector's dream, ranking second only to Sanibel's. You'll find a golf course, tennis courts and movies twice a week in winter only.

Housekeeping need not be expensive. Oysters can be gathered by the bushel. You can make delicious salads from the heart of wild cabbage palms. And dishes like broiled pompano amandine (costing $4 in restaurants) cost no more than the effort of catching and cooking the fish.

Summer and fall rates at smaller hotels and guest homes average $8-$10 daily for two while housekeeping units run about $60-$85 a week, with considerable reductions by the month.

If you're seeking a real escapist spot, 100-acre Cabbage Key, a short boat ride from Gasparilla, is made to order. On sloping lawns among its towering coconut trees, stand the Bermuda type houses and cottages of The Inn on Cabbage Key. From June 1 to January 1 you can rent a housekeeping cottage accommodating two for $55 a week, or one accommodating four people at $70, with use of a boat and canoe thrown in. Full board is $14 a day. The inn has its own art studio and art classes at $16 for four lessons. References are required.

Gasparilla's climate is identical to that of Sanibel, with fewer mosquitoes. Rates are naturally lower for a longer stay. In Boca Grande village are smart resort shops, drug and variety stores, liquor shops, good restaurants, grocery stores, gift shops and other basic facilities including a doctor. But there's no Chamber of Commerce and the only way to seek out reasonably priced accommodation is to go there and inquire.

Eventually the causeway may shatter Gasparilla's idyllic seclusion. Meanwhile you can reach the island by train or by taxi from Tampa or Fort Myers. By car you drive down State 771 or 775 from U.S. 41 south of Venice.

PUERTO RICO. For $51 you can fly in 3–4 hours from New York to this Connecticut-sized piece of mountainous United States soil in the tropical Caribbean. From Miami, fares are cheaper still, and all flights are tax free. Spanish-speaking Puerto Rico is like being abroad at home. You'll find all the foreign atmosphere of Spanish towns and churches, cockfights, lotteries, and a rich Spanish tradition combined with American efficiency, money, postal service, hygiene, and medical facilities.

Despite the booming industrial progress of its "Operation Bootstrap," out on the island in rural Puerto Rico you can still see thatched cottages, barefooted children, men cutting endless fields of sugar cane with machetes, and women washing clothes in streams. Excellent roads wind through verdant, precipitous mountains, often under canopies of arching trees, to old Spanish towns and unspoiled fishing villages. Palm-lined white beaches scallop the island's 360 miles of shore, which is dotted with reefs, cays, and islets. There are deserts, coffee fincas, a tropical rain forest, and scores of beauty spots bright with flamboyant African tulip trees, breadfruit, royal palms, and feathery bamboo.

You will eat native Creole dishes like arroz con pollo, tostones (fried bananas), jueyes (land crabs), pasteles, and lechon asado. Hospitable islanders welcome visitors at their frequent fiestas, where you'll hear traditional Spanish songs to the accompaniment of mandolin and guitar and, very probably, be invited to a lechonada (pig barcecue with exotic tropical fruits). Like the Virgin Islands, Puerto Rico basks in a climate of perpetual summer, and though the summer months are slightly warmer and more humid, temperatures of over 90° are extremely rare. Yet during these summer and fall months, most hotels and guest homes reduce their rates by 20%-30%. Thus summer and fall are the ideal seasons to discover Puerto Rico on a budget.

Here are some atmospheric places to stay where you'll experience the true flavor of Puerto Rico. Many towns have inexpensive guest homes—often in former mansions—while for real island ambiance, you should try Puerto Rico's ordinary commercial hotels; most are right in the center of Puerto Rican towns, yet nowhere are you far from beaches. While it's true that many of these hostelries are stronger on atmosphere than comfort, by staying at them you can vacation in pleasant surroundings on about $10-$12 a day, with a constant round of well cooked native food at every meal.

Arecibo, an ancient north shore town, has superb beaches and you can stay inexpensively at its commercial type Mir Hotel on the plaza, famed for native foods. In the hills southeast of Arecibo, on Route 140 between Florida and Utuado, is Hacienda Roses, a 75-acre coffee plantation which takes guests at $15 a day including meals—a rare opportunity to sample the real Puerto Rico. (Write: Hacienda Roses, Utuado.)

Barranquitas, together with nearby Aibonito, are two cool mountain villages in the heart of the island. Both are ideal for retirement. You can take your pick of the small island style guest homes or hotels. But you'll probably prefer to stay at the relaxing Treasure Island Resort at Cidra nearby. Summer rates are only $15-$18 daily for two in a cottage. At Cayey, near Aibonito, you can live on a coffee plantation high in the mountains: it's called Plantation Guest House and rates are reasonable.

Boqueron, on the southwest coast, has a magnificent sweep of beach and a village of old, gingerbread-adorned houses. Its modest Villa del Mar Hotel serves good island seafood.

Guanica, on the south shore near La Parguera is a lovely old Spanish town near a superb beach; the Copa Marina Resort Hotel here is priced right. Nearby, in the cooler hills, is the coffee town of Yauco where you can live well at the inexpensive Casa Roig.

Guayama, at the foot of the moutains on the southwest shore, is a charming town and summer resort, ideal for a quiet sojourn or for retirement. Accommodations are available locally.

La Parguera, in the dry southwest corner, is a typical native fishing village at the foot of rolling, cactus covered hills on the Caribbean shore. In this unspoiled spot, more than anywhere else, you will quickly meet the native Puerto Ricans and get the feel of the island. There are few 'phones and fishing schooners daily disgorge an abundance of tasty seafood. For 50¢ boat fare you can swim in the crystal clear waters of Mata de La Gata reef, at $15 a day hire a powered skiff for superb bonefishing, or weekends take the boat trip over to Maguey Islands and its unique zoo. There are dozens of mangrove islands, reefs, and fascinating underwater gardens which you can comb for driftwood and shells. And on moonless nights you'll join everyone else for the amazing cruise across Bahia Fosforescente, a phenomenal bay ablaze with phosphorescent lights.

Rates at the smart La Parguera Guest House run $5-$10 single, $7-$14 double without meals; across the street is the Casa Blanca Guest House, also reasonably priced.

Loiza Aldea, a historic seacoast village, lies east of San Juan at the mouth of the Rio Grande. Long isolated, its culture remains the purest in Puerto Rico. Here you'll find colorful fiestas, an ancient church, and the island's only hand-operated ferry. The small Charron's Beach House offers inexpensive hospitality.

Mayaguez, on the west coast, is an attractive tropical university town with a splendid beach to the south. Here you can stay at the budget priced La Palma Hotel in the city while just outside, high in the hills among cool coffee plantations, is the Rosario Mountain Resort, charging a flat $25 daily for two including all meals and many extras.

Rincon, the island's most westerly community, has a lovely palm-shaded shore. Here the Sea Beach Colony Resort provides reasonably priced accommodation.

Ponce. To sample city life, spend some time in this colorful second city of Puerto Rico. Two charming plazas separated by a cathedral form the city center and all around are elegant old houses. You'll enjoy shopping in the lively market and Ponce also has a splendid Art Museum. Excellent beaches, fishing and skindiving are nearby. Hostelries like the Melia, San José Guest House and El Coche in La Rambla are reasonably priced.

San German, Puerto Rico's most picturesque hill village, is a real little Spanish town. Founded in 1519, it clusters around massive Porta Coeli church, oldest in the Western Hemisphere, and the grounds of its Polytechnic Institute are a paradise of lush tropical foliage. On Sunday nights, the traditional Spanish *paseo* is held on the plaza: to band music, the town's eligible senoritas stroll in an outer circle anticlockwise while the caballeros walk facing them in an inner ring.

For $9 a day, two can stay at Costello Hall Guest House on the campus of the Inter American University; meals are extra.

Retirement in any of the resorts we've just mentioned can be delightful and not expensive. All these places are within easy reach of San Juan's splendid cultural activities: the winter Drama Festival; the spring Theater Festival; the summer Casals Festival; and the fall symphony season. (Incidentally, there are a dozen comfortable guest homes in San Juan with summer rates of $7-$12 a day for two.) Since 1956, the IBEC Housing Corporation has built thousands of attractive new homes in the hills around San Juan, priced at $12,000-$16,000 with low down payments. Other huge housing developments like those in Florida, underway almost everywhere, have helped bring living costs down to reasonable levels while rentals are now available at most places for $85-$110 a month. Likewise, modern meat packing and food processing plants, big stores and even discount houses, have brought down living costs to where you need spend only 5%-10% more than in Florida. For the outdoorsman, Puerto Rico also has a cross island hiking trail (La Ruta) with overnight shelters and there are delightful hikes in El Yunque Rain Forest.

Income taxes are also slightly lower than in the United States. For details, write the Department of Treasury, Office of Research and Statistics, San Juan, for their free booklet "What you should know about taxes in Puerto Rico."

Subtropical Fishing Village: Chokoloskee Island, Florida

From its settlement in the 1870s until 1955 Chokoloskee Island remained isolated by six miles of water from the town of Everglades on Florida's West Coast. Now a causeway links this outpost of Americana to Everglades and the Tamiami Trail. Several motels, electricity and telephone service are signs of the island's new life. But it may be many years before creeping modernity spoils this picturesque fishing village.

Chokolosee, rising in some places to 20 feet above sea level, is one huge Indian shell mound. Since 100 B.C., several Indian cultures have occupied the island. Nowadays, shell-paved roads link the scattered houses of some 35 fishing families. Rickety wooden piers, fish houses, boats and drying nets line the curving shore. And in Smallwood's general store—a genuine bit of Everglades island life—the musty shelves are piled with relics of an earlier day.

Chokoloskee, one of Florida's Ten Thousand Islands, is probably the least spoiled, most unusual village this far south in Florida. Sharing the same climate as Miami, it's a fine spot for a winter vacation with atmosphere or a summer fishing hideaway. Average rates at the motels are $65 a week, slightly more for housekeeping units. In Chokoloskee, which means old house in Seminole, most homes are built on pilings.

Flying is the most convenient way to reach Puerto Rico. From New York the fare is $51 (economy night flight), from Miami $52 (economy night flight).

More information: Puerto Rico Division of Tourism, 666 Fifth Ave., New York, N.Y. 10019.

THE FLORIDA KEYS. Slowly but surely the bulldozers and dredges are destroying the wild mangrove beauty of this subtropic island necklace. Only the rich shoal greens and deeper blues of the sea remain as a natural background to the bare, barrack-like levittowns which are springing up on island after island. But for the time being, at least, you can still get away from it all simply by leaving the main highway, U.S. 1. At some places a mile or two away from U.S. 1, the Keys are still so unchanged and undeveloped you could swear you were on a remote Bahamian cay.

Try driving northeast up Key Largo on Route 905 to the Angler's Club, where you can cross by boat to Elliot Key, one of the largest and most beautiful of the keys, with a slim white beach and outstanding beachcombing and skindiving. Another delightful experience is to rent a sailboat at Miami's Dinner Key (about $20 a day) and cruise through the roadless "Islandia" Keys to Ragged Sands Key and to Elliot, Totters and Old Rhodes Keys, so beautiful and unspoiled they may become a National Monument.

Big Pine Key, beyond Marathon, is still largely undeveloped and its small communities and trailer parks offer restful living and vacationing. Lastly, you might consider Key West which, despite its busy streets and Navy base, remains a town of character and charm with a population that is openly nonconformist. Summer rates are inexpensive everywhere and in May, the tarpon fishing ranks with the world's best.

For retirement, the Keys come closer to offering more real outdoor Florida living than any other part of the state. Temperatures are lower in summer, warmer in winter than anywhere else in Florida and waterfront lots are priced lower than most mainland towns. But for the ultimate in Keys living, thousands have found the answer in a house trailer. For under $1,000 you can make a downpayment on a large, modern used trailer and have it parked in a waterfront lot at a choice of trailer parks with a boat dock at your door. Year around rates at such parks average $30 a month and though haulage adds slightly to all prices, $200 a month should more than cover all basic necessities for two (including park rent but excluding trailer payments). There are trailer parks on every island, including Big Pine Key, which lies just across the famous Seven Mile Bridge from the supermarkets and other urban facilities of Marathon.

More information: Write the CoCs at Key West, Marathon or Tavernier, Florida.

AMERICA'S LEAST KNOWN TROPICAL ISLAND

How good is your geography? Isabela Segunda is the capital of an island over which the stars and strips have flown for nearly seventy years. What is the name of that island and where is it?

Like 99 out of 100 other Americans, you'll be surprised to learn that Isabela Segunda is the slumbering, one-street village capital of the island of Vieques, one of the Spanish Virgin Islands located in the Caribbean just nine miles off the southeast side of Puerto Rico (described earlier in this chapter). You can fly there from San Juan, Puerto Rico, via a short, 25-minute hop. Or you can take the older freight ferry or the fast, new, 60-passenger hydrofoil which makes the trip from Fajardo, Puerto Rico, in about an hour.

Ambitious plans for developing Vieques into a swank tourist resort have failed. So for a few more years it seems the island will remain a seductive hideaway from tourist ballyhoo. Whichever way you get there, you're headed off the beaten tourist track.

From the air, Vieques is a long, green hilly island 20 miles from east to west and six miles across, entirely ringed by white sand beaches and obviously one of the most beautiful islands in the northern Caribbean. As your plane drops down to pelican-diving height, you'll see cattle grazing among rich plantations of sugar, pineapple, bananas and other exotic tropical produce. All this is in the central sector of the island south of Isabela Segunda. The U.S. Navy owns both the eastern and western tips, which it uses occasionally for landings during Atlantic Fleet maneuvers.

Timeworn Isabela Segunda reminds you of Mexico. Horses are more common than automobiles, and there seems an air of French colonialism about the main plaza which is heightened by the architecture and the open drainage system. Looming above the village is an unfinished fort, one of the last Spanish fortresses ever built in the Caribbean. Since restored in the original manner, it offers a superb view from the top. From it, you can see a score of outlying islands including lofty St. Thomas in the Virgin Islands, 40 miles away.

Isabela Segunda was named for Queen Isabella II of Spain, daughter of Ferdinand VII, and other picturesque Spanish place names freckle the map. But Vieques probably comes from the Carib Indian word for crab, *Biaques*—hence the island is often referred to as Crab Island. Spanish is the mother tongue of all Viequesans but most speak a little English. For Vieques was originally settled by the English before the Spaniards took it over in 1753. In 1834, Isabela Segunda was built by order of Don Santiago Mendez de Vigo, governor of Puerto Rico, and the whole island remained Spanish until it fell, along with Puerto Rico, during the Spanish American War. Since 1898 the island has been American territory.

Don't look for night life or casinos yet, although they may come. To date, Vieques is the perfect get-away-from-it-all Caribbean island. Only during the comparatively rare visits of the Atlantic Fleet does Isabela Segunda spring briefly to life. The rest of the year, this peaceful port dozes in the Caribbean sun.

For a sojourn or vacation, Vieques has a sprinkling of guest houses which charge five-to-six dollars a day, meals extra. But for the time being, the island's best hostelry is Sportman's House, a delightful old colonial manor perched atop a high bluff in a sugar plantation overlooking the sea. Here you'll discover all the charm and easy formality of a French colonial inn. Sportman's House is not exactly a bargain but considering the luxury, the fine cuisine, the swimming pool and all the other adjuncts, the weekly rates are far less than you would pay in San Juan or Miami Beach. For a less pretentious hostelry, there's the Carmen in town, a typical island hotel, clean but short on private baths and hot water. The Carmen has no restaurant but you can breakfast at a *loncheria* and dine at a choice of small restaurants. There are also several modest guest homes.

For a longer stay, you can occasionally find simple island-style, two-bedroom houses for around $100 a month. But there is no central registry and finding a rental may take some persistence. Also here are the beginnings of an ambitious subdivision that failed to get off the ground. Its one hundred lots cluster around a sheltered lagoon just east of the crescent shaped beach of Ensenada Sombre (to be called Sun Bay). Night time phosphorescence turns this lagoon into a pyrotechnic sea of fire much like that of La Parguera in Puerto Rico. And just around the corner lies a really outstanding tropical beach, Playa Navia. Although much of Vieques' water is tepid, water is far more abundant than in the rest of the Virgin Islands and engineers predict that wells will more than provide an ample supply for the new subdivision. Since no lots had been priced as this was written, the only clue to land prices was that most of Vieques' remaining private land was recently valued at around $2,000 per acre. Local labor seems in plentiful supply for building and household help. And undoubtedly, two could retire at this idyllic retreat on about the same sized budget as they'd need for St. Croix (described earlier in this chapter). The climate falls midway between that of St. Croix and Puerto Rico.

Isabela Segunda abounds with small bars where you can meet the friendly islanders over a jigger of good, low cost Puerto Rican rum. And there are gay weekend dances and occasional cockfights. Apart from that, you make your own amusements. It goes without saying that Vieques' pellucid waters are superb for fishing and skindiving and riding is popular, too. Both small boats and horses can be found for rent. There's small Spanish-English library. And that's about it.

More information: Economic Development Administration, Commonwealth of Puerto Rico, 666 Fifth Ave., New York, N.Y. 10019. Provided you intend to stay there, Sportman's House will be glad to send information on the island; and the larger real estate firms in Puerto Rico may also have island listings.

GUAM, U.S.A. Even if you're a serviceman who put in a hitch there, you may be surprised to know that you can land on Guam without any formality, stay as long as you like—even retire there—and get a job or start a business, all without any red tape. Because Guam was quietly made an unincorporated territory of the United States in 1950 and all its people given U.S. citizenship, few Americans are aware that since 1961, when the Navy relinquished government of the island, they have been able to go freely to this beautiful tropical isle and enjoy privileges identical to those available in the U.S. Virgin Islands.

Despite the fact that one third of the island is a U.S. military preserve and is covered with military installations, Guam is almost completely untouristed and largely uncommercialized. The largest of the 18 Marianna Islands, it is actually the top of an immense mountain that rises 37,500' from the floor of the Pacific. From the miles of white, palm-shaded beaches that encircle its shore, Guam rises a further 1,334' above sea level to the cloud-capped peak of Mount Lamlam. Verdant coconut and banana plantations follow the valley contours and lush jungle cloaks the southern half of the island. Apart from the military bases, Guam resembles Hawaii. Located 5,800 miles west of San Francisco (and only 1,500 miles south of Tokyo) it is actually west of the international date line and, as a result, is the place where America's day begins.

Within its 209 square miles, this 30 x 8 mile island is home to some 94,000 Americans; about 35,000 servicemen and their families and some 59,000 Guamanians. Short and stolid with dark, round features and narrow eyes, the handsome Guamanians greet you with a "Hafa adai"—*aloha* in their Chamorro tongue—and though completely modern in outlook and education, they retain all the traditional friendliness and hospitality of the South Seas. Guamanians also speak English, are Catholic by religion and the majority still follow the leisurely Latin way of life first introduced here by the Spaniards.

Like Puerto Rico, Guam became American by right of conquest after the Spanish-American War of 1898. Japan held it between 1941 and 1944. In 1950, it became an unincorporated U.S. territory with most of the self-governing attributes of a state but with the residents, though full U.S. citizens, being unable to vote in presidential elections. Since 1961, any U.S. citizen has been free to enter Guam without any formality—and with only a vaccination certificate, you can continue anywhere into the U.S. Trust Territories of the Pacific that lie beyond.

Agana, Guam's capital, is a transplanted American city, mainly interesting for its free port shops, where the luxuries of the world sell duty free at prices which are often lower than those in Hongkong. Because Guam is U.S. territory, you may bring back $200 worth of duty free purchases instead of the usual $100 allowance. But to discover the charm of Guam you must visit some of its 19 villages. You'll find, clustered beside blue coves along the island highway, picturesque villages like Umatac, Inarajan or Merizo—draped with fishing nets and fragrant with the blooms of the ylang-ylang trees which drift down from the hillsides.

Umatac flanks a bay brillant with palms and tropical flowers. Gardens and lawns are decorated with large sea shells and the scene is made colorful by the women and children constantly bathing off the beach. Magellan landed here in 1521.

Merizo, a beautiful village, lies beside the sea within sight of the offshore Cocos Islands. Occupying the village center is an ancient Spanish church and monastery while in the hills above are caves with lamp-lit shrines. Merizo is a splendid beach resort and islanders will take you over to Cocos Island for skindiving and picnics.

Inarajan is a charming village of quaint old Spanish houses on narrow streets. The villages are famed for their cockfights and water buffalo races.

In these and other villages, Guamanians hold frequent fiestas. Visit one and you'll be offered *fanihi* or fruit bat, a succulent delicacy, or such native dishes as venison and chicken *kelaguen*. Another thing to see are Guam's jungle ranches; the owners often invite visiting Americans to dinner and you'll be served such typical island fare as baked yams, taro, coconut crab and fresh baked *tuba* bread.

Best way to explore Guam is to rent a car (standard U.S. rates apply) and drive around the island. En route, you'll see all the villages plus crumbling Japanese pillboxes and rusting tanks and such archeological curiosities as *latte* stones, probably the coral pillars of ancient temples.

Guam's most flavorful hostelry is the Micronesian, an inexpensive hotel with a lot of South Seas flavor. Tony's Travel Lodge is also fairly reasonable. More modern inns and motels with air conditioning and pools charge $15-$18 double, meals extra. However, while permanent rentals are not abundant, with a little persistence you can find a reasonably priced apartment for rent.

But—lying in the Orient, 3,600 miles west of Hawaii, Guam is the most off-the-beaten-path bit of U.S. territory described in this book. It's not a place you can look over on a weekend vacation. Yet if you'd really like to get away from it all to a tropical island in the Pacific, Guam has lots to offer. Besides Hawaii, it's the only island in the Pacific where Americans are free to settle, work or start a business under the U.S. flag. More vacation cottages, small motels, guest homes and resorts are badly needed, not only for visiting Americans but for the hundreds of Japanese who are expected to become Guam's number one tourists. For Guam is the closest tropical island to Japan and today's prosperous Japanese can easily turn Guam into a popular resort. Guam also offers good opportunities to start smaller businesses —scuba diving, fishing tackle, and boat rental stores—to serve the small but growing tourist trade.

So—start a small guest house or launch a small store or repair business in one of Guam's picturesque villages and you can lead a leisurely South Seas life the rest of your days.

Guam is also aerial gateway to the American administered Trust Territory of Micronesia. New airlines and hotels are about to open up these scattered Pacific atolls, on some of which females still go topless in Edenlike simplicity. Very soon, such little known islands as the Truk, Yap, Mariannas and Caroline groups will be open to visiting Americans at special air fares and should offer splendid opportunities to get away from it all on American administered soil.

The dry season, January through June, is the best time for a visit. Although subject to almost daily showers (annual rainfall 90"), Guam is cooled by constant trade winds and the temperature ranges between 72° and 88°. In this latitude (13° North) typhoons can be damaging but no more so than in the Florida Keys.

From the U.S. Pacific Coast, air fare to Guam is $317 o.w., $602.30 r.t. If you are visiting Guam, you can take in Japan and Hongkong at only slightly higher fare. Freighter service is also available.

More information: Guam Tourist Commission, Box 3520, Agana, Guam 96910.

CHAPTER 8

Island Idylls in the Southern Sun

L ooking for an island where two bits buys a dollar's worth of vacationing in the winter sun? Here are four accessible islands in the Southland where you can do just that. While prices soar to astronomical heights in southern Florida and at desert resorts, rates at these empty islands *drop* as much as 50%. Each of the islands has more color, flavor, and atmosphere than the crowded winter resorts. And more amazing, several of the islands actually have a better climate than some resorts which up their rates for winter tourists.

EDISTO ISLAND, SOUTH CAROLINA. It sounds unbelievable but on Edisto Island, mules still draw wagons, Negroes sing old slave lullabies, and lush plantations still thrive in queenly groves of gnarled oaks and magnolia. The same aura of old plantation days hangs over the little resort of Edisto Beach, a spindly community of some 350 houses on stilts lining a shell packed beach among subtropical palms and myrtle overlooking the Atlantic between Beaufort and Charleston.

Even in summer, the island is inexpensive. But after the summer visitors leave, a blissful indolence descends over Edisto and tranquility reigns till the following May. Yet winters are mild and sunny, and it's then that fishing is best. From Labor Day on, you can rent a nicely furnished housekeeping cottage or apartment for $35-$65 a week including heat; at Ocean Villas apartments for three run $35, 2-bedroom apartments for seven are $50, and 2-bedroom beach housekeeping cottages accommodating eight are just $55 a week. Delicious oysters sell for $3.50 a bushel and all the crabs and clams you need are here for the taking.

The hinterland is full of deer, wildfowl, and turkey; and bass, bluefish, trout, and mackerel swarm in nearby rivers. Edisto is also a bird watcher's paradise; the Carolina Bird Club counted 106 species in a single day. Beachcombing can be rewarding too; priceless relics of corsair days are occasionally washed ashore. Some of the surrounding plantations can be visited and there are longer trips to take you to famous gardens such as Magnolia and Middleton. Night life is nonexistent in uncommercialized Edisto, but there's dancing some evenings and you can meet the islanders over a beer at the Pavilion Restaurant.

Adjoining community is exotic Edisto Beach State Park, one of the most beautiful beach parks on the entire Atlantic coast. A particularly pleasant hostelry here is Hutson's Landing, five miles down the beach, a quiet and picturesque yachtsman's retreat with some of the best and freshest seafood in the South.

If you fall under the spell of this picture book island, and decide you'd like to live here, you'll discover some real bargains in lots and homes for sale. For as little as $9,000 you can buy a furnished 3-bedroom house on the beach, a 4-bedroom one from $12,000.

More information: Collin's Pavilion Motel; H. Lybrand, Ocean Villa Apartments and Cottages; Atwood Agency; or Hutson's Landing Club, Box 139-A, Route 1; all at Edisto Beach, S.C. 29438.

CATALINA ISLAND, CALIFORNIA. It costs $475 for steamer fare to Europe and back. But for $6.25-$7.50 r.t. you can board a motor cruiser at Long Beach or Newport Beach—or a steamer at Wilmington—and cruise across the blue Pacific to a rugged isle reminiscent of the French Riviera. All summer long Catalina hums with tourist throngs. But after Labor Day, the population dwindles to a mere 1,600 gracious islanders and Catalina settles down to eight whole months of secluded tranquility. Until the following May, the Islanders enjoy their own vacation, hotels cut rates 20%, and Catalina basks in a mild sunny climate that never knows frost.

Though Catalina is only 25 miles offshore and part of Los Angeles County, it is undeniably different. Descending the gangplank is like entering a foreign land—Catalina, which many rank with the choicest spots on earth, presents the picturesque, beautiful, and unusual all in one. Picture if you will a rugged mountainous island with murmuring surf washing high cliffs, headlands, and great rock pillars dotted with cozy coves and bays. Inland, sweeping up to lofty Mount Orizaba, tortured canyons form a captivating background to a real oldtime ranching country where buffalo, boar, wild sheep, and goats roam untamed. And nestling in a canyon between precipitous hills, the red-tiled roofs and soft white walls of Avalon town reach back from a blue crescent bay through winding streets lined with palms and eucalyptus.

There's a quiet beauty about Avalon in the off-season. Even in mid-winter, bowers of semitropical foliage bloom and through the still air, the bells of Chimes Tower mark the passage of the hours and quarters. Geraniums grow wild, garbage cans boast gay colors, and horseback riders mingle with the handful of cars. But you won't need transportation. Everything from horseshoes to fishing and riding can be found within five minutes walk. Strolling Avalon's color-splashed streets is a never ending delight, each bend revealing a fresh inspiring view. White hulled boats swing at anchor in the deep blue bay all winter long. Some evenings fog drifts in, shrouding Avalon in a cloak of silence broken only by the plaintive moan of the foghorn and the wild cries of swooping gulls and cormorants. It's then you experience your deepest contentment with this secluded paradise just 17 minutes by air from frenzied Los Angeles.

But most days are bright and clear and you can bicycle over miles of shoreline roads that wind and twist above the sea. All winter you can sun on the beach and watch the busy shore boats. You can play golf on an interesting 9-hole course, visit the Historic Museum and the Bird

Park, sail or play tennis, hike across hilltops in the exhilarating breeze and fish off the pier or from a rowboat. Nights, the town comes to life with a variety of night spots that stay open all year and with get-togethers of all kinds where you'll meet the friendly islanders and join in their fun. There are movies, a weekly newspaper, the "Islander" and many clubs and lodges. Catalina seldom has crime and juvenile delinquency is limited to visiting summer tourists.

Costs? Several hotels stay open in winter and you can get a comfortable double room for $55 a week. Apartments start at around $65 a week and for not much more, you can get a deluxe bungalow. For a longer stay, you'll find winter rentals going begging, with small apartments from $100 and small homes from $160 a month. Utilities are expensive and freight adds to cost but overall, prices are little higher than on the mainland.

Because everything you can possibly need lies within five minutes' walk, a car is unnecessary and this makes retirement costs lower than on the adjacent mainland. Taxes, payable in a lump sum that may be as low as $75 a year, cover all city facilities including fire department, police, and hospital. There are also churches. Retirees live in two main areas of Avalon: the level central section where closely grouped 2-3-bedroom furnished homes sell from $22,500, larger ones with rental accommodations up to $50,000.

That is Catalina today. But in 1963, a new Master Plan was drawn up to provide for more resorts and for new retirement subdivisions throughout the island's 75 square miles. Heart of the plan will be a series of lovely contoured homesites rising in tiers above Avalon and the community of Two Harbors. Homesites here can be leased on a lifetime basis but none will be sold. Automobiles and ugly forms of commercialism or suburban conformity will be strongly discouraged. Instead, funiculars and electric trams will provide transportation. Only smokeless native industry will be permitted. And numerous cultural activities are to be introduced to make Catalina a replica of culturally oriented Santa Barbara. For more about this splendid island retirement development, write to Santa Catalina Island Co., Avalon, Calif. 90733.

More information: Avalon Catalina Island CoC, Box Eye, Avalon, Calif. 90733.

MUSTANG ISLAND, TEXAS. It's only 45 minutes out over the bridge and causeway from Corpus Christi, but lonely, primitive Mustang Island and its picturesque fishing village of Port Aransas are worlds away from the big Texas city. Mountainous sand dunes, cloaked in purple morning glory and garish sea beans, flank a broad, white, surf-pounded beach, which stretches an unbroken 130 miles clear down to Mexico. Thousands of wildfowl blacken the skies, rare roseate spoonbills and herons stalk the placid back bays, and clumsy pelicans doze on posts in the colorful fishing boat haven. At the island's eastern tip, tall palms cluster around Port Aransas, a languorous village of

1,200 individualistic islanders who earn a living as fishermen and guides.

Once called Tarpon, Port Aransas lives for fishing. In the historic Tarpon Inn, over 7,500 kingly scales bear autographs of F.D. Roosevelt and hundreds of celebrities who caught tarpon here. And in summer, fish-hungry anglers by the thousands embark at the docks seemingly without noticing the island's dazzling, shell-packed beach and the peace and solitude surrounding the village. The result? Port Aransas is probably the most overlooked island paradise on the Gulf with the least-used beach in America.

Although the village is crowded in the summer by fishermen and surfers, in late fall, winter and spring, only a handful of canny Midwesterners who have discovered the mild, dry climate and low off-season rates are in evidence at all. During these sunny, rainless months, rates drop 25%-50% so that motels and housekeeping cottages can be had for $45 a week or $120 a month, some for still less. Yet Mustang Island lies on the same latitude as St. Petersburg, Florida, and enjoys a similar climate marred only by rare northers and still rarer frost. So inexpensive is seafood that for $2 island restaurants serve such enormous seafood dinners they customarily present each diner with a paper bag to take home the uneaten portion. And for $7 you can spend the day deepsea fishing on a party boat.

As an escapist spot to just loaf in the sun you'll find it ideal. You can comb the beaches for hundreds of different shells and weird driftwood, and it's not unheard of to pick up an occasional Spanish doubloon. Crabs and oysters are here for the taking, bay fishing is tops all winter, you can spear flounders by torchlight or hunt geese and duck. Winter weekends see informal fishing tournaments followed by jolly evening shrimp boils and square dances to which everyone is welcome. There are cozy little bars, a movie, and less than an hour away, Corpus Christi's symphony, art activities, and night life. Many couples have retired in this New England-like fishing village; cottages and homes sell from $10-14,000. More fashionable homes and some condominiums are available and you'll find a well equipped county park with cabanas. Its heavy summer patronage is bringing gradual change to Port Aransas. But for a fall through spring sojourn, it's still ideal.

Much the same sort of thing can be found at neighboring Rockport on its lovely peninsula of windblown oaks. A school of fine arts flourishes in fall, but Rockport's harbor and deep water reefs were made for painting at any time of year.

More information: Corpus Christi Area Tourist Bureau, Box 1147, Corpus Christi, Texas 78403.

BEAUFORT, SOUTH CAROLINA. Not more than one tourist in a thousand driving south on U.S. 17 ever turns off at Garden Corners and takes the winding dead end road that tunnels for miles through moss-hung oaks and out across two islands to picturesque Beaufort.

The few who do suddenly discover themselves in a green-blue mosaic of Carolina Sea Islands and a crinoline-flavored background of grisly pirate lore and belvedered mansions. Brackish rivers coil around green, wooded islands with names like Dahtah, Ashepoo, Tachassa King, and Little Pon Pon, and near the road you pass praise houses where Gullah Negroes still sing the purest spirituals in America. The Sea Islands were settled by white men 60 years before the Pilgrims landed and Beaufort itself dates from 1711. Ox carts still rumble over Sea Island roads. And Beaufort has changed little since the old plantation days.

Ancient houses with tabby foundations, some still with musket slots, slumber under a perennial green mantle of moss-shrouded live oak, magnolia, chinaberry, and wild jasmine. Every house in Beaufort carries a legend, like Marshlands, home of Emily in Francis Griswold's *Sea Island Lady*. Some still have slave quarters in the rear. Stately gardens riotous with camellias and azaleas surround hoary graveyards and ancient St. Helena Church. And all of Beaufort looks out over wooden piers gay with shrimp boats to endless miles of timeless islands and tidewater marsh.

Contentment comes naturally here. There are no tourist crowds, night life, or bars. Only a few artists and writers have so far discovered Beaufort as an unspoiled paradise. From September 1 till May 31 accommodations become vacant and rates are inexpensive. During the long fall-to-spring off-season, small apartments can be had at $100-$125 and two-bedroom homes at $125-$150 fully furnished.

There's plenty to see in the history-steeped Low Country: you can visit innumerable plantations, churches, graveyards, and other historical shrines, as well as the U.S. Marine Base on nearby Parris Island. The waters teem with fish and almost anywhere you can take enough oysters, blue crabs, clams, and terrapin in half a day to stock the average restaurant for a week. Just imagine yourself feasting on huge sizzling bowls of crab meat and hush puppies at practically no cost at all. There are deer and wildfowl in abundance, yet no one but natives ever hunts them. After dark, you'll find winter art classes, square dances, and movies, but not much else.

Constant southwest winds blowing across limitless water keep Beaufort cool in summer, and winters are balmy and bright. If all you want to do is to get away from it all in an atmospheric little waterside town, Beaufort is the place.

As you might expect, Beaufort ranks high for retirement. Despite gnats and mosquitoes being troublesome at times, and summers tending to be humid, life is quiet and living costs inexpensive. For year around rental, small unfurnished apartments are numerous at $100 a month, and there are two-bedroom unfurnished homes at $125. Older two-bedroom homes sell for $15,000, new ones $18,000. Many ex-Merchant Marine and Navy men have discovered contentment here in the later years. Taxes are very low.

More information: Beaufort County CoC, Beaufort, S. C. 29902.

CHAPTER 9

Hideaways Steeped in Americana

Here are six corners rich in Americana where you can relive the past free of clicking turnstiles and advertising stickers on your bumpers. Not only were these historic places chosen for their freedom from commercialism but also for their *living* history. At three of them you can vacation in perfect comfort among some of the most colorful, most unspoiled Indian tribal life remaining on this continent. And in New Mexico there's an added bonus in an equally rich Spanish-American culture. In this historic Southwestern state are the oldest cities in America— several antedate Columbus.

Elsewhere, you can blaze the trail of early fur traders to a strange land where you'll see fur trading being carried on in exactly the same way today. You can recapture the rough, tough days of the California Gold Rush, sample a forgotten corner of colonial American, or live the life of a wealthy Southern aristocrat in an authentic atmosphere of taffeta and lace. All are primarily for your summer vacation.

NEW MEXICO'S OLD SPANISH TOWNS. If you're *really* seeking something different: escape from the machine age to a timeless land where every man is an artist and you can find fulfillment through self-expression, consider New Mexico's age-old Spanish towns and mountain villages. Drawn by its colors and moods, its intense sunshine and limitless horizons, more Ph.D.s, writers and artists settle in New Mexico than in perhaps any other state. Scores of imaginative men and women, tired of worrisome city living, have come here to master that most elusive of arts, the art of living.

By and large, New Mexico's villages have been discovered only by those who seek to understand and live in the past. In 18 living pueblos scattered along the Rio Grande, you will find Indians living exactly as did their ancestors when Coronado came in 1540. Atop mountain peaks or in cool valleys, descendants of 18th century Spanish colonists pursue their quiet traditional way of life in tiny remote villages of quaint adobe homes under lacy cottonwoods and aspen trees. Here, among the mountains and mesas, the brown and tan adobe villages, you will discover a way of life unique in America: a land where progress has been halted, where old traditions are revered. People live, think, and worship as their ancestors did, often in weathered missions built in the sixteenth century; soft Castilian Spanish drifts across plazas; bread is still baked in outdoor earthen ovens, horses and wagons creak through narrow streets, and at Christmas or fiesta times, ancient *creches* and *luminarias* decorate buildings, shepherds' fires burn before houses, and the pueblos resound to primitive Indian dances.

To walk into one of these old Spanish towns is like stepping back 200 years in time. Not infrequently, you'll still see women in black *rebozos* mingling with Indians in deerskin boots and checkered headbands. Proud Spanish Americans, descendants of Spanish Dons, are as friendly and gracious as the people of Mallorca or Andalucia. But don't expect them to come skipping out to meet you. Give them time. In the mountain villages, especially, the people are shy of strangers. Stay around a few days, and you'll meet everyone; try hurry them or be patronizing and you will return home disappointed.

Whether you stay in Santa Fe or in a mountain village without plumbing, you'll find plenty to do. Sightseeing opportunities are inexhaustible. Within a day's drive of most places you can visit 18 living Indian pueblos—more foreign than anything in Europe—where craftsmen busily weave or create ceramics and jewelry, no two pieces are ever alike. At fiesta times there are colorful ceremonial dances to chants and drum rhythms. You can fish, ride, play golf, hunt, ski in winter, and attend square dances. You can meet artists and writers or old time prospectors. There are Indian ruins and cliff dwellings to explore for potshards, metates, arrowheads and skeletons, and you can pick up almost every kind of known rock. Remote trading posts sell genuine ceramics, paintings, blankets, pottery, jewelry, and handsome moccasins ($9-$14) that never reach the tourist shops. And in small inns and dining rooms far off the beaten path you can sample enchiladas, tortillas, tacos, tamales, and guacamole salads, all liberally sprinkled with green and red chili.

High, dry, cool, and bracing, New Mexico is a natural therapy for tension, its constant year around sunshine a frequent cure for asthma, arthritis, and bronchitis. Golf is played nine months of the year, and even in winter when snow silhouettes the pinon and manzanita, sparkling dry sunshine and crisp air make outdoor activities pleasant and invigorating. Year around retirement or sojourning can be surprisingly inexpensive.

Here's how. In the smaller towns and villages, old adobe homes on large tracts of land can still be picked up for the proverbial song. It's not unheard of for large old haciendas to sell for under $3,500. And if you're a do-it-yourself addict, you can install plumbing and fix these places up like palaces for a few hundred dollars. There's nothing like a thick walled adobe for winter warmth and summer coolness. Too, you'll soon learn to trade for apples, apricots, blue cornmeal, beans, chili, dried corn and other staples from farmers or village stores—prices are surprisingly low. Unskilled labor can be had for $10 a day, maids for $20-$25 a week, and in some places (but not all) you can still get a haircut for $1, a shave for less. Laundering is quite cheap. Near Indian villages you can hire bands of Indians who will build you a brand new adobe home for less than you'd pay for a pre-cut frame house elsewhere.

Adopt local customs and you'll live better and for less than in most other states. Try to import supermarket standards and you'll pay through the nose.

A word about staying at small mountain villages. This book is a guide to off-beat America. But frankly, New Mexico's Spanish mountain villages are so offbeat, they are not for the average tourist. Few have any commercial accommodations at all. Drinking water is some-times piped in through hand hewn log troughs laid end to end and in some places, plumbing is a luxury. If you go, be prepared for some mild adventure. And learn a few Spanish words. In most villages, you'll meet a few American escapists or artists for congenial company; but you can't count on it. And for the first few days, companionship could be a problem.

Don't be too easily discouraged when you are told a village has no visitor accommodations. A few inquiries may direct you to a family willing to take boarders. Some ranches also take paying guests.

Because of the abrupt change, we suggest you ease gradually into New Mexican life. Don't head straight for a small village. Instead, go first to Santa Fe. Even Santa Fe, with its narrow streets and heavy adobe homes, will seem unreal at first. But this historic city—founded in 1610 as the capital of New Spain and today, America's oldest state capital—also boasts every modern comfort plus an ample supply of hotels, motels, rentals and homes for sale. Make your base here. Proud of its Spanish heritage, quiet, unhurried and peacefully untrammelled, Santa Fe has long been called the "City Different." Here, thinking is prized, intellectualism valued, and conformity alien. Thus, like hundreds of other people with alert and imaginative minds, you may find that Santa Fe offers everything you seek.

Otherwise, make day trips from Santa Fe to nearby villages. At some villages, you can stay overnight at motels in the area. Feel your way along and play it by ear. At some villages, you may find a home for rent, recently vacated by a writer or painter who has moved on. Or ou may find an inn or a private family willing to take guests.

Starting with Santa Fe, one of America's most charming residential cities, here is our handpicked selection of New Mexico's most unspoiled escapist retreats. It's best to avoid July and August, when tourist traffic is heavy and rates higher. However, camping is good at or near most villages (though sites are sometimes short on wood and water).

Santa Fe, New Mexico's capital, is an easygoing, overgrown pueblo where the primitive mingles with sophisticated culture and wealthy homes are intentionally indistinguishable from the modest adobes of the intelligentsia. For its size (45,000) no other American city is so essentially different and few are so tolerant. Notwithstanding several gaudy miles of motels, gas stations and franchised tacos and fried chicken stands along busy US85, and a 4-laned highway loop through the lower city, most of Santa Fe is still relatively untouched and unchanged. The real Santa Fe begins with territorial architecture surrounding the plaza and spreads east through winding unpaved roads bordered with tan adobe homes to restful, pinon-studded hills. Apart from a few traffic lights, the downtown area is still thankfully free of such common eyesores as neon signs and telephone booths. Nor does Santa Fe have any monotonous suburbia. Stroll a mile or so from the edge of town to a hilltop and you can see thousands of acres of virgin country. Away from garish US85 and its endless traffic, no hotdog stands, gas stations, billboards or trash dumps mar the roads. Nor is there any big city crime: women can walk safely anywhere at night. Most of the paperbacks we saw in the supermarkets were scholarly classics; paintings from pop to primitive adorn dozens of art galleries and shops; corner fireplaces and massive beamed ceilings are taken for granted in most homes; and Santa Fe is nationally renowned for its high quality concerts and summer stock and for its outdoor opera theater, high on a hill, at which nine different operas are presented each summer, with many American premieres, each sung in English by world famous voices.

Emphasizing Santa Fe's distinct and unique way of life is the fact that the State Art Museum occupies the town center while the State Capitol lies on the loop highway. Downtown, costumed Navajos mingle with tweed-clad citizens under ancient Spanish colonial *portales*. And for block after block, from the plaza up Canyon Road to Cristo del Rey church, is a solid succession of writers' homes and artists' studios. To walk through the city is to walk through nearly four centuries of history. Tucked away downtown are old stores full of lamps, harness, *ristras* of chile, saddle irons and things you haven't seen for 30 years. The fragrance of burning pinon and juniper wood drifts through the narrow streets. No one blows a horn at a pedestrian. On Santa Fe's narrow streets, you often see a car stop to let someone in or out. A line of cars may form behind him. But no one toots his horn.

In spring, lilacs burst into blazing blue, red, purple and white. Unlike the situation in most other cities, Nature here is ever at hand and even city dwellers live close to the soil. With unfurnished apartments available at around $100 a month and modern two-bedroom homes from $12,000, Santa Fe can be safely recommended to any retiree with a creative hobby and an interest in the arts. Despite cold winter days and a light cover of midwinter snow, the city offers zestful retirement in a sunny, dry and healthful climate. You'll find dozens of clubs and groups that welcome newcomers.

But don't expect to step into the rich, full life of Santa Fe in July or August. During these months, painters and writers, fearful of tourist hordes, stay hidden or take to the hills. However, your best passport to quick acceptance by the art colony is to become a painter yourself. "Get a sketch book and pastels," a local artist advises. "And if anyone asks what you're doing, say 'abstractions'." In no time at all, you'll be flooded with invitations to social gatherings. Another way is to visit studios to see paintings for sale. Eventually, you might have to buy a canvas or two but by that time, you could know half the colony.

Then, too, whenever a local author publishes a book, it's common practice to hold a *soiree* at a local bookshop. Again, if you attend opening nights of plays by Santa Fe playwrights, invariably there'll be people in the lobby who can present you to the playwright—a not unnatural request. One way or another, you can swiftly enter the thriving art and intellectual life of this fascinating town.

Now for the villages. Here they are, from A to Z.

Abiquiu: many writers and artists have lived chapters of their lives in this Spanish-American town overlooking green Chama Valley. Fields of corn and chili, cedar-cloaked mesas and red cliffs, surround the adobe village and its colorful plaza. Abiquiu's massive mission church, embellished with fine tin handicrafts and an inspiring *viga* ceiling, is one of New Mexico's most handsome. Terraced flower gardens climb the steep hillsides and in spring, flowers pour over low adobe walls. Abiquiu is 40 miles north of Santa Fe.

Acoma, the "Skytop City," is the oldest and undoubtedly the strangest town in America. Built before Columbus crossed the Atlantic, Acoma is perched atop a 400-foot-high mesa in a vast valley rimmed by buff-walled cliffs. The whole scene is utterly fantastic. You park below the towering mesa and ascend either over a newly built automobile ramp, or up wooden ladders and rock niches hewn from a fissure in the face of the mesa.

The entrance is dramatic. Passing through a low rock arch, you suddenly emerge on the windswept mesa-top to find yourself in an unbelievable town of terraced adobe homes, some 3 stories high. There are houses as old as the pueblo itself: you will see windows made of mica slabs, ancient Spanish T-doors, earth ovens, carved door lintels, and the largest mission church in New Mexico. Every ounce of 'dobe in its ten foot walls was hauled up the burro trail from the valley below. Inside, Indian women in blue *rebozos*, kneel in penitence on the cold stone floor. The painting on the wall was given by the King of Spain in 1629.

Acoma is barren. Nothing grows in this forlorn Shangri-La. Everything—water, food, firewood, oil—must be brought up by burro train from the plains below. Walled yards are piled with corn, strings of red chili, beans, fodder, and dried meat. There is no electricity, no plumbing. Wooden toilets stand in windblown isolation around the mesa's outer rim. But the views would amply repay far more inconvenience. To the east, rising wraith-like from the plain, the pink walls of Enchanted Mesa tower higher than Acoma itself. And as far as the eye can see stretches an endless jumbled sea of gigantic buttes and mesas. Despite its being only 14 miles from busy U.S. 66, Acoma is as remote as a monastery in Tibet.

Some 2,000 Keresan Indians call Acoma home. Time was when they made fine jewelry, pottery, and rugs. And some still do. But there is no school in Acoma and during school months, most of the Indians move to Acomita village, 12 miles away. Thus most of the time there are empty houses for rent in Acoma. Rates are $2-$3 a day or $35 a month. A maid, indispensable for Acoma's woodburning stoves, adds a further $50-$60 a month. For a short stay, you can rent a single room for $1.50-$2.50 a day.

Nowhere else in America can you find another village so utterly out-of-this-world as Acoma. You will see pagan dances at Easter and from time to time, superstitious Indians make secret pilgrimages to the top of Katsim—the Enchanted Mesa. A day, a week, a month here is an unforgettable experience. But before you can stay, you must secure permission from the Governor of the pueblo, who lives at Acomita. This may take a day or two and a gift helps. If officialdom still frowns on your sleeping in Acoma, you can rent a room at nearby Acomita, Santa Maria de Acoma, or in the motel at Laguna on U.S. 66. *Warning: Acoma is definitely not for the average tourist.*

Anton Chico, one of New Mexico's oldest towns, nestles in a beautiful valley beside the Pecos River. Actually, there are two towns or plazas: the Old Town or upper plaza with its stone-walled Sangre de Cristo church was the home of Dons; the lower village three miles distant, still *agreste*, boasts a later church with wonderful stained glass windows. Both plazas are steeped in rich Spanish traditions. Some haciendas are ruined; most are crumbling. But inside you will find delightful corner fireplaces and split log and rush ceilings in traditional pueblo style. *Santos* stand in wall niches and Sangre de Cristo Church is filled with figurines. Today, Anton Chico is a ghost town; only 125 families remain. But there are absolutely no tourists. To get there, take the paved side road off U.S. 84 between Las Vegas and Santa Rosa.

Bandelier National Monument is a camper's paradise. In magnificent canyon country, you will find 93 well planned campsites with toilets, surrounded by hundreds of ruined Indian home sites dating from the 12th century. There are organized trails and ranger-conducted sightseeing programs and you can explore over 300 hand hewn caves, hillside kivas, and towering cliff dwellings of 400-1,200 rooms. Also here are a park lodge, saddle horses, and trailer sites. To reach this fabulous 500-year old city, leave U.S. 64, 84, or 285 west on State 4; Bandelier is about 45 miles from Santa Fe.

Chaco Canyon: if you've ever seen those magazine photos of weird ruined Indian apartment houses, here's where you can get in the picture and explore them yourself. Chaco Canyon is ten miles of camper's heaven in the wildest, most primitive part of New Mexico's Navajo Reservation. Its ancient Pueblo Bonito apartment houses built in 919 A.D. are the largest and finest Indian ruins this side of Mexico City. There are 32 ruined kivas alone. Under red cliffs lies one of America's most remote campsites, with modern facilities and a trading post and filling station nearby for supplies. (Tip: bring your own cooking fuel; firewood is scarce.) Get there by turning off State 44 at the Blanco Trading Post near Otis and going south 28 miles over a graded gravel road.

Chamita is a storybook Spanish village among lonely hills and mesas beside the cottonwood-dotted Rio Chama. There are tiny orchards, old adobe houses, covered wells, earth ovens, and your shaving water arrives via hand hewn log troughs. The wooden crosses studding the village are there to remind residents of long dead ancestors. It's a strange place, remote and fantastically different—no place for ordinary tourists, a Mecca for the true escapist, a paradise for artists. You arrange your own accommodations. Chamita is north of Riverside just off U.S. 64.

Chimayo dozes in its sun-soaked valley, a village of weavers, where handlooms stand inside many a cottage door and craftsmen dream up patterns to the rhythm of swinging shuttles. For Chimayo is home of the famed Chimayo blankets, a craft brought from Spain and preserved in the valley by the Ortega Master Weavers. Chimayo itself, an unhurried village of colorful adobe homes, color-splashed by strings of red chili suspended from the eaves, nestles in the canyons of the Sangre de Cristo range. You can visit ancient cliff dwellings and the old Spanish churches of Santa Cruz, Cordova, and Trampas in neighboring Penitente country. And in the center of Chimayo is the famous Santuario, called the Lourdes of America, where pilgrims come to scoop sacred earth from a miracle hole. True, there are TV antennas in Chimayo and tourists come to buy the famous blankets but Chimayo still lives on in the days of the Dons. And the blanket industry has saved it from economic decay. The ideal strategy is to establish a base at Riverside or Espanola on U.S. 84 or 64 while arranging accommodation in the village.

Cloudcroft among pinewoods at 9,000 feet is a summer art colony with the highest and coolest golf course in the 50 states. The fussiest tourist can count on finding comfort here while here are also unpretentious cabins available. Quiet and relaxing with magnificent panoramas, Cloudcroft is home of Cloudcroft Art Colony, where you can attend classes in painting, weaving, and ceramics conducted by nationally known craftsmen. After classes, there are chuck wagon suppers, hay rides, and campfire sings with none of the hoopla of the average tourist resort.

Cundiyo, a perfect Shangri-La, is a picturesque adobe village precariously clinging to a mountainside 30 miles north of Santa Fe. So remote and secluded is Cundiyo, that through intermarriage, all but three of its residents bear the family name of Vigil. This is a village of Spanish weavers and it's . . . well, it's primitive . . . don't come here if you're a sybarite. From Santa Fe you reach Cundiyo by way of Pojoaque and Nambé.

El Rito's single neon sign is inexcusable but detracts little from the beauty of this serene old Spanish village. Years ago, El Rito was a rough, tough Western town (blood stains of vintage 1939—a murder of passion at a wedding dance—still stain its saloon) but nowadays artists replace the desperadoes of yesteryear. Strung out for miles along a creek, El Rito's rustic architecture harmonizes wonderfully with the unspoiled scenery of surrounding Carson National Forest. There are paintings on display in stores and if you like a rural setting, retirement here is tops. El Rito is 60 miles north of Santa Fe by paved highway.

Galisteo lives by its reputation as the least spoiled village in all New Mexico. Here you have only to spend a moment to relive its elegant past. Residents have sworn that nothing will ever be permitted to spoil Galisteo's atmosphere and charm. In massive adobe homes, you can view private collections of treasured Spanish antiquities and there are elaborately carved Spanish doorways, ancient flower-adorned patios, and lacy wrought iron gates.

Despite several rusting automobile bodies scattered around, we can recommend Galisteo as a genuine discovery!

You get the timeless feel of the place best by wandering among the *santos* in the plaza church beneath the fleckering light of a Georgian candelabra. Best of all, Galisteo has simple housekeeping accommodations at $65 a month and—get this—for around $8,500, you can buy an attractive two-bedroom adobe home. Others (slightly crumbled but cheap to fix up) cost even less. If you would like to retire at low cost in an authentic Spanish village, Galisteo is the answer. It's just 21 miles from Santa Fe. Eat at the atmospheric La Mancha Restaurant.

Hillsboro, a one-time mining town in the Black Range Mountains, boasts a lurid outlaw past and an authentic Western cowtown flavor. Green cottonwoods arch over Hillsboro's sleepy main street and among the walled patios or beside blue *casita* doors, old settlers and prospectors sit eager to yarn with anyone who'll listen. The Hatcher Hotel provides inexpensive accommodation and if you'd like to retire amid rich local color, Hillsboro has lots to offer. You'll find it near Truth or Consequences just down State 180 from U.S. 85.

Kingston lies in the bosom of the mountains six miles from the Black Range summit, a small ghost mining town of false fronted stores and old frame houses in trim flower gardens. As New Mexican towns go, Kingston is not old, yet in its stillness there's a nostalgic feeling of long ago. Typical of Kingston is the post office bell, rung as in early days to herald arrival of the mail. It's a small summer resort and an ideal place if you are seeking a hideaway. Two can stay at the Black Range Lodge quite inexpensively, and there are other accommodations. Kingston is near Hillsboro.

Manzano, a little Spanish town near Mountainair, occupies a beautiful setting below the wooded Manzano Mountains. Each night and morning the mission bells toll out across the ancient apple orchard planted in 1800 and the little 'dobe houses with their crimson-splashed flower gardens. Not far away is the ruined mission of Gran Quivira where you can camp, and the country abounds with ruined Indian villages littered with arrowheads and shards. Accommodations are available in private homes, and, occasionally, small homes in the area rent at $55-$65 a month. Several retired couples have purchased old Spanish adobe or rock homes at low cost and cleverly remodelled them into attractive pueblo style residences worth $6-8,000 (without any increase in the original low tax assessments). Upon arrival you can stay at Mountainair's hotels, motels, or cottages, which last run about $100-$125 a month out of season.

The Mogollon Mountains in southern New Mexico offer unsurpassed wilderness camping in a rugged unfrequented area rich in Indian lore, ghost towns, cliff dwellings, temple caves, and old battle sites. If you're a rock hound, or would like to relive the life of an early day prospector, you can do it here on a two week vacation. You'll find three magnificent camp sites beside Willow Creek and nearby you can explore Gila Cliff Dwellings National Monument.

Pena Blanca, strictly out of the 17th century, is another crumbling Spanish village where the sweet sound of mission bells mingles with soft fragrant cedar smoke. Typically New Mexican down to dying haciendas, covered wells, and rambling garden walls, Pena Blanca is a ranching village close to the Cochiti Indian Reservation. You must arrange accommodations on arrival. It's northwest of U.S. 85.

Taos has been a popular haven for writers and artists since 1898. For years it was one of those rare places where independence and individualism flourished while the machine age passed it by. Until the late 1960s, Taos successfully resisted change. But since then it has gradually turned into a sleek emporium of shophisticated dress shops and art galleries. On winter weekends, its streets echo to the *après ski* life of a gay young crowd and in summer, five hundred tourists a day flood accommodations and drive prices up. The artists have become rich. New homes are going up. Parking meters rim the plaza. Weekend traffic is maddening. Worst of all is the mile of utterly tasteless and disturbing motels, auto agencies and franchised hamburger and root beer stands that line the road between Taos and neighboring Ranchos de Taos. Flourishing hippie communes have appeared on the outskirts and so many long haired followers of Eastern philosophies are around that some stores refuse to serve anyone not wearing shoes.

Despite these changes, Taos may still merit consideration. Driving along a main road a few miles from the plaza recently, we had to stop for several minutes while a band of Indians on horseback drove a vast herd of sheep across the road. Personally, we'd avoid Taos itself. But neighboring Ranchos de Taos appears still relatively unspoiled and hundreds of people live in complete tranquility in country homes a mile or two from Taos plaza.

Ranchos de Taos sprawls in a huddle of adobe homes and artists' studios clustered around the ancient bastioned walls of San Francisco de Assisi Mission, built in 1772. New homes, most in pueblo style, are appearing on the outskirts. But there is none of the blatant commercialism of Taos.

So popular is Taos that homes or apartments for rent in the area are non-existent. Best plan is to rent a motel efficiency unit or—for permanent residence—to buy or build. Worst time to arrive is during the frantic July-August period or during the midwinter ski season. During summer, you can attend a famous art school, hear lectures on art and philosophy, enjoy summer stock, foreign movies and the music festival at nearby Twining. Taos has its own individual culture, art, music and dress. Several first class French and Mexican restaurants boast well stocked cellars. In few other places in America will you find such a sophisticated small town in such a primitive setting. Even today, you'll probably find more art, beauty, color and atmosphere, more individualists, more stimulating people, more original thinking per capita in Taos than in almost any other American community.

Tesuque, ten miles north of Santa Fe, is a small art colony and suburb, fine for retirement. Small pueblo-style homes with corner fireplaces can sometimes be rented quite reasonably.

Truchas, largest and highest of the old Spanish villages, nestles among the Truchas peaks at 8,000 feet. This is Penitente country and in Lent, you'll see strange rites and ceremonies in the village and in their *morada.* You'll find electricity, grammar schools, and a modern water supply but beneath the surface, life has changed little since Truchas was founded 200 years ago. When you move in with one of the 300 families, you're heading for the most unusual type of living you have experienced.

More information: for Santa Fe, write the CoC. For other places, write Tourist Division, Dept. of Development, State Capitol, Santa Fe, N. M. 87501.

GOLD RUSH TOWNS OF CALIFORNIA. The discovery of gold at Sutter's Mill in 1848 touched off an era of turbulent Gold Rush days that changed the history of California. Boom towns sprang up overnight and many died just as quickly. Fire overwhelmed most; others remain as melancholy ruins. But for one reason or another, a handful of these towns has survived. Here, among the rocks and hills of the Sierra's western slope, you can relive the days of '49 in as pleasant a setting as anyone could wish for.

Heart of this colorful heritage is the Mother Lode country, 100 square miles of green forests and apple orchards, deep canyons and high mountains. Pioneer day structures still cast a romantic spell over once roaring old camps, many immortalized by Mark Twain and Bret Harte. At some towns you can stay at balconied, Victorian style hotels where both of these writers once signed the guest book. And you'll find plenty of Gold Rush Americana in the form of decrepit old houses and gardens, early day churches, and preserved saloons, faro banks, firehouses, and Chinese stores. Mountains of tailings and rock from placer mines line rivers and creeks and you'll see whole hillsides washed away by early hydraulic mining. Occasionally you can still meet a grizzled prospector who never gave up, and every old hotel has its character with yarns of earlier days. Vivid place names such as Brandy City, Port Wine, Poverty Hill, Poker Flat, Tragedy Springs, Murderer's Bar, and Squabbletown are sprinkled across the map.

Whether you just like to poke about in old places or drive scenic highways, you'll find plenty to explore. There are caves, historic churches, gigantic trees, pioneer museums, old theaters, and, within easy reach, jewel Lake Tahoe and the grandeur of Yosemite National Park. You can pan for gold (and find it) or fish for trout in the same chill streams. In summer, you'll find art shows, summer theaters, and old time square dances. Food ranges from imported French cooking to Hangtown Fry—oysters, eggs, and bacon fried together. And you can shop for low priced handset jewelry—pieces made of local gold and gems run only $2.50-$5—and uncut gems are plentiful for as little as 25¢.

Prices are lower than they were in 1849 (when whiskey cost $16 a fifth; eggs were $3 each, and knives fetched $30). But don't expect anything fantastically cheap. For real flavor, sample the old hotels. Several are still as they were in the '50s down to the same groaning floorboards, high ceilings, and musty odor. Alternatively there are plenty of housekeeping motels and cottages, and inexpensive mountain fruits help lower grocery costs. Any ranch will sell you a whole lug of fine Bartlettt pears or a box of sweet apples for $3.00. Attractive camp-sites are also abundant; many are in state parks where the charge is just $1 a day.

At an elevation averaging 2,000 feet most of the Mother Lode towns lie above the fog and below the snow. Occasionally there'll be light snow in winter but summer days are far cooler than in central California and blankets at night are the rule. This salubrious foothill climate is recommended for asthma, bronchitis, and respiratory ailments, and for retirement can hardly be exceeded. If you look, forward to owning a little 3-5 acre place during the Golden Years, you'll find numerous small fruit farms to choose from. For $20,000 you can buy an attractive 3-acre rancho with a nice two-bedroom home. Others run as low as $15,000.

For a week, a month or a lifetime, you'll find the following towns packed with Gold Rush memories. They're all easily located on any road map of California and all have accommodation in or near.

Auburn, built on the Mother Lode in 1848, stands on hills above a deep river gorge. In the lower town around the plaza you'll find many picturesque pioneer day buildings including an astonishingly photogenic firehouse. Tourists come all year to visit its gift and antique shops but spring and fall are relatively uncrowded. Several motels supply very reasonably priced accommodation and there are attractive homesites if you're about to retire. Auburn is within a very short distance of Lake Tahoe and the High Sierras.

Grass Valley, a larger and more modern town today, lies in the heart of gold mining country and has many picturesque historical buildings. Nearby are the atmospheric old gold rush community of Downieville and the Rough and Ready mining camp. Grass Valley makes a good center for exploring the Mother Lode, or for retirement. Small apartments rent from $100 a month; older two-bedroom houses sell from $12,500, new ones from $17,500. The Bret Harte Inn charges $65-$70 a month for two, meals additional.

Mokelumne Hill, on State 49, has a lot of history, a small white church built in 1850, and various ghost-like Gold Rush buildings. But its real charm lies in the Hotel Leger, formerly the Hotel de L'Europe and, before that, the Leger Beer Hall. Although modernized, it still retains an authentic 19th century flavor. Rates are $62-$68 a week for two with semi-private bath.

Murphy's, where Randolph Hearst's mine was located, is an interesting ghost town near Mercer's Caves (which you can explore). Here is the unspoiled pioneer-day Murphy's Hotel complete with bullet-riddled doorway and a bar where the call was "Name your poison!" Built in 1856, the hotel is replete with original iron shutters and balconies, and the names of Mark Twain, John J. Astor, and Ulysses S. Grant can be seen in the guest book. Rates in the old section are $30 weekly for two.

Nevada City, a peaceful little town built on seven hills among beautiful trees, teems with gold mining history. Landmarks include Stewart Mansion on Piety Hill (home of pioneer lawyer William A. Stewart), Red Castle on steep Prospect Hill—a red brick monument of pioneer architecture, the Wells Fargo Express Building, and the Ott Assay Office which is still in business. The bricks of the gracious old National Hotel have housed many of the West's most colorful characters, and you'll still find traditional mountain hospitality in its high ceilinged rooms and lobby furnished with antiques. Rates are $70 double per week (and substantially reduced by the month). Meals add about $5 per day.

At 2,500 feet, fog-free and dry, romantic Nevada City is one of California's most atractive retirement towns.

Paradise, just north of the Mother Lode, is surrounded by historic Western settlements and the huge Willard Nugget came from nearby Sawmill Peak. Since those days, Paradise has grown into a garden community of some 22,000. Occupying an uncrowded 17 square miles on a ridge between the Feather River and Butte Creek, Paradise is a community of homes scattered through orchards and meadows under giant pine and oak trees. Despite its modern conveniences and well stocked shops, Paradise retains all the beauty and atmosphere of a rustic Western village. It's not uncommon to find deer on your lawn while squirrels and songbirds are everywhere. Trout abound in rivers and streams and in nearby Oroville Dam; hiking and riding trails lead straight into the High Sierras; and local clubs sponsor frequent rock hunting trips, square dances and arts and crafts classes. With its climate free of smog and fog—cool summers and mild winters—Paradise is tops for vacationing or retirement. You'll find motels, apartments and trailer courts in all price brackets and a wide choice of homes at reasonable prices.

Volcano is probably the most picturesque of the Mother Lode ghost towns. Daffodils carpet the surrounding hills in spring and you can visit the largest Indian grinding grounds in the United States. Equally atmospheric is the St. George Hotel built in 1862. Its unnumbered rooms, bearing names like Sutter's Creek and Rough and Ready, look out over vine-tangled 19th century balconies. In neighboring Amador County are the colorful towns of Amador City, Drytown and Fiddletown, all rich in reminders of gold rush days and offering quiet vacationing or retirement.

Weaverville, northern California's Trinity Alps, with its picket fences, honey locusts, and Victorian air, is another old mining town well worth your time. There is traffic on U.S. 299 but just off the highway you'll discover an aura of romance in the quiet, tree-shaded old brick houses with their iron doors and shutters. Here, too, is an old joss house where 3,000 Chinese laborers once worshipped.

More information: write the CoC's at individual towns.

MOOSONEE, ONTARIO. Whenever you're ready for a startlingly different summer vacation, whip up a little of that spirit of adventure and crank up the family car for a real voyage of discovery. To Moosonee you ask? Where's that? Never mind now. Just drive up to Toronto and keep going north up Highway 400. At Barrie switch to Highway 11 and keep going north. You're going a long way north. *You're bound for Canada's Hudson Bay on the edge of the Arctic.*

As far as Cochrane the highway is paved and well maintained. Leave your car here. The railroad staff will see that it's safe. People are friendly here. Already you're in the Northland. No one's a stranger. The rest of the way you go by train. No car can reach Moosonee. Buy a ticket—it's only $7.45 each way.

As you step aboard the train, a mixed one consisting of work-stained coaches and boxcars, you sense that this is a train with character and personality. Her name is the *Polar Bear* and the Northland is her home. Glancing around you see your fellow passengers: lumberjacks headed for lonely outposts in the woods; Indians headed home after a visit to the bright lights; khaki-coated Mounties; and missionaries, doctors, nurses, and fur traders bound for the Arctic. There's no formality and soon you've made a host of acquaintances.

All day the *Polar Bear* rattles northways across the limitless muskeg, making leisurely calls at lonely frontier posts and logging camps. During the 186-mile trip you enjoy a hearty buffet lunch with your newfound acquaintances. And you learn the pros and cons of frontier life. Finally, 670 miles north of Toronto, the train pulls into Moosonee—most easily accessible point in Ontario's Northland.

You step out into a strange new world. Immediately you are greeted by a reception committee of Indians who stare at you as at a visitor from Mars. Crowds of Indian children swarm aboard the dining car for a feast of ice cream, a rarity at Moosonee. You investigate a cinder sidewalk raised above the muskeg. It leads down to mighty Moose River a quarter of a mile away. Then you're met and ushered aboard the Log Lodge "Limousine," converted school bus which slowly but surely negotiates the snowless summer roads to your vacation home— Log Lodge.

Log Lodge is no resort hotel but it lacks nothing in plumbing or homelike comforts. Hearty outdoor meals are served thrice daily and you can live here for $7 double per day without meals (or with private facilities for $11 a day per couple). Believe us, these are very reasonable prices for a remote area where everything must be shipped in. The Ontario Northland Railway purposely keeps all rates as low as possible to encourage more people to see the great potentialities of this part of Ontario. Alternative accommodations can be arranged at the Hudson Bay Staff House at Moose Factory or in summer at the modern campground.

You'll find no neon signs, juke boxes, bars, or liquor stores at Moosonee. Save for some new construction projects, a few outboard motors and an occasional bush plane, this frontier outpost hasn't changed a great deal since the first white man arrived 300 years ago. All transportation is by big 22-foot outboard-powered canoes. And that's how you cross to Moose Factory, a $2 r.t. ride to an island three miles out in Moose River.

Moose Factory was old when the American Revolution occurred. It's been an old spot in Canadian history since the Adventurers of England established the first Hudson Bay post here in 1673. This is a BIG Hudson Bay Post. Half the supplies of the Arctic roll from its wide, sturdy doors. You can buy anything from lipstick to sled dog harness, not to mention those beautiful Hudson Bay blankets. Indian tents and tepees cluster around the Anglican mission and you may see some Eskimos. The blacksmith's shop has seen daily service since 1800 and in the Anglican church the altar drapes are moosehide and the prayer books are in Cree. This is the untouched Far North and you get here for approximately $15 in round trip fare plus gas.

At Moose Factory you'll be cordially welcomed at the big Hudson Bay store where they sell exquisite Eskimo carvings, Indian leatherwork, and native handicrafts at rather attractive prices. The Indian village reaches a mile along the shore and the little ships passing continuously ply to every corner of James Bay and far into Hudson Bay. There are trappers and sled dogs galore. In fact there are so many husky dogs, we suggest bringing ear plugs (how they can howl in the long evening twilight!)

Don't come here for a lightning visit. You'll regret it. You can spend days just exploring Moose Factory, the outpost weather station, the busy waterfront, and the Mountie headquarters. All day, every day, you'll see primeval Indians with tribal customs and traditions unchanged till recent years. It's superfluous to suggest bringing your camera. There are two exciting boat trips costing $5 per person. Downstream, you can go to Ship Sand on James Bay, an arm of Hudson Bay, where thousands of blue geese rendezvous in fall. And upstream, among myriad islands, you'll visit the primitive Indian encampment at French River, home of an Indian tribe living in blissful ignorance of the 20th century. Fishing isn't outstanding but it's worth bringing your rod along. Best time for a visit is in August, when the weather is finest and flies fewest. Hayfever is unknown.

Moosonee itself was virtually inaccessible before the railway was built in 1932. When you go back next day on the *Polar Bear* you'll travel with scores of newfound friends. And when you reach your car again, you'll have earned the right to go home and brag about North America's most fantastic vacation. (One day roundtrip excursions are available June 15-September 14 on Sunday, Wednesday and Friday from and back to Cochrane, $12 r.t.)

More information: (you can also go by rail direct from Toronto. All reservations *must* be made ahead.) Write Mr. L. F. Dobberman, Passenger Service Supervisor, Ontario Northland Railway, North Bay, Ontario, Canada.

QUEBEC CITY, P. Q. It isn't always necessary to seek history and charm far from urban comforts. For just across the Canadian border, in French speaking Quebec City, you can stay in a replica of a Left Bank *pension* and enjoy all the history and romance of the only walled city still standing on this continent north of Mexico.

Of course, you've seen calendar pictures of Quebec, perched high on a lofty cliff with its oblique grey roofs and dormer windows crowding down to the St. Lawrence. Champlain chose this site in 1608 because, from the heights of Quebec, his cannon could reach across the mile wide St. Lawrence. Barracks and houses were built behind a massive stone wall that encircled the city. And Quebec became capital of New France. But the city was not impregnable. In 1759, the British under

Wolffe scaled the Heights of Abraham, took Quebec intact and gave the French a peace treaty which has permitted French law and culture to continue unchanged to the present day.

Quebec is still capital of Canada's largest province—home of five million French speaking Roman Catholics—and 92% of the city's population are ethnically French. French is universally spoken, all signs are in French and French menus betoken the tempting French cooking you will receive in such typically named *pensions* as Au Pigeon Voyageur, Manoir des Chenes and the Pension Blais.

From the Province of Quebec Tourist Office in Parliament Buildings you can obtain a giveaway list of tourist accommodations. Scan its pages and you will find the addresses of comfortable *pensions* located all over the Upper Town. Often, these *pensions* are in mellowed houses two centuries old. And a few steps away are such imposing panoramas as that from the rue des Remparts.

Stand on the rue des Remparts, where ancient French cannon still poke out over the St. Lawrence, and you see at once why Quebec is called the "split level city with two voices." From the Upper Town in which you are standing, Quebec drops abruptly down a cliff to Lower Town, a sea of high, steep roofs and medieval grey stone buildings crowding the St. Lawrence. An iron staircase called Breakneck Steps connects the two towns. Or you can take the elevator that runs between Dufferin Terrace and Joliet's House.

From your vantage point in the Upper Town, you can stroll along the city walls. Below, you watch busy bus traffic passing through archways, relics of the former city gates of Saint-Louis, Saint-Jean and Kent. A full square mile of Upper Town still lies within these crenellated walls. As you walk along Dufferin Terrace, under the bulk of Chateau Frontenac, you note the enchanting river panoramas: the St. Lawrence busy with liners and freighters. Then, just beyond, you see the Citadel, guarded by French speaking soldiers in battledress. Past the Citadel's historic walls, two-wheeled horse-drawn carriages clip clop into Battlefields Park, where Quebec fell to the British in 1759.

Hayfever: Unknown

Most of the places in this book are havens for ragweed sufferers. Free booklets giving hayfever indices for most parts of the United States and Canada can be obtained by sending a postcard to the following addresses.

For the United States—Oren C. Durham, Chief Botanist, Abbott Laboratories, North Chicago, Ill. Ask for *Hay Fever Holiday*.

For Canada—Canadian Government Travel Bureau, Ottawa, Canada. Ask for booklet *Canadian Havens from Hayfever*.

Despite the cars and buses, old Quebec continues to be a living museum. You can spend days exploring it all on foot, with the free walking tour map and brochure available from the Tourist Office. During fall, the whole St. Lawrence country becomes a flaming pageant of autumn colors. But the true Quebec is revealed only to those who remain in the city throughout winter.

Under its blanket of snow, Quebec is completely transformed. Skiers glide on the slopes of Battlefields Park while ice skaters cut fancy figures and waltz to band music by the chute of Dufferin Terrace toboggan slide. For two weeks preceding Lent, *Bonhomme Carnaval*

Medieval Retreat: in a Monastery

Scattered about the eastern United States and Canada are a number of monasteries which welcome guests seeking retreat and seclusion. Within their medieval walls you can enjoy a few days of restful re-creation and renewed spiritual health. Most monasteries conduct regularly scheduled retreats of from 3-7 days. During this time, withdrawn from the world in the peaceful confines of the monastery, most people discover a new peace and understanding. There is usually a friendly spiritual director to guide you. Here are several monasteries which welcome male guests for this purpose.

Saint Leo Abbey, Saint Leo, Fla. 33574. A Benedictine Abbey encircled by orange groves on the shores of lovely Jovita Lake. Anyone is welcome to spend a few days; costs run $20 for 2-3 days, all-inclusive. St. Leo's has an 18-hole golf course.

Monastery of the Holy Ghost, Conyers, Ga. 30207. Retreats last 3-6 days; accommodations are in a comfortable guest house.

Abbey of Our Lady of New Melleray, Dubuque, Iowa 52001. A Trappist monastery, one of only four in North America. Guests can stay from Sunday evening until Friday evening; scheduled retreats are arranged at weekends. Payment is by free will offering.

Abbey of Gethsemane, Trappist, Ky. 40073. A Trappist monastery founded in 1848 by French monks, possesses a truly medieval flavor. Scheduled retreats are conducted all year from Sunday to Friday. Payment is by voluntary offering.

Abbey Cistercienne, La Trappe, Province of Quebec. This is the famous Oka monastery which produces Canada's best known cheese. It lies among densely wooded hills. Male guests only are received for week-long retreats any time but Holy Week. There is no set fee.

More information: for reservations, etc., address the Father Guest Master at the monastery of your choice.

presides over a succession of festivities climaxed by a Mardi Gras second only to that of New Orleans. Sleighs pop and curling *bonspiels* and hockey matches are daily events. During these frenzied Mardi Gras days you will see the international dog sled derby, a thrilling canoe race across the St. Lawrence and a round of masquerades and balls and street festivities. Because none of this is staged for tourists, the entire population participates wholeheartedly. Unlike Paris, Quebec is not a night club town. A few supper clubs present distinctively French entertainment until 1 a.m. But that's all. Summer entertainment is limited to harness races and an occasional concert on the Terrace. But for under $5 you can enjoy an all day river cruise to Sainte-Anne de Beaupré shrine.

Perhaps you wouldn't want to retire in Quebec but six months or a year spent living in a *pension* here could turn out to be the most interesting chapter in your life. You'll quickly learn to speak French and even the lowliest eaterie prides itself on its cooking. Quebec is also a good place to load up on British imports: English doeskin gloves are only $3 a pair, fine Harris tweed sports jackets just $35.

More information: Office Municipale du Tourisme, Place de L'Esplanade, Quebec City, P.Q., Canada.

THE TURTLE MOUNTAINS OF NORTH DAKOTA. To find an unusual vacation you must look in an unusual place. Certainly, the average American seldom thinks of spending a vacation in unromantic-sounding North Dakota. But on the Canadian border, midway between Atlantic and Pacific, that state's Turtle Mountains offer a low-cost vacation where outposts of the 20th century rub shoulders with pre-Columbia culture. Sixteen thousand Chippewa, Cree, and Metis Indians living among these lake-studded, timbered hills add a unique background that brings you close to the real American Indian while enjoying a quiet, relaxing and uncommercialized vacation. Through interpreters, you can speak with some of the nation's oldest Indian chiefs, attend Sun Dances and Indian gatherings, and, in July, witness the mile-long religious procession of mixed bloods at the feast of St. Anne.

The Turtle Mountains rise out of the prairie, a 40 x 50 mile chunk of wooded hills studded with oak-bordered lakes and laced by scores of silvery streams. Almost at the geographical center of North America, here Western and Eastern wildlife overlap: the black-chinned western humming birds meet the ruby-throated eastern humming birds and the woods abound with deer, elk, coyotes, bobcat, and coon, while deep in the forest lurk the toy fan-tailed deer. Here the Mound Builders "vanished," and today "Folsoms," "Yumas," and other prehistoric types of arrowheads can still be found.

The summer cottages of local people dot the shores of islands and peninsulas on sparkling Lake Metigoshe, largest of the many lakes. But Metigoshe is still uncrowded. You will find no honky tonks, neon signs, or juke boxes in the Turtle Mountains. Just to the southeast,

Long Lake is even more secluded. In midsummer housekeeping cottages rent for $40-$50 a week and if you pay $50, a boat is often included.

Prices are so low you will hardly believe them. Eggs sell as cheaply as 23¢ a dozen, whole chickens for $1, and vegetables can be bought from farmers at below market prices. In June, you can gather bushels of choke berries, pin cherries, wild raspberries, and huge bush cranberries and for $1 you can add a quart of the lushest, richest cream you ever saw.

Out of season—September and October are beautiful months—prices are even lower. If you'd like to enjoy the long sunny warm summer days and cool, refreshing nights in a cottage of your own, you'll find miles of lakefront land at bargain prices ready for building.

Of course, all the usual water sports are here: boating, bathing, water skiing, and fishing for walleyed pike and perch. There are frequent Indian dances. You can shop for whittled lamp stands, cured and mounted skins, crocheted slippers, and patchwork quilts sold by natives at uncommercialized prices and you can cross into Canada and buy English woolens, china and silver at well below United States prices. And if you're keen for good cooking, you'll ferret out those rural places where country women serve mouth-watering Scandina-

---

Old fashioned family vacation: at low-cost farms

Wherever you live in the East or Midwest, there are probably a dozen nearby farms at which you, your wife, and two children can spend a vacation for $150 a week for all four. You can pick your farm from an easily obtainable list by the mouth-watering descriptions of the food served; a typical farm offers "charcoal steaks, smoked pork chops, chicken dinners, buttermilk pancakes, hot biscuits and honey." Children get unlimited milk and farm produce. All farms have inside plumbing and electricity and specialize in rural hospitality. Some are modernized colonial homesteads beside New England lakes; others are near golf links, art colonies, and beaches. Children, of course, revel in the hay rides, wiener roasts, picnics and swimming holes—and there's always a baby sitter handy.

Listings of farms taking guests are obtainable from: Farm Vacations and Holidays, Inc., 36 E. 57th St., New York, N.Y. 10022 (enclose $1.95, also on sale in bookshops); Pennsylvania Farm Vacations, Travel Development Bureau, Pennsylvania Department of Commerce, Harrisburg, Penna. 17120; Ohio Farm Vacation Association, Route 1, Quaker City, Ohio 43773; and the state tourist information bureaus of Connecticut, Vermont, Maryland, West Virginia and other Northeastern and Midwestern states as listed at the end of each state write-up in Chapter 10. Most listings are not ready until May.

vian, German, and Bohemian meals. A full T-bone steak dinner with all the trimmings costs only $2.50. There are miles of riding trails and woodland hiking trails where you can find arrowheads, meet veteran trappers running lines, and study nature close up. And not far away are the famous International Peace Gardens on the Canadian border.

But in this unspoiled country where hospitality is a by-word, your most memorable experiences will be in meeting people like Henry Klebe and Edward A. Milligan, men who know the Indian as few other Americans do. Henry Klebe, caretaker of a private museum, will explain his unique theories about the origin and spread of mankind and the Indian in particular. And Edward A. Milligan, called He Topa (Four Horns) by the Indians, has spent a lifetime in association with the Indians of the West, has performed two major Sun Dances, and is the adopted son of One Bull and Whitebull, warrior nephews of Sitting Bull.

You can easily meet Milligan by staying at his lodge, Timberwolf Up, a beautiful lakeside guest house jammed with collectors' items, where rates are $50-$60 a week for modern housekeeping accommodations with a boat. Through him, you can talk to all the colorful Indian personalities who still perform their ancient tribal rites and Sun Dances.

To locate the Turtle Mountains, head for Bottineau, North Dakota, then ask directions.

More information: Edward A. Milligan, Timberwolf Up, Lake Metigoshe, Bottineau, N.D. 58318.

TO LABRADOR

Few people know it, but you can drive most of the way to Labrador and continue your journey by train. Only in recent years have new highways and a railroad made this trip possible. To get there, you drive first to Quebec City, then take Highway 15—the Côte Nord Highway—to Tadoussac and Sept Iles. Leaving Quebec City, the road winds through 150 miles of picturesque Laurentian villages and charming countryside. You cross the fiord-like Saguenay River to Tadoussac. Then for hundreds of miles, the road takes you through a sea green forest to the busy frontier iron ore port of Sept Iles. From here, on Tuesdays and Fridays, a train of the Quebec and North Shore Railroad sets out on its 300 mile crossing of the western Labrador wilderness to Schefferville. For hours the train winds north beside the Nipissis River to the mining towns of Wabush and Labrador City. At Wabush, you can stay in the rather expensive Sir William Grenfell Hotel. But for greater economy, you'll want to continue on the train while it crosses the northern boundary of Labrador and goes two or three miles into Quebec, to the isolated town of Schefferville. At Schefferville are two somewhat less expensive guest homes: the Royal and Montaignes.

More information: Newfoundland Tourist Development Office, St. John's, Newfoundland (for Labrador); Tourist Branch, Department of Tourism, Fish and Game, Parliament Bldgs., Quebec City, P.Q.

ST. LAWRENCE ISLAND. Few people know it but without leaving the United States, you can vacation in an Eskimo village within sight of Siberia. St. Lawrence Island is the place, a 100 x 60 mile slice of the State of Alaska surrounded by the often chill waters of Bering Straits.

To get there, you first fly or drive to Fairbanks, then you buy an onward ticket by Wien Air Alaska. From Fairbanks, you fly to Nome, a frontier town that retains much of its gold rush appearance and heritage and where you can pan for gold and still strike color within minutes almost anywhere. But Nome, with its late model cars and tour buses and jumping night life, is a far cry from the Eskimo village you're seeking. You realize this as you switch from the big prop jet that brought you to Nome to the ancient DC-3 that flies through snow fleeced clouds to St. Lawrence Island.

The plane touches down twice on St. Lawrence Island—at Northeast Cape and at Savoonga to land supplies—before bumping to a stop on the landing field at Gambell Village, the island capital. Eskimos in fur-trimmed parkas turn out by the dozens to welcome the plane and many have dog sleds, even in summer. Untouched by commercialism or the tourist boom, the Eskimos consider every stranger a V.I.P. and you'll be plied with friendly questions about life "outside."

That this in an unspoiled Eskimo village is apparent from the dozens of *oomiaks* or skinboats that dot the shore, each laboriously covered with walrus hide. Huge six foot whalebones, some a century old, serve as fenceposts and walrus bones are scattered everywhere. Ask for a toothpick and you'll be handed a walrus whisker. Many Eskimos live by hunting whales and walrus from their skinboats—visitors are welcome to go along—while others make a living by herding reindeer.

On a clear day, you can view the coast of Siberia, a bare forty miles away, and from time to time, empty skin boats blow across from Eskimo villages on the U.S.S.R. shore.

Don't look for a martini before dinner (Gambell Village is dry, so bring your own liquor) but one enterprising Eskimo offers clean basic rooms in a Quonset hut plus all meals at $15 a day. For an even more interesting experience, however, you can stay with an Eskimo family at approximately the same price.

More information: Alaska Travel Division, Pouch E, Juneau, Alaska 99801.

CHAPTER 10

Guide To Getting Away From It All

Whatever other kind of place you're seeking if it's different, unusual and in North America you'll find it in this chapter.

Fed up with the regimentation of 20th Century living? Then here are scores of Old World towns and villages rich in history. Tired of fighting tourist hordes? Here are places where a tourist is a curiosity. Like to do something really different on your summer vacation? Then how about exploring the West's ghost towns, camping beside a glacier, staying at an Eskimo village or a Hudson Bay post?

You'll find brief descriptions of all of these plus many more. This chapter is a run down of almost every place in North America which is unique, colorful, atmospheric and uncrowded.

You will read of authentic frontier towns, cow towns, logging towns, fishing villages, mining camps, river towns, colonial villages, and old ante bellum Southern towns where you can spend an entirely different vacation far from the artifical atmosphere of commercialized resorts. There are camping Utopias, handpicked state parks, more island paradises, and hideaways galore. If you'd like to find a foreign background without leaving North America, here are Scandinavian, French, German, Swiss and even Eskimo towns and villages.

Both in this and in earlier chapters you'll find many references to art and literary colonies. Main reason is that artists and writers have a nose for uncrowded beauty spots heavy with atmosphere. Art colonies do not remain in a place which is spoiled. Wherever there is an art colony you can be pretty sure of finding at least the fundamentals of a Utopia: atmosphere and beauty with a minimum of commercialism. And in many cases, these art and literary colonies are the sites of summer theaters and schools of arts and crafts or writing; and they frequently offer lectures, concerts and other cultural activities. Within this chapter we have tried to mention the best of these cultural towns; places where you can combine natural beauty and atmosphere with stimulating new ideas and intellectually satisfying company.

Among these places you will read of many which are ideal for a longer stay or for permanent retirement. But space prevents us from going into the detail of preceding chapters. Thus we urge you to write for further information before deciding any one place is for you.

In most cases you can obtain this by writing to the state and provincial bureaus listed. But for larger towns you should address the Chamber of Commerce in that city (no street address necessary). And for national parks and national monuments, address the Superintendent at the specific park or monument. Information on state parks and forests can be had by writing the State Park or State Forest Commission at the capital of the state concerned. For Canada, the provincial bureaus listed will provide all the information you require.

ALASKA. To discover the real pioneer Alaska, sample a week or more at one of the following places; all abound in magnificent scenery and fishing. Many of these places are accessible by car over the Alaska Highway or via the passenger and auto ferries that operate from Seattle and Vancouver Island to Prince Rupert, B.C., Ketchikan, Petersburg, Sitka, Haines and Skagway.

Chitina is a friendly, colorful pioneer ghost town where you'll find reasonable rates at its comfortable Chitina Hotel.

Cordova, not over-touristed, is a typical friendly old Alaska town with board sidewalks and several hotels. Nestled among pinewoods and framed by the mountains of Prince William Sound, it is the most beautifully located city in Alaska.

For a hideaway without peer, take the 45 minute flight from Juneau to Glacier Bay National Monument. Glacier Bay Lodge has comfortable cabins at $18 a day with views of the glacier-dotted coastline and you can take a cruise up Glacier Bay through waters flecked with icebergs, teeming with bird colonies and dotted with seals on floating ice cubes.

Few tourists visit Katmai National Monument, an hour by air from Anchorage. Here you'll find the Brooks River Lodge, set amidst superlative scenery with excellent food and lodging. Thousands of smoking fumaroles dot the monument while the rivers and waterfalls are literally jammed with leaping salmon and trout.

Haines, Alaska's Shangri-La, is a lovely little town attractive to artists; there are medium-priced accommodations but reservations are advised during midsumer.

The nearest Alaskan city to Seattle, so isolated it is reached only by steamer, ferry or seaplane, is Ketchikan, a flavorful commercial fishing center where the streets cling to mountain slopes overlooking the Inside Passage. It has the world's largest collection of totem poles.

For $65 each way you can fly from Fairbanks to Kotzebue inside the Arctic Circle, a flourishing Eskimo village where you'll see authentic native dress and culture, reindeer herds, seal and white whale hunting, and the blanket-tossing dances. Kotzebue is 90% native and beluga whale hunts are held in summer. Much the same can be seen at Point Barrow, most northerly point in mainland North America and only 1,200 miles from the North Pole. Wien Air Alaska offers tours to both places with comfortable accommodation guaranteed.

To sample life in an unspoiled Eskimo village, take Wien Air Alaska to Point Hope. This isn't the place to find a French restaurant but there's a tiny modest hotel and among the village's 300 Eskimos you'll discover the true timelessness of the Arctic.

In Southeast Alaska's Tongass National Forest, the U.S. Forest Service maintains over 100 vacation cabins, available to anyone at $2 a day. Write: U.S. Forest Service, Box 1631, Juneau.

Camping is a cheap way to enjoy Mt. McKinley National Park, primeval Alpine country surrounding the highest mountain in North America. You can drive right into the park and view caribou, Dall sheep, moose and even wolves and grizzly bear which roam through the park's stark beauty. You'll find two modern campgrounds and several others. Don't miss Camp Denali, a superb wilderness retreat, with rustic chalets and tent cabins at around $70 a week.

Ninilchik village on the Kenai Peninsula is a flavorful old Russian village with an original Russian church, an attractive campground and plenty of housekeeping cabins.

At Petersburg, a bit of Old Scandinavia—a fishing village rimmed by gigantic snow-peaked mountains—icebergs are a common sight; you can stay at the Mitkof Hotel or the Tides Inn.

Seward, located on a beautiful fiord, has kept its frontier flavor preserved in false-fronted stores, unpainted buildings, steepled churches, and unpaved streets; there are hotels and motels.

Sitka, the old Russian capital, has an Old World air and a lover's lane between totem poles. There are a hotel and a motel.

Skagway, once a rip roaring town, still retains a frontier atmosphere. Several inns and a hotel offer an adequate choice of accommodations.

Among more modern towns, Seward and Valdez lie in dramatic fiord settings. They're both small and hospitable with a lot of social gatherings and home entertainment for visitors.

More information: Alaska Travel Division, Pouch E, Juneau, Alaska 99801.

ALBERTA. For a cultural vacation amid unsurpassed mountain beauty and grandeur, enroll in the School of Fine Arts held at Banff each summer. Rates run about $10 a day with meals; month-long courses in music, weaving, painting, etc., $50-$100.

At incomparable Banff National Park, you'll probably linger at the 6,200' Moraine Lake Lodge. Rooms are $10-$12 a day, limit of 22 guests. But you can hike or ride a pony to reach the delightful Plain of Six Glaciers, a mountain hideaway only four miles from Chateau Lake Louise, serene with knowledge that there's room only for four guests. Rates: $5 daily per couple plus meals.

More inspiring mountain panoramas than seen from the timberline Mount Assiniboine Lodge can't exist. For rising sheer from mirror-smooth Lake Magog is the jagged peak of Canada's Matterhorn, Mount Assiniboine. You won't be bothered by neighbors. It's 34 miles to the nearest highway and railroad and the only way to get there is by a two day pack horse trip. Rates are $16-$17 daily all inclusive (write Mount Assiniboine Lodge, via Banff, Alta.).

Another true Shangri-La high in the Rockies is Lake O'Hara Lodge (address, Lake Louise P.O.) accessible only by special bus. Open June 27-Sept. 4; rates are $30-$35 daily for two.

A bargain in beauty is the improved camp-site at Maligne Lake, gem of the Canadian Rockies. Encircled by 10,000-foot peaks, this tantalizing lake defies description. Cheapest regular accommodations are tents at $12 a day with meals. But for a $1.50 permit you can camp for a full two weeks. Allow $11.50 for transportation by special cars into this almost inaccessible mountain hideaway.

For 50¢ a day you can enjoy a choice of other alluring camp-sites among the calendar-picture mountains, lakes and glaciers of Banff and Jasper National Parks. For something really different, try Jasper Park's camp-site at the Columbia Icefield.

More information: Alberta Travel Bureau, 331 Highways Bldg., Edmonton, Alta.

ARIZONA. To step into another world of solitude and vast distances, head for Kayenta on the Navajo Reservation, your base for visiting Monument Valley. Mighty mesas tower like sentinels over the Valley while awesome pinnacles, arches and spires cast deep shadows across the brilliantly colored landscape. You can camp or stay at a motel or at Goulding's Lodge.

For an unforgettable camping vacation in Arizona's most picturesque Indian country, drive up to Canyon de Chelly on the Navajo Reservation. You'll see cliff dweller ruins and mummy caves and meet shy, friendly Navajos, excellent weavers. The women wear squaw dresses. Unannounced Sings and Squaw Dances lasting three days and nights are often held. There are two camp-grounds and other lodgings at Thunderbird Ranch; and also at an Indian-run motel at nearby Window Rock.

Another escapist camping spot is lovely Bonita Canyon at Chiricahua National Monument, a wonderland of towering monoliths and steep canyon walls. There are also cabins at Maraway Ranch.

Every year, millions of tourists swarm over Grand Canyon National Park and Lake Mead Recreation Area but a bare 3-4 a day visit Grand Canyon National Monument, which lies between them. To get there, drive from Fredonia to Toroweap Overlook, a sheer 3,000' above the Colorado River in a brillantly colored world of cliffs, chasms and forests—it's like the end of the world ... a real experience!

For a wonderful summer vacation, drive to Show Low and onto the Apache Indian Reservation. Twenty-five per cent of the 5,000 odd Apaches still live in wickie-ups made of branches and you'll find magnificent fishing streams among the cool Ponderosa forests. Fort Apache hasn't changed much since the days when U.S. troops hunted Geronimo and nearby at Kinishba, a ruined pueblo site, you can hunt for shards and arrowheads on the mesa tops. Cheapest way to enjoy this reservation in the White Mountains is to camp. Several campgrounds near lakes and streams are only 75¢ a night.

If you're seeking Southwestern charm, sample Tubac, a tiny colony of writers and artists on US19 between Tucson and the Mexican border.

On the Hopi Reservation you can visit ancient mesa-top pueblos continuously inhabited for 900 years. Storybook villages like Walpi and Old Oraibi, perched high on stark mesa outcrops, date from 1100 A. D. Three thousand Hopis living on the reservation weave magnificent baskets and make fine jewelry. While the Hopis themselves cannot put you up, Mrs. Elizabeth White at Oraibi will, and odd trading posts are able to. Write the Superintendent, Hopi Reservation, Keams Canyon, Arizona, if you'd like to stay here awhile. Also recommended is the remote Navajo Mountain Trading Post situated 65 miles from its post office and 160 miles north of highway and railroad at Flagstaff. Dealing exclusively with Indians, you get a ringside experience from your $6 a day cabin. Meals are $1.25-$2 each additional; and there are pack trips.

When its last copper mine closed in 1953, Jerome became America's youngest and largest ghost town. Picturesque, sagging and crumbling down a mountainside, but still alive, Jerome would be an atmospheric place to linger awhile. You can camp at neighboring Mingus Mountain Recreation Area. Some old houses can be rented cheaply in Jerome or at nearby Clarksdale, another mining town. For camping out, a better bet in summer, try Horsethief Basin. Other rewarding locales are: campsites and sporting lodges along US666 between Clifton and Springerville (summer and fall only); Forestdale Trading Post near Show Low; pleasant undeveloped camp sites in the Huachaca Mountains west of Bisbee; and Cochise's Stronghold, a welter-world of giant rock formations; Payson under the Mogollon Rim; and thrilling Aravaipa Canyon (permission necessary from neighboring ranches).

For a rich camping adventure amid primitive Indian culture, head for Cibecue Creek, a wondrous 45-mile canyon of multicolored cliffs in the Apache Country. There are Indian ruins galore, good fishing and costumed Apaches still living in grass roofed wickieups. To get there, drive US60 north from Globe to 16 miles north of Salt River Canyon, thence fork left into Cibecue village and creek.

More accessible, tourist conscious, but still one of America's most beautiful canyons, Oak Creek Canyon in the red rock country offers camping galore. There are also motels and it's least crowded in fall.

Healing mud packs and invigorating spa bathing in the bright Arizona sunshine may be enjoyed in Old World style at the trim 3-story Indian Hot Springs Hotel at Pima. Complete hotel facilities, including meals, averages $9-$11 a day.

An off-beat place where you can sample a real subtropical Southwestern desert camping vacation is at Organ Pipe Cactus National Monument near the Mexican border. You'll see huge saguaro cactus, palo verde and Gila monsters in a magnificent desert setting. Bring cooking fuel.

If you're a painter or rockhound or just want to retire in a remote old mining town, try Oatman in northwestern Arizona. Access is from Kingman over the Oatman Grade, a paved but sinuous mountain road that serpentines for miles past abandoned mines and weird eroded rocks and ore dumps.

More information: Arizona Development Board, 1500 W. Jefferson, Phoenix, Ariz. 85007.

ARKANSAS. Two outstandingly beautiful state parks offer low cost camping at $1 a day or housekeeping cottages at $25-$60 a week. Devils Den State Park in the most rugged part of the Boston Mountains is famed for its grotesque caves, giant rock formations, and picturesque cliff paths. Petit Jean State Park, on a mountaintop among tall trees, is a fairyland of canyons, waterfalls, palisades and Indian picture rocks.

Among the least crowded state parks are Lake Ouachita (most accommodations are open year around) and Buffalo River, where steep grassy banks offer cataclysmic river-gorge views framed by pines. Both have cabins.

Near Huntsville lies the Land of the Crossbow where fall pageantry recreates life around the period of the crossbow. Crossbow instruction and target practice are available daily, plus a deer hunt. Farther east, about ten miles north of Mountain View, take to the back roads for undiluted Ozarkian flavor. Scattered here are typical hill country homesteads and the last of the pioneer log cabins and rail fences. Local craftsmen produce artistic items of native Ozark hardwoods. Tiny clearings amid the endless tapestry of forest green are a paradise for campers and trailer owners. Or you'll find modest cabins for $3-$5 a day.

For a cool vacation high atop Arkansas' highest mountain, 2,890-foot Mount Magazine, try a few days at the non-profit Mount Magazine Lodge ($5-$6.50 double). Exhilarating views.

To write a book, paint or just relax in an atmospheric mountain village, Winslow on U.S. 71 in the jumbled Boston Mountains will repay a sojourn. Part art center and poets' retreat, part ghost town and smart club center,

Winslow is a pioneer resort village of many facets. It's ideal for retirement.

More information: Publicity and Parks Commission, 412 State Capitol Bldg., Little Rock, Ark. 72201.

BRITISH COLUMBIA. Like being in Switzerland is spending some time in Garibaldi Park north of Vancouver, a scenic Alpine wilderness of wild, tumbled volcanic mountains, glaciers, craters and high meadows carpeted with wild flowers. Chalets charge about $60 weekly single with meals. Write for park booklet to British Columbia Forest Service, Parks and Recreation Division, Parliament Bldgs., Victoria, B.C., Canada.

Edens and Shangri-Las abound in this big northwestern province. Don't overlook the fishing lodges in the Cariboo and Chilcotin country and in the vast unsettled areas of northern and central British Columbia. All are ideal for family rest and relaxation while Dad and the boys enjoy fabulous fishing. A few you'll like include Ruth Lake Lodge and Sandpoint Resort on lovely Canim Lake in the virgin wilderness of the green Cariboo Mountains; and Bowren Lake Lodge at Barkerville. All are inexpensive.

Set in B.C.'s matchless Inside Passage are other attractive resorts. Write: Minstrel Hotel, Minstrel Island; Shoal Bay Lodge, East Thurlow Island; and Stuart Island Resort, Stuart Island.

It's not untouristed but close to the United States border is lovely Okanagan Valley, a fruit-and-flower-laden lakeside Eden framed by blue mountains. You'll probably enjoy the smaller resorts best, Naramata is a gem. You can camp on the lake shore or stay at housekeeping cottages starting at $45 a week. Warm and dry, Okanagan is fine in late September and October when tourists are few .

British Columbia is dotted with idyllic camp-sites including many in Yoho, Kootenay, Glacier and Mount Revelstoke National Parks. Get full details of each from address below.

More information: B.C. Government Travel Bureau, 626 Superior St., Victoria, B.C., Canada.

CALIFORNIA. For a state park vacation Big Basin Redwood Park, 25 miles from Santa Cruz, is easily outstanding; big redwoods, camp-sites and a lodge.

Borrego Springs is not low-priced but neither is it as expensive as the more fashionable desert winter resorts. In this mountain-rimmed oasis you can discover the true quiet and serenity of the Southwestern desert and soak up its flawless winter sun. There are plenty of camp sites and reasonably priced accommodations.

One of the most beautiful, cultural and unspoiled villages in America is Carmel, nestled among trees on a hill above its enchanting fan-shaped beach. Cosmopolitan and unhurried, Carmel is an atmospheric village of small flower-festooned shops and studios, winding streets and colorful patios. Neon signs, industry, and street lights are banned. Over 500 artists and associates belong to its art association; there are art galleries, instruction in all the fine arts, live theater at both an indoor and an outdoor theater, and Shakespearean and Bach Festivals each summer. Living here is no bargain but in neighboring Carmel Highlands rentals are less costly.

Equally interesting is Big Sur, a rural community of hippies, writers, artists and others interested in Oriental philosophies. You'll find it south of Carmel, amid powerful vistas of mountains and sea. Here is the Esalen Institute, an experimental school in exploring human awareness. Reservations are needed to enroll but it's a most rewarding experience.

If you're a desert lover, you'll like weird Death Valley National Monument, site of more phenomena than any other United States desert. There are badlands, ghost towns, volcanoes, sand dunes and Scotty's million-dollar Castle. You can soak up winter sunshine on little at Texas Spring campground or stay at hotel for a minimum of $10.50 double daily without meals.

Alternatively, for trailerites, a good winter sunshine hideaway is Palo Verde, south of Blythe on US60; others lie north of Blythe along the Colorado at Parker Dam.

In California's High Sierras you can hike for weeks without coming across a human habitation. There are recognized trails with campgrounds about every ten miles. Among outstanding camping spots in the state are Tuolumne Meadows, above Yosemite Park, and the two unimproved sites near Feather Falls. Near Oroville, Feather Falls are higher than Yosemite's Bridal Veil, yet seldom visited and at their best May 1 to June 15.

Less frequented than better known parks, Lassen Volcanic National Park, home of America's most recently active volcano, possesses many of the features of Yellowstone Park. There are several scenic camp-grounds. Offering access to the seldom-explored eastern reaches of the park is offbeat Drakesbad Resort Lodge. Lodge and cabin bedrooms run $11-$15 daily with meals. Farther north, Lava Beds National Monument and its Indian Well camp-ground are equally attractive and packed with geological interest.

For a vacation in an old world inn, try the Benbow Inn on the Eel River near Garberville. To further escape human contact, wend your way north, for the off-beat Mendocino Coast offers an escapist setting in its cliff-lined shores and old logging towns with their flavorful New England architecture. You'll see huge redwood forests and surf-pounded rocks and reefs and you can fish, hunt abalone, or beachcomb for agates and jade. You can stay at inns or motels or camp. Best places include Fort Bragg, Elk, Mendocino, Little River, Point Arena and Gualala. More information: CoC, Fort Bragg, Calif.

For fun and friendship away from the turmoil of city life, plan to vacation at Glacier Lodge located at 7,769' amid a wonderland of trout streams and glacial peaks in the High Sierras. Rates are only

$63-$79 a week with two meals daily. Write: Glacier Lodge, Big Pine, California 93513.

Winter rates drop to attractively low levels along the Southern California coast at Laguna Beach, Newport, Oceanside, and Santa Barbara. On Oceanside's 4-mile strand $45 a week nets a first-class motel efficiency fronting the blue-white Pacific surf. All along the coast, residents swear winter is their finest season and in mountain-girded Santa Barbara they prove it by staging every type of cultural activity. Music, lectures, symphony concerts and road show successes are all here to divert you from the incomparable views and sun-swept beaches (occasional days *are* rainy). Yet through June 1 rates drop 20%-30% and housekeeping apartments and motels go from $45 a week.

Would you like to live for a while in Denmark? Then go to Solvang near Santa Barbara. Called "Little Denmark," Solvang is a completely Danish town with a Danish college, church and school. Danish costumes are worn on holidays.

Time has almost stood still in the Sacramento Delta country around Crockett off US 40. Nostalgic Port Costa has been discovered by artists and gift shop operators but you can still cross Steamboat Slough on a cable-driven ferry to Locke, an unbelievable town of false fronted stores and wooden sidewalks inhabited entirely by Chinese. The ideal way to explore Delta is by a houseboat rented at Antioch.

More information: Redwood Empire Assn., 476 Post St., San Francisco, Calif. 94102; All Year Club of Southern California, 705 W. 7th St., Los Angeles, Calif. 90017; San Diego Convention and Tourist Bureau, 330 A St., San Diego, Calif. 92101; Division of Beaches and Parks, 1416 Ninth St., Sacramento, Calif. 95811.

COLORADO. For a different vacation, try the Aspen Summer Festival at Aspen. From June 27 to September 4, there's an unending round of lectures, public discussions and concerts. Between mental bouts you can ride the chairlift to the summit of Ajax Mountain and join arists and students in the heated outdoor swimming pools, or sample some of the area's other attractions: riding, climbing, wildlife study, and short car trips to ghost towns, hot springs, silver mines and Glenwood Canyon. Admissions ranging from $1.25 to $3 push costs up but with housekeeping accommodations starting at $55 a week, a vacation at Aspen is within easy reach of most families.

Called the "Switzerland of America," Ouray in western Colorado is a small alpine resort of 800 people surrounded by some of the most spectacular mountains in the Rockies—within 15 miles are 38 peaks exceeding 13,000' ... a grand sojourning or retirement spot if you appreciate scenic grandeur and mountain hiking.

Eldora, an even smaller alpine community 20 miles west of Boulder, lies on a dead-end road in a Shangri-La setting close to the mighty snow-clad peaks of the continental divide. Untouristed and unchanged, Eldora is a community of year around and summer chalets and log houses with unexcelled opportunities for mountain hiking, rock hunting, skiing and fishing. There are cabins for rent and a motel nearby.

To step back into the roaring 80s, we recommend a sojourn at the historic Hotel Splendide in Empire. Built in 1872, this one time stagecoach stop still has all the gay warmth of the elegant eighties. There are claret red carpets, walnut furniture with gold leafed mirrors and carved maple beds. Using the hotel as base, you can take easy drives through Colorado's most scenic mountain country. Rates are $8 double and up.

Nostalgic shades of '83 still hang over Silverton in Southwestern Colorado, so high in the San Juan Mountains—9,300 feet—it is often snowed in for weeks. False-fronted stores, a Western frontier flavor and operating gold mines lend an authentic pioneer atmosphere. Equally intriguing and amazingly unchanged are the three delightful towns of Telluride, Creede and Lake City, all in southwest Colorado and not too touristed.

You won't escape tourists altogether but you can still get away from it all by camping in the magnificent settings of Black Canyon of the Gunnison, Dinosaur or Colorado National Monuments or at Mesa Verde or Rocky Mountain National Parks. Many other campgrounds and lodges provide offbeat vacationing in the intriguing Grand Mesa, high above the Colorado River near Grand Junction.

If you'd like to "drop out" of the world and its problems and reside in a Utopian community with a modern Oriental-type philosophy, write to Drop City, Trinidad, Colo. 81082. It's mainly for younger people and intellectuals.

Colorado also boasts many of the West's best preserved ghost towns. Write the address below for its "Ghost Towns and Mining Camps" literature.

More information: Advertising and Publicity Department, 600 State Services Bldg., Denver, Colo. 80203.

CONNECTICUT. Too near large cities to be untouristed or low-priced, Connecticut nonetheless has many charming corners where you can recapture the flavor of colonial New England. Art colonies flourish at many of them.

The Cornwalls, a series of delightful rural villages among wooded hills, are popular with artistic folk. Room and board: from $60 weekly, in summer.

Essex, on the Connecticut River, with its sea captains' houses, village smithy and colorful yacht harbor, preserves much of the air of 1840. Inns charge from $8 double daily plus meals.

Farmington, west of Hartford, is also alluring with its historic homes, herb gardens and brick walks.

Guilford, a tranquil and unspoiled center of New England antiquities, has scores of pre-Revolutionary homes. There are beautiful old churches and an active Art League; also tourist homes and a motel.

Kent, in the Litchfield Hills, has a sizeable art colony.

Litchfield has many fine old colonial homes and Lebanon's village green is unchanged from pre-Revolutionary days. Both towns are historic, have lodges and village inns. Two additional communities to discover: Woodbury in the fertile Pomperaug vale, charmingly situated on an Indian trail where maple-shaded 18th century homes are worlds away from modern cares; and, hillside Colebrook in the upper Connecticut River valley region.

Silvermine, a historic village with colonial homes clinging to the hillsides above the river, overflows with charm. Artists' houses line the winding streets and their works are displayed at the Silvermine Guild Gallery.

You'll also get the atmosphere of quaint old maritime Connecticut in the fishing village of Noank. There are fishing, docks, a lobster hatchery, and an art school. Accommodations include tourist homes and cottages.

Old Lyme, a former wooden-ship-building center, has the oldest summer art colony in America and a splendid art gallery. There are country inns.

Slightly more off-beat is the unchanged New England village of Somers, among scenic hills and forests.

Stonington is a typical New England fishing village. There are motels.

Washington is an enchanting little village on a hill with its own 700-acre woodland recreation area. Local accommodations are available.

More information: Connecticut Development Commission, State Office Bldg., Hartford, Conn. 06115.

DELAWARE. A pleasant spot to linger a while is New Castle, a charming village of time-mellowed Georgian mansions on shady Old World streets. Dover, the state capital, has similar architectural treasures and flavor. The old shore resort of Lewes and historic Milford are other atmospheric towns. All are ideal for leisurely retirement.

Bethel is an atmospheric old village of small white houses built by ship captains and carpenters. Their descendents still live here. Well kept white picket fences line the winding lanes and you'll discover many historic relics.

For a bargain priced vacation preceding June 15 or after Labor Day, sample White House Farm Cabins along Indian River Bay on Long Neck Road near Rehoboth Beach.

More information: Delaware State Development Department, 45 The Green, Dover, Del. 19901.

FLORIDA. From May 15 to November 1, practically every resort south of Daytona Beach is brimming with bargains. During winter, rates drop at all resorts north of Daytona Beach and west along the Panhandle's Gulf Coast.

Looking for unspoiled Florida hideaways? Here's a selection: 1. a unique charm of bygone days overhangs Everglades City, a frontier fishing village at the gateway to Florida's labyrinthine Ten Thousand Islands. There are no movies, golf or tennis and few cars. Throughout the long, tropical summer, from May to November, rates are inexpensive at the local lodge and motels. 2. Off Carrabelle, itself a picturesque old North Florida fishing village, lies Dog Island, linked by ferry; there are miles of fine beaches and also cottages renting at $75 a week. 3. Just south of Tallahassee, near the old river port of St. Marks, is Shell Island with its comfortable Bullock Cottages—a real fishing vacation hideaway.

Far down in peninsula Florida, south of and warmer than either St. Petersburg or Sarasota, is the friendly, peaceful oak-shaded, non-resort community of Arcadia. Here you can bask in the warm winter sun, gossip with the friendly inhabitants, play shuffleboard, fish, or watch cowboys at work or citrus groves in operation. Throughout winter, while rates soar everywhere within 100 miles, you can housekeep or stay at guest homes very economically. If you'd like a healthful vacation, the Orange Grove Health Ranch here offers a delightful and restful vacation in the sun for about $77 a week.

Built like Rome on seven hills and surrounded by high rolling country reminiscent of Kentucky, Brooksville is a charming inland vacation spot only 19 miles from the Gulf, among lakes, streams and rivers with the finest of bass fishing. Although winters are warm, rates remain soothingly low.

Just off Pine Island, near Fort Myers, is tiny Demere Key and here, surrounded by a luxuriant botanical garden, is Sea Grape Lodge, one of the most charming and delightful escapist havens in Florida. Rates aren't rockbottom but for a real island vacation in the sun, Sea Grape Lodge is unsurpassed. (Write: Sea Grape Lodge, Demere Key, Pine Island via Matlacha Station, Fla.)

Now for a brief rundown on more hideaways; seven miles west of Bradenton on Route 684 is the picturesque, uncommercialized fishing village of Cortez, a delightfully unspoiled Florida retreat; 75 miles north of St. Petersburg you'll find old Homassassa, a picturesque riverside village with a budget priced inn dating from 1882; six miles north, peaceful Crystal River offers quiet vacationing and retirement in a river-coiled setting. Just north (20 miles southwest of Cross City) you'll find Horseshoe Beach, a budget priced seashore village. Then to the south, watery old Aripeka on the Gulf is an atmospheric, low cost vacation and retirement village. Along Florida's Panhandle Coast, the old antebellum oyster fishing town of Apalachicola offers low costs and is linked by road to beautiful St. George's Island.

Over on the East Coast, we'd suggest these places; Fernandina Beach near Jacksonville, on the 14-mile beach-lined sweep of historic Amelia Island; and for a fishing vacation, either Moore Haven or Okeechobee on Lake Okeechobee. For atmosphere, you should try the old Gulf Hammock Lodge near Inglis or the Sportsman's Lodge at Welaka. In Central Florida, such small communities as Ocoee, Winter Garden, Apopka, Gotha, Lake Mary and Windermere offer attractively quiet living among blue lakes and rolling orange groves. On the West Coast just north of Napels is Vanderbilt Beach, a small resort reminiscent of Cape Cod with one of Florida's finest beaches.

For a quiet, reasonably priced beach vacation, try Englewood on the Gulf Coast in summer, and Flagler Beach, on the upper Atlantic Coast, in winter.

More information: Florida Development Commission, Adams and Gaines St., Tallahassee, Fla. 32304.

GEORGIA. Uncrowded outside the summer season and warm enough to rank as a winter resort, Crooked River State Park 7 miles from the ocean, lies in an area teeming with early American history. Nearby you can explore tabby ruins and the colorful fishing village of St. Mary's, and enjoy excellent fishing. Housekeeping cottages for two are available all year for $48 a week, boats at $2 a day.

Back in 1828 Dahlonega, in the heart of Georgia's Blue Ridge Mountains, was the scene of America's first gold rush. Panning for gold is still a profitable pastime, especially in fall when the mountains blaze with autumn colors. And today, you can enjoy this unspoiled mountain wonderland at bargain prices. For just $91 a week covers full board for two at Dahlonega's flavorful Smith House Hotel. Alternatively, you can make your headquarters in comfortable housekeeping cottages at beautiful mountain-rimmed Lake Winfield Scott or at scenic Vogel State Park; rates are $45-$50 a week. Around here are lots of bargains in abandoned farms, many ideal for conversion into retirement estates.

Looking for a charming Old Southern town deep in the heart of Dixie? Then try Washington. There's still an air of crinoline and Southern chivalry about its stately colonial homes lining narrow, heavily shaded streets. Much the same could be said for Thomasville near the Florida line. Or for the opposite, a completely New England village deep in Dixie, look over historic Midway, south of Savannah.

Savannah is unique among medium sized cities, a gracious town of quiet squares and dignified town houses with a subdued European air. Life is still unhurried, a far cry from America's maddening turnpike civilization. Yet centuries-old houses can still be picked up inexpensively and turned into charming and lovely homes.

More information: Georgia Department of Industry and Trade, 100 State Capitol, Atlanta, Ga. 30334.

IDAHO. An unusual vacation suggestion: spend some time exploring Hells Canyon in southwest Idaho—deepest gorge in the world where the Snake River has chiseled a path between perpendicular lava walls an incredible 8,000 feet deep. Besides driving down into the canyon (or taking jeep trips) and fishing for giant 200-pound sturgeon bulging with caviar, you'll find scores of remote fishing streams and lakes. Long inaccessible, the canyon is reached over forest roads from Weiser, Idaho or Baker, Oregon. You can stay at Indian Creek Lodge at Cuprum, Idaho; or at motels or a hotel in Halfway, Oregon. But to really get to know this fabulous canyon country, we suggest your camping at one of the Forest Service Campgrounds like the alluring Seven Devil's Campsite in Idaho, or at the ghost town of Cornucopia in Oregon where rustic cabins are sometimes available for $60 a month.

Less commercialized, less expensive, and more remote than most Western resorts, McCall on Big Payette Lake is a gem set off by wooded mountains and granite peaks. Few but local people vacation in this idyllic spot. At nearby Ponderosa State Park, you can camp or park a trailer free for two weeks, or pay only $25 for the entire season rental.

Reached by a thrilling mountain road probing the vast wilderness region bordering the River of No Return (Salmon River), is the semi-ghost gold mining town of Warren. Accommodations are quite modest but it'll be a sojourn you'll never forget.

Rich in National Forests, Idaho is

fairly dotted with hideaway mountain camp-sites. Among the more accessible are many beautiful camp-grounds in Howell Canyon near Lake Cleveland at 8,000 feet on Mount Harrison in Sawtooth National Forest. And among the headwaters of Salmon River you'll discover scores of untrammelled streams. For a guide to Idaho's wilderness lakes, write the Idaho Department of Fish and Game, Boise, Idaho. The Forest Service Building, McCall, Idaho, will also send you guides to getting away from it all.

More information: Department of Commerce and Development, 108 State Capitol, Boise, Idaho 83702.

ILLINOIS. A combination of old architectural treasures and scenic beauty, Galena offers a quiet charm and a memento-crammed background of its stirring past. Since its colorful riverboat heyday, a succession of famous personages—Lincoln, Grant, McKinley, Dolly Madison and many more—have been familiar figures on bow-shaped Main Street and among the levees. You'll find an abundance of scenic and historical areas surrounding Galena. Plan to stay at historic DeSoto House Hotel.

A fascinating variety of scenic and historic attractions clings to the lower Ohio River. Towns bear vestiges of pioneer days and Shawneetown and Cairo are interesting places to sojourn awhile.

In spring, Pere Marquette State Park is colorful with blossoming trees and shrubs and its lodge offers solid comfort at medium cost. Much the same can be found at Starved Rock State Park. During weekdays in spring, both offer quiet serenity far from the turmoil of modern civilization.

More information: Illinois Information Service, Room 406, State Capitol, Springfield, Ill. 62706.

INDIANA. Here are five picturesque, historic villages where you can discover quiet, peace and quaint old Hoosier living.

Brookville lies in the lovely Whitewater Valley, a charming, small old Indiana town.

Nashville, in the Brown County hills, is another picturesque village dotted with artists' studios. Resident artists and craftsmen produce superb landscape paintings, weaving, pottery, wrought iron work, dolls and woodcraft. You can see their work at the several thriving art galleries. You can easily spend a week discovering Brown County and such attractive towns as Helmsburg, where you can stay in railroad cabooses remodelled into vacation cottages. Prices are moderate and it's especially beautiful and unspoiled in fall.

New Harmony was founded by Harmonists in the early 1800's as a Utopia of pastoral celibacy. Their big communal buildings of red brick and black walnut beams still stand. Later, Robert Owen, Welsh reformer, tried his "universal happiness through universal education" experiment here. Both projects failed but left their marks in old buildings, a large library, an art gallery and a wealth of sidewalk philosophers. Especially in June, when Golden Rain trees shower blooms, you too, will enjoy the unique harmony of this flavorful place. Adding to New Harmony's attractions is nearby Vincennes, a historic town with a decided French flavor.

Vevey, settled in the early 1800's by Swiss immigrants, still bears the flavor of Switzerland's Vevey and Montreux. Background is provided by many quaint old Swiss-style homes.

Berne, bordering the fabled Limberlost Swamp in the farm-dotted Wabash Valley, was settled by Swiss immigrant Mennonites a century ago. And you'll discover Amish people carrying on identical traditions of the Plain People to this day. Nappanee, an art center in the Amish country, is an alluring place to retire or vacation. For more nostalgia, you should take in the Pioneer Threshermen's Convention at Rushville, held annually in early August, when old fashioned steam threshing machines puff into action as they did half a century ago.

For a thoroughly unique vacation, sign up for a week or two at Camp Chesterfield, world famous spiritualist center, open June 20th through Labor Day. Here the philosophy and religion of spiritualism are taught and demonstrated while resident mediums display their gifts.

More information: Public Information & Education Division, Room 612, State Office Bldg., Indianapolis, Ind. 46204.

IOWA. From the 1850s until 1932, life in the seven villages of Amana was on a completely communial basis. Although there is now a joint stock ownership invested in the villagers themselves, the Amanas still flourish as the oldest living communal society in the United States. German is still widely spoken, women attend Sunday church in the black costumes of the 1850's, and handicraft shops and bakeries continue to produce beautiful handmade furniture and home-cooked foods in a spirit of practical idealism.

Despite the introduction of modern equipment and the infiltration of neon signs, much of the old simple beauty and mode of living persists. All medical attention, old-age benefits and burials are free. You'll see big flower-garlanded homes of early Dutch and German architecture furnished with antiques, there are old churches with rows of pegged seats, and original German crafts are still practiced in the shops. Local restaurants with gourmet ratings serve huge home-cooked German meals and Old World specialties like Westphalian-style ham and "Schwartenmagen" head-cheese.

Tourists rubberneck around the villages in August but you can do better. *You can actually live here*, sleep and eat in the old homes, live the unchanged life of a typical Amana German family, feast on prodigious German cooking, and discover a thousand curious facts about this unique community. Several families in each village accept boarders at $8 a day, room and meals. If, however, as often happens, they are unavailable, try the Die Heimet Hotel at Homestead. Meals are available at the Ox Yoke Inn, the Colony Inn, and Ronnebwig and Zubers, and at sandwich shops. Amana lies on U.S. 6 and Route 149 southwest of Cedar Rapids.

Less engrossing sociologically but infinitely more scenic are the Great Lakes resort region with cottages from $35 weekly, and the rolling wooded hills of Little Switzerland bordering the Mississippi at McGregor.

A highly atmospheric ghost town is the old river port of Bentonsport with its 19th century homes and buildings.

More information: Iowa Development Commission, 250 Jewett Bldg., Des Moines, Iowa 50309.

KANSAS. Settled by Swedish pioneers, Lindsborg in the beautiful Smoky Valley, retains much Swedish atmosphere and ambiance. Arborvitae trees line the business district sidewalks and Swedish influence is apparent in the famous Birger Sandzen Memorial Art Gallery and in the numerous other art galleries and Swedish craft shops, the Swedish Crown Restaurant, and the Swedish bakery. Each fall in odd-numbered years sees the Svensk Hyllings Festival, with public smorgasbords and street dances. Swedish is still widely understood and Swedish customs are still followed, especially at Christmas.

More information: Kansas Department of Economic Development, State Office Bldg., Topeka, Ks. 66612.

KENTUCKY. Bardstown, with its fine old Georgian homes and art filled St. Joseph's Cathedral, would be an atmospheric place to stay a while. Much of Kentucky's best whiskey is made here. Famous mansions include Wickland and My Old Kentucky Home State Park. Nearby you can camp in typical Kentucky knobland.

More information: Travel Division, Capitol Annex Bldg., Frankfort, Ky. 40601.

LOUISIANA. Part of the apprenticeship of many a writer and artists seems to include a stint in the French Quarter of Old New Orleans. For something entirely different, you might try the stimulating experience of living in the Quarter for a vacation or longer stay. Really to know the Quarter, *you must live in it.* This is not recommended for tourists. But for $75-$150 a month you can rent a small studio apartment somewhere on the old squares between the river and Rampart Street. Once established, you'll soon make an interesting circle of acquaintances—long haired intellectuals, artists, poets, writers and other curious characters—who will provide your orientation to the art colony and its Bohemian way of life.

Besides sketching the hidden courtyards and the historic French buildings with their lacy Spanish balconies, you'll enjoy the sidewalk art shows, the aromatic French coffee and Creole cooking, and the real New Orleans jazz. And especially in winter, when New Orleans basks in mild Indian summer weather, there are symphony concerts, first class live theater, and occasional opera, lectures and concerts with good seats for less than $2.

Really to get away from it all down in the French-speaking Bayou Country, there is no better place than Pecan Island, an interesting and unique spot on the Gulf reached over a graded road from Kaplan. There are excellent hunting and fishing, a good climate all year, many unusual characters and homey accommodations at very reasonable cost.

Or to sample rural French living you might try spending some time in St. Martinville or St. Francisville. St. Martinville, settled by Acadians in 1765, is an atmospheric old Louisiana town of stately ante bellum homes, quaint stores and a beautiful Catholic church. St. Francisville, on the Mississippi in West

Feliciana Parish, is also surrounded by historic Southern homes and plantations including Rosedown and Oakley. You'll find motels and tourist homes, or you can board with a French family. You might also try living at one of the picturesque villages along the shores of watery Bayou LaFourche. Another pleasant community where you'll meet congenial people is Covington in the Ozone Belt.

More information: Tourist Development Commission, Box 4291, Baton Rouge, La. 70804.

MAINE. During the weeks immediately preceding June 15 and after Labor Day, when rates are 25%-40% lower than in summer, southern Maine's beach resorts are unusually attractive. September, usually the sunniest month of the year with sea temperatures at maximum, is especially nice. Here is our handpicked selection of beauty spots.

Kennebunkport, a quaint New England fishing village with picturesque streets, lies on the rockbound shores of Cape Arundel. During summer, there are an active art and literary colony and an opera company. Adjacent to Kennebunkport is the picturesque shoreside village and art colony of Cape Porpoise where you can stay inexpensively.

Ogunquit, between a rocky coast and a long sand beach with dunes, is an alluring summer resort village near surf-pounded Bald Head Cliff. A sizeable art colony paints here all summer and there is a summer playhouse.

Other historic Maine towns rich in colonial homes and seafaring legends are Bath, South Berwick, Thomaston, Harpswell, and York. China is a shady lakeside community ideal for sojourning before or after summer visitors arrive.

Offbeat island retreats are numerous, along the rocky Atlantic shore and at inland lakes. Salt water vacationers find complete resort facilities at Camp Eggemoggin near Brunswick and the 2½ by ½ mile island is only six miles from the open sea. Full board runs $56 a week single. Quieter and accessible by highway bridge is island-tip Coveside Inn on picture postcard Christmas Cove. Another homey oceanfront hostelry is Ocean Reef Inn, at Chamberlain, open May 26-October 15 for ten adults only.

For about $100 a week including meals, you can enjoy a vacation of sailing, canoeing and waterskiing at Linekin Bay Resort, Boothbay Harbor, Me. 04538. Unlimited use of all watersport equipment, sailboats and canoes is free, including cruises on a schooner.

Inland near the Quebec border, in a wilderness paradise of lakes and streams, you'll find Attean Lake. No cottage or summer camp mars its shores. But tucked away on one of its 42 islands is a delightful group of log cabins called Attcan Camps (address: Attean Lake Resort, Jackman, Me. 04945). Here in summer, $90 a week covers full board in your own private cabin with fireplace and you can fish, enjoy canoe trips or just relax in this wild and lovely mountain country "far from the madding crowd."

For an outdoor vacation, the less frequented parts of Maine's enormous Baxter State Park merit consideration. Within the park are 45 mountain peaks, countless lakes with excellent trout fishing, and a wealth of wildlife including many, many deer and bear. Camping costs but 25¢ a day; shelters can be rented for 75¢.

More information: Department of Economic Development, State House, Augusta, Me. 04340.

MANITOBA. By train you can go from Winnipeg to Churchill on Hudson Bay, a summer grain port and colorful frontier outpost of the Far North occupying a rocky barren river mouth location. Weatherworn downtown facades overlook unpaved streets. If you're lucky you'll see natives harpooning the great white whale from frail canoes and there are an Eskimo Museum, rebuilt Fort Prince of Wales, Anglican and Catholic missions, and a whaling plant. Each

August, special trains make the trip for $229 per week all inclusive. Costs on the regular thrice weekly service would be similar.

New highways opening up Manitoba's Northland give easy access to a Far Northern wilderness of beautiful lakes fringed by a silent wilderness of pines, muskeg and rocks. Fishing in these virgin waters is an angler's dream. You can camp, stay at housekeeping cabins for as little as $25 a week, or at more elaborate motels and lodges.

For an off-the-beaten-path motoring adventure, drive up Route 10 to Flin Flon and The Pas (from where you can continue to Churchill by train—see above). Another rewarding car adventure is to drive north to seldom visited but unusually beautiful Prince Albert National Park.

A more accessible escapist area is huge Whiteshell Provincial Park 100 miles east of Winnipeg, a thousand square miles of magnificent rugged forest land dotted with countless fishing lakes. Accommodations range from camping at $2 per week to staying at housekeeping cottages for $25-$80 a week.

For an escapist vacation in the Far North, sample a week at Norway House on Ross Island at the remote head of Lake Winnipeg. Close to this busy Hudson Bay post are the Playgreen Inn, a Cree village, Indian schools and missions, and the stone jail and log warehouses built for the booming fur trade of a century ago. You reach Ross Island by a 2½-day steamer cruise on the M.S. *Lord Selkirk*, which sails weekly from Winnipeg each summer.

More information: Tourist Development Branch, Department of Tourism & Recreation, 408 Norquay Bldg., Winnipeg 1, Manitoba.

MARYLAND. Drive down almost any dead-end state road on Maryland's Eastern Shore and you'll discover at least one fishing village remote from the cares of civilization. Just south of the giant Chesapeake Bay Bridge, for example, you'll discover leisurely paced

Talbot County with its two historic towns of Easton and Oxford, both atmospheric vacation centers and fine for budget priced retirement. For a visit, don't fail to stop at one of Talbot County's two country inns. The Pasadena, at Royal Oak, Md. 21662, offers a homey atmosphere by the water and provides room and a huge, family style breakfast and dinner for $60-$65 a week. The Oakwood, at St. Michael's, Md. 21663, offers a swimming pool, room and three whopping meals a day for a weekly rate of just $59-$62.

Relatively undiscovered and untouristed is St. Mary's County, a long, ragged peninsula stabbing out into Chesapeake Bay. Though it is only an hour from Washington, D.C., motorists avoid driving down this dead end peninsula. Hence, away from the towns, much of St. Mary's still looks as it did in the 17th century, when the county gave birth to the manorial system in America. Opulent mansions and hoary churches still dot the countryside, horse-drawn Amish carriages still clip-clop along the roads, and farmers' markets offer farm-fresh produce at bargain prices. You'll especially enjoy the twice weekly church suppers with their groaning tables of fried chicken, country stuffed ham, turkey and oysters—all you can eat for $1.75. St. Mary's has 4½ miles of beach at Lookout Point Park, some of America's best fishing (charter boats are a good buy) and in spring and fall, large fully furnished waterside cottages rent for $35-$40 a week. St. Mary's is also attractive for retirement. A good buy is the 4-day Monday-through-Thursday package at the Point Lookout Hotel for $65 for two people, including breakfast and dinner—it's an Old World beach hotel far from turnpike bustle. The Seven Gables Hotel at nearby Hollywood offers much the same. (For information about St. Mary's, write: St. Mary's County Development Committee, Compton, Md. 20627.)

Another good spot for an unregimented vacation is Solomons Island,

about 90 minutes southeast of Washington, D.C. One street wide, it's a fishing village with sandy beaches and a motel, hotel and several boarding houses. Yet it's completely innocent of night clubs, movies or other forms of canned time killer.

A really colorful island you can reach by car—across a lift bridge tended by a woman—is Tilghman's Island near Easton. Center of activity is busy Fisherman's Wharf, where you can feast on the finest fried oysters and steamed crabs this side of heaven. There are boats everywhere—rakish-masted skipjacks, oyster trollers and sports fishermen. Island families have been isolated so long there are only a few family names: almost everyone is a Sinclair, a Harrison or a Haddaway. Comfortable boarding houses exist.

Historic spots for retirement with charm and atmosphere include Annapolis, Frederick, beautiful Princess Anne, St. Michael's fishing village, unspoiled Kent Island and Betterton.

For an untramelled spring or fall vacation, sample a week at the Schley Inn at Braddock Heights near Frederick. Rooms overlook a spacious garden with huge swimming pool and beautiful views, and the inn is famed for its cuisine. Yet at this charming inn, rates are only $72 weekly including all meals (address: Schley Inn, Braddock Heights, Md. 21714).

Surrounded by mountainous Garrett County, historic Grantsville in western Maryland is a rewarding place for a different vacation. Its Casselman Hotel has been in business since 1824 and many rooms have open fireplaces. Rates are only $37 a week for two (some rooms higher). But for a real experience, you must eat at Penn Alps, a European style pension-restaurant that serves huge meals of Amish dishes prepared from fresh farm produce. The house commands sweeping views of mountains and river and through its Amish management, you can contact and experience the culture of the Plain People at first hand. It's priced right, too! (Both the

Casselman Hotel and Penn Alps are at Grantsville, Md. 21536.)

More information: Department of Economic Development, State Office Bldg., Annapolis, Md. 21401.

MASSACHUSETTS. Rich in history and atmosphere, seascapes and fishing villages, many a Bay State beauty spot seems the ideal setting for a first-rate bargain paradise. Summer's human tidal wave of tourists and the consequent upsurge of prices transform them during July and August into something considerably short of Utopia. But after Labor Day, when tourists are few and rates drop as much as 50%, you can enjoy these same places free of crowds and with the added bonus of riotous fall colors. Here are some places you're certain to like.

After Labor Day historic Cape Cod resumes its unhurried, tranquil way of life. Here are dozens of Old World towns, tall white lighthouses and ancient sea captains' homes, colossal sand dunes, moody moors, green cranberry bogs and panoramic sea views galore. Each village offers its own special atmosphere and way of life. Those on Cape Cod Bay retain more historic flavor, those on the Sounds are livelier. Comparatively mild winters and cool summers make all ideal for retirement.

Dennis, with its muraled Cape Playhouse, is especially delightful. Full of flavor, too, is Falmouth on Vineyard Sound, an old seaport with an elm-shaded village green and an ancient church. Provincetown, capital of the Cape, is quieter in September and you can enjoy its beautiful dunes and harbor, meet Portuguese fishermen and perhaps some of its resident artists and playwrights. But for the ultimate in atmosphere, we like Sandwich, oldest village on the Cape; it's a quaint old town with a charming flavor, nestled on low hills by the bay.

Across Nantucket Sound, the Old Colony's twin islands, Martha's Vineyard and Nantucket, preserve much of the air of old whaling days. Even in summer you can find guest homes charging $6-$9 daily, but in September rates are cut in half. You won't see a billboard, parking meter or traffic light on Martha's Vineyard and you can bicycle over winding roads to the cliffs at Gay Head and to all its shore villages. Edgartown, the oldest settlement, is a real New England seafaring village of white sea captains' houses on narrow, picket-fenced lanes. An especially good buy in June is the Menemsha Inn near Gay Head charging $70-$90 single weekly for full board.

Fall is also the best time to enjoy Nantucket. Of all places in America, Nantucket has most successfully resisted change. It is happily free from parking meters, billboards, traffic lights and just about every other form of ugly commercialism and featureless American standardization. Though only 12 x 3 miles in extent, this quaint New England stronghold features miles of moody moors, fields of wildflowers, endless beaches with rolling sandhills, and high bluffs with majestic sea views. Cobbled village streets lead past quaint rose covered cottages with neat picket fences. And the sense of isolation is heightened by the difficulty of bringing cars over on the ferry and by the fogs which not infrequently close down the dribble of light plane traffic, As a result, the smaller villages like Siasconset, Quidnet, Madaket and Wauwinet remain delightful little Edens 30 miles across the sea from "America" as the islanders still call the mainland.

Over in "America," historic Cape Anne is lovely in fall. Between its magnificent seascapes, the two fishing harbors of Rockport and Gloucester are among the most "paintable" and most painted in this country. Summer rates are lower here than on Cape Cod and especially in Gloucester, you'll find many reasonably priced artists' apartments for rent along the wharves. This is headquarters for the North Shore Art Association and Rockport boasts a first rate art school.

Other unusually pleasant seashore

spots include: Cohasset, an alluring South Shore village; Duxbury, an attractive Pilgrim village, once home of John Alden; and the delightful old colonial town of Ipswich.

Inland, serenity is the most cherished possession of Deerfield, considered to be the best-preserved colonial village in New England. Spend some time here and you'll fall under the spell of its carved weatherbeaten doorways, huge elms, and hoary houses; many writers, painters and poets live in Deerfield and craftsmen work here year around. Sheffield in the Berkshires is another historic beauty spot while delightfully preserved elm-arched Stockbridge attracts writers and artists, many enjoying permanent resident status.

More information: Massachusetts Department of Commerce & Development, 100 Cambridge St., Boston, Mass. 02202.

MICHIGAN. For summer cultural entertainment, Interlochen in north Michigan is the place to head for. During July and August the National Music Camp presents a constant round of orchestra and band concerts, recitals, dance, drama, and operatic performances. Special adult sessions are offered at the end of August. Old fashioned Bay View on Little Traverse Bay is also location of a summer music school. Charmingly set in ghost town solitude at the abandoned lumbering village of Pequaming on Lake Superior is the Kitchigam School of Arts. There are dormitory accommodations for students. Other visitors stay at Henry Ford's former summer home, Pequaming Resort; for reservations, write c/o Postmaster, L'Anse, Mich.

Mackinac Island, too, is crowded until Labor Day but thereafter this historic island resumes its normal leisurely, peaceful tempo. During the balmy fall weeks you can bicycle or be driven in a horsedrawn carriage over the island's uncrowded roads to high cliffs, peculiar rock formations, old homes and buildings, and to ancient forts. You'll be pleasantly surprised to find

Mackinac (pronounced Mackinaw) free of all modern distractions; even cars are banned. The result is a quiet island charm as venerable as the ornate Grand Hotel with its colonnaded porch fully two blocks long. Some 36 tourist homes charge $30-$45 a week double; full board after Labor Day runs about $60 a week single.

You can't escape vacationing crowds altogether at Saugatuck, but this Lake Michigan resort among huge sand dunes is so picturesque, it has become the Midwest's largest art colony. Cottages are $35-$60 a week, guest homes $30 double, and full board can be had for under $50 single.

Almost entirely forested, brimming with crystal clear trout streams and lakes and dotted with atmospheric mining communities, is Michigan's Upper Peninsula wilderness playground. For outdoor living in summer away from the Joneses it's ideal. Beautiful waterfalls abound while the beaches and old mine tailings are rich in rare gemstones.

Frankenmuth, north of Flint, is a solidly German community which has preserved its European heritage, customs and language. Made here are German beer and ales while the town is also famous for its German style chicken dinners. Holland, on Lake Michigan southwest of Grand Rapids, also retains much of its original Dutch flavor and characteristics. A stay at either would be interesting out of season.

More information: Michigan Tourist Council, Stevens T. Mason Bldg., Lansing, Mich. 48926.

MINNESOTA. Getting away from it all is no problem in this lake-spangled northwoods state. Perhaps the surest way is to rent a canoe-camping outfit from outfitting bases at Ely or International Falls. Within minutes, you'll be in a calendar-picture world of boundless lakes and forests where there are no man-made sounds except your own and once there, it's impossible to spend any money. For roughly $7 a day, outfitters equip you with canoes, food, tent and everything you'll need for carefree days or weeks deep in the woods. You can escape civilization with equal ease and in greater comfort by renting a fully equipped houseboat with guide-cook from Pete's Cabin Boats at Ely. Rates run about $22 a day each for parties of four, all inclusive. Or if you prefer to camp with your car, you can almost duplicate a canoe trip by camping along the Gunflint Trail, near Grand Marais.

Minnesota's two top state parks, Interstate known for its geological features and scenic Dalles of the St. Croix River, and Itasca among 157 lakes at the head of the Mississippi, are also both tops for camping. Itasca has cabins. Among larger resorts Glenwood is probably the most picturesque.

Everyone knows the 49th parallel is the northern boundary of the United States. But through an error of geography, the United States flag waves over several islands and an isolated piece of land *north of this boundary.* Oak Island, the largest of these islands and the most northerly island in the continental United States, lies far out in enormous Lake of the Woods. And if you take the ferry there from Warroad, Minnesota, you're headed for a unique little paradise. Beautifully forested with spruce and pine and ankle deep in carpet moss, Oak Island is surrounded by the best muskie fishing grounds in the entire United States. On this quaint island are a general store, a post office and two small summer resorts. Chippewa Indian guides lead you to fine fishing while resort operators furnish ice locker space for your catch. Boat trips take you among an island maze where you make a canoe portage or in season gather unlimited wild raspberries and blueberries. Oak Island Resort provides a free boat and the finest recreational facilities for $84 a week single with meals. Manzke Pine Island Resort on 35-acre Pine Island (Ray, Minn. 56669) also hugs the Canadian border and is reached after a

five-mile boat trip from Kabetogama landing. Weekly rates for a cabin for 4 people with your own boat are $50-$65 per person. Other resorts on or among islands include Ludlow's Island Lodge and Chap's Lodge, both on Lake Vermilion at Cook, Minn. 55723.

More information: Vacation Information Center, State Capitol, St. Paul, Minn. 55101.

MISSISSIPPI. You can still find an air of pre-Civil War days among Old World streets of ante bellum mansions in such historic towns as Holly Springs, Iuka, Natchez, Columbus and Port Gibson. Near Iuka, among the rolling hills and woods of extreme NE Mississippi, is attractive Tishamingo State Park, interesting for its Indian lore and wealth of wild flowers. The park offers housekeeping cabins, a dining room, swimpool and fishing.

Two picturesque Gulf beach resorts are Bay St. Louis and Pass Christian. Bay St. Louis has many of the attributes of Biloxi while Pass Christian is a changeless old Southern town and a real gem for budget priced retirement. Ocean Springs is another Gulf beach resort with quiet charm while Moss Point is renowned for its tradition and fine old homes.

More information: Mississippi Agricultural & Industrial Board, 1504 State Office Bldg., Jackson, Miss. 39201.

MISSOURI. All costs are low in the Show Me State and the Missouri Ozarks rank as one of America's cheapest summer resort areas. An interesting place in the Ozark's Lake Taneycomo region is Hollister for its resemblance to a charming Old English village.

Two picturesque river towns are Clarksville on the Mississippi and Hermann on the Missouri. Founded by early German settlers, Hermann possesses numerous historic homes and a decidedly Old World flavor at its colorful and exciting peak during the gay annual Maifest. Yet another fascinating river town where passing time has wrought little change is St. Genevieve, Missouri's oldest settlement. Many of its charming older homes are jammed with priceless French heirlooms and treasures. An appealing tranquility abides and morning, noon and eventide you'll find yourself anticipating the church bells chiming their regular calls.

More information: Commerce & Industrial Development, Jefferson Bldg., Jefferson City, Mo. 65101.

MONTANA. An uncrowded vacation spot is the lovely Bitteroot Valley, threaded by a sparkling river between two mountain ranges. You'll find comfortable motels and two hot springs resorts.

Cradled between two high mountain ranges, Flathead Lake is a favorite Rocky Mountain resort area. Yet you can avoid most of the tourist traffic by staying at Polson, where costs are also lower. For camping, Yellow Bay State Park on the eastern shore occupies one of the lake's loveliest settings.

Another really overlooked beauty spot with magnificent scenery and modest accommodation is Swan Lake.

When you're tired of the same old thing in vacations, try exploring Montana's mysterious ghost towns. Because Montana's mining towns were abandoned more recently, most are better preserved than those in other parts of the West.

For example, at Bannack you can still stroll down Hangman's Gulch and there are many old buildings including a log jail. Cooke, near Yellowstone Park, until recently a ghost town, is living again as a rejuvenated mining center. Elkhorn, near Boulder, is full of crumbling dwellings, an old general store and fraternity hall—all worth seeing. At Marysville, near Helena, you can see the famous Drumlummon Mine, store buildings, a weed-grown graveyard and beautiful mountain views. Also, with wonderful mountain views, Rimini is an interesting relic of numerous cabins and abandoned mines.

Somewhere on your tour include

Virginia City, completely restored to its 1860 appearance. It's touristed but a day in this living museum of Western history is worth the crowds. You'll see saloons with player pianos and nickel movies, the restored 19th century Fairweather Inn, the neighboring mining camp of Nevada City, and old time melodrama. Other ghost towns are Silver Star and Rochester in Madison County, Kendall in central Montana and Maiden in beautiful Maiden Canyon.

For real Western atmosphere, try one of the following four towns. Even in the summer tourist season, Browning, home of the Blackfeet Indians, with its numerous cowboys and grizzled pioneers possesses a distinct Old West flavor. Another real Western town is Enis in Madison County; motel accommodations start at $4 per couple. A typical cowtown is Jackson in the mountain-rimmed Big Hole Basin. Outside July and August or the skiing season, you can find a lot of atmosphere by staying at the Diamond Bar Inn (housekeeping cabins $48 weekly for two). Nearby Wisdom is also a real frontier town complete with boardwalks, unpainted false-fronted buildings, general stores and saloons. There are a modest hotel and cabins.

Yet another of Montana's untrammelled beauty spots is the Kootenai River country between Libby and Eureka on Route 37. This beautiful riverside area has fine budget priced accommodations at Troy, Libby or Eureka.

Montana also offers two uncrowded spas: the Camas Bathhouse at Hot Springs, an all year spa operated by the Flathead Indians, with inexpensive accommodations available; and Medicine Hot Springs on Route 93 near Hamilton—mineral baths with cabins, meals and campsites.

More information: Travel and Advertising Department, State Highway Commission, Helena, Mont. 59601.

NEBRASKA. You won't find dramatic scenery in this wide plains state but because tourists are relatively few, Nebraska offers a variety of unique, uncrowded vacation spots far from the madding crowd. From high, pinestudded buttes to the rolling, lakedotted Sand Hills, you'll find a wide choice of unspoiled settings. Uniqueness is a byword here and if you're seeking a western brand of uncrowded relaxation, Nebraska has it. This is truly a land of wide open spaces with well equipped campsites offering modern comfort in the wilderness.

Ponca State Park on the Missouri River Bluffs offers campers grounds on high hilltops or in snug little canyons. Nearby, at Lewis and Clark Lake, you can explore the Devil's Nest Country, rich in relics of Jesse James, Doc Middleton and other western outlaws.

History buffs will also enjoy the old river town of Brownville. On the banks of the rolling Missouri, this old town lives on today much as it did a century ago when it was a bustling embarkation point for settlers heading West.

Nebraska is surprisingly Western. At Macy and Winnebago, Indians still pow wow in their ancient regalia and you'll thrill to the colorful spectacle of their age old rituals. Tom toms throb and ankle bells jingle as the tribes meet for their ancient conclaves.

In the wide, spacious Sand Hills, cowboys still rope and brand in real western country. In towns like Hyannis and Thedford, cowboys walk the streets in Stetsons and jeans, lending a genuine Western touch. The unique Sand Hills is also a land of many lakes with delightful campsites and fishing lakes.

In the far western Panhandle, pine studded buttes rise above the plains, many of the strange formations figuring in the rich Indian lore of the region. Fort Robinson State Park awaits you here, an army post during the wild frontier days. You'll stay in cabins that were originally the adobe officers' quarters in the fort's heydey, or in barracks which have been converted into a comfortable lodge. Then, at nearby Chadron, you'll find Chadron State Park where you can camp among pine studded hills and buttes with excellent riding and trout fishing right outside.

In the far northwestern Panhandle, Nebraska's Badlands offer an unforgettable spectacle. Wind and rain have carved Toadstool Park into weird rock formations rich in fossils and relics of early Indian Days. Also in the Panhandle are the Wildcat Hills where buffalo and elk still roam on special game preserves. The hills are filled with secluded untouched beauty spots for camping.

More information: Nebraskaland, State Capitol. Lincoln, Neb. 68509.

NEVADA. Like Montana, Nevada is a happy hunting ground for ghost-town exploring. A score of historic mining camps, some totally abandoned, some still populated, abound in the legends, landmarks and ghosts of bonanza years.

Biggest, best preserved and certainly the liveliest is Virginia City, Queen of the Comstock. Once the richest city in America, Virginia City is abuzz around the clock with tourist crowds and non-stop gambling. Yet it's worth visiting to see Piper's Opera House, the twenty ornate saloons, the historic hotel and silver nabobs' mansions, and the false-fronted main street. The "Territorial Enterprise" has continued publication since the earliest days.

Drive for half a day southwards, and you'll enter quieter ghost towns like Aurora, Candelaria, and Rawhide. Southward again are Bullfrog and Rhyolite, the latter abondoned only in 1912 and still well preserved. Among present day mining towns, nearby Beatty is probably the most picturesque. Half a day east of here lie Manhattan and Round Mountain, two ghost towns located in the central sector of the Toiyable National Forest. Just north on U.S. 50 is Austin with pioneer era relics. Farther east are Eureka and reached by dirt road off

U.S. 50, Hamilton, which had 101 saloons and 23 lawyers. Another ghost town reached by dirt road is Delamar, off U.S. 93 near Caliente. And if you're traveling on U.S. 40 through northern Nevada, dirt roads take you to these forgotten communities: Tuscacora and Jarbidge in the Elko region; and Unionville, near Winnemucca. In all instances, inquire locally before embarking along dirt roads to some of the older mining camps. Often dangerous after cloudbursts, they also offer a serious challenge to drivers of modern low-slung cars.

For the camper, Nevada also offers numerous camp-sites in remote mountain and desert areas, in Humboldt, Nevada and Toiyable National Forests, and on Lake Tahoe. You'll find really off-the-beaten-path camping in the Lincoln County area of eastern Nevada with three outstanding state parks to pick from and first class fishing. And no review of this part of the West should omit Wheeler Park Recreation Area near Ely, where you can camp or rent cabins near a glacier, the highest peak in the Great Basin, and gigantic Lehman Caves.

A charming western village is Paradise Valley, 40 miles north of Winnemuca on State 8-B. Nestled among poplars and cottonwoods, Paradise Valley is a century old western town of false fronted stores with a population of 50 and a traditional general store still in business. Life in this sleepy village among the Santa Rosa Mountains hasn't changed much since the 1920s.

More information: Department of Economic Development, Carson City, Nev. 89701.

NEW HAMPSHIRE. A charming spot is Cornish, home of a sizeable summer artists and writers colony and site of the Saint Gaudens National Historic Site where the great sculptor lived and worked.

It's difficult to avoid summer tourists altogether but three overlooked regions are: the Warner-Bradford area; Canaan; and Warren and Wentworth among magnificent scenery on Route 25. After Labor Day, you can find bargains galore at most of New Hampshire's lake-shore resorts.

Places with atmosphere include Amherst, picturesque birthplace of Horace Greeley where a whipping post still stands on the village common. Portsmouth on the coast and Lancaster and Wolfeboro inland possess numerous stately old colonial homes and an aura of yesterday.

There's only one place in America where you can walk for several days through grand apline scenery without seeing a car or town yet stay every night at comfortable lodgings. This is the stretch of Appalachian Trail between Franconia and Pinkham Notches. Day after day, you thrill to exhilarating panoramas as you walk, high above timberline, across the rugged Presidential Range. Each night you stay at one of a series of Appalachian Mountain Club huts which provide snug sleeping accommodation and hearty outdoor meals for about $9 all inclusive.

New Hampshire possesses a multitude of beautiful campsites. Write the address below for their free brochure on Family Camping.

More information: Division of Economic Development, State House Annex, Concord, N.H. 03301.

NEW JERSEY. Unhurried rural vacationing in Upstate New Jersey is attractive when you stay at Old World Newton or at leisurely Swartswood, beside a lake. Here, only 70 miles from Manhattan, is an unspoiled countryside of rich dairy farms and villages; you can stay at inns or tourist homes.

For a flavorful Southern version of Cape Cod, try Cape May—an old time resort with the largest concentration of Victorian buildings east of the Mississippi. Row upon row of white clapboard homes and hotels—adorned with ornate balconies, Corinthian pillars and black shutters—overlook manicured lawns that slope down to picket and spindle fences bordering tree-shaded streets. All is well preserved and no change is permitted. Every night, a lamplighter makes his rounds to light the gas street lamps. Already, Cape May has lured a sizeable permanent art colony and the cultural flavor is enhanced by a summer playhouse. You'll find over 50 guest homes, many with inexpensive rates. Despite the surfers, there in all seasons, Cape May offers genuine quiet and tranquillity from mid-September until early June.

You can find all the flavor of a working fishing village at Bivalve on Delaware Bay, a busy little port teeming with oyster luggers and all the sights, sounds and smells of oyster fishing.

Ocean Grove, near Asbury Park, is a devoutly religious beach resort where cars are banned on Sundays and life hasn't changed too much in the past 50 years.

More information: Department of Conservation and Development, Box 1889, Trenton, N.J. 08625.

NEW MEXICO. Out in the middle of the vast Navajo Reservation, immense Ship Rock literally floats like a ship in a sea of jumbled sand and red hued rock. You can sample a week or more of interesting Indian life in this primitive area by staying at the Hotel Shiprock. Rates are $3.50-$6 per day for two, excellent Western style meals extra (some rooms cost more).

Or if you yearn to ride a vast landscape of wind and rock, make your headquarters at Vogt Ranch, Ramah, N.M. 87301—the only guest ranch in the mile high Navajo Indian country. All inclusive rates are $101 per week including unlimited riding.

New Mexico is also rich in ghost towns. Write the address below for their "Ghost Town Map."

More information: State Dept. of Development, Tourist Division, 302 Galisteo, Santa Fe, N.M. 87501.

NEW YORK. Proximity to large cities poses problems in avoiding tourists but after Labor Day crowds thin out, rates go down, the woods become a pageant of fall colors and the weather normally stays balmy.

Surprisingly, however, unspoiled pockets persist within 100 miles of Times Square. One such unspoiled area is the eastern tip of Long Island, which forks into two peninsulas divided by Peconic Bay. Between the North and South Forks lies Shelter Island, a still comparatively untouched vacation island with at least one reasonably priced, old time resort hotel. Of the forks, the North Fork is cheapest: here are historic hamlets and villages with saltbox cottages and you can vacation at reasonably priced guest homes close to the beach. More stylish and expensive, the South Fork boasts several of America's most graceful villages, among which East Hampton, with its summer theater, is outstanding. During fall, when rates are reduced, a vacation here is like turning back the clock 300 years.

Many state parks in the Thousand Islands offer fine camping in an archipelago of more than 1,700 varied, colorful river islands. Accessible only by boat are Mary Island, Canoe-Picnic Point and Cedar Isld. State Parks. After the summer crowds have gone, camping—or staying at a local motel—is a fine way to enjoy four other beautiful parks: Letchworth, Taughannock Falls and Watkins Glen, each with misty glens and waterfalls; and Allegany Park, renowned for sylvan charm and prolific wildlife.

Lake Pleasant, a tiny overlooked hamlet on two lovely Adirondack lakes, hasn't changed much since the 1800s. You can camp, rent a cottage or stay at a choice of lodges, all inexpensive.

Outstanding culturally is Chautauqua where in July and August one may attend plays, opera, symphony concerts and lectures or join classes in music, the arts and crafts and the theater; and the artists' colony at Woodstock, which also has a summer playhouse.

A unique vacation is offered at Lily Dale, N.Y. 14752—a beauty spot and the world's largest spiritual center. Lectures, demonstrations and seances go on all through July and August.

More information: State Department of Commerce, 112 State St., Albany, NY. 12207.

NORTH CAROLINA. Looking for a leisurely beauty spot on the Southland's coast? Beaufort might well be that place. You'll discover an antique 18th century charm in its narrow oakshaded streets lined by time-mellowed colonial homes. Rates are low, fishing excellent and the weather so mild it's pleasant from February to November. Beaufort is a topflight retirement spot with very reasonable living costs.

From Harker's Island, a short drive from Beaufort, you can explore the unchanged Core Banks. At Harker's Island, you board America's only sail-powered ferry for a daylong cruise to Cape Lookout and back. En route, you'll discover miles of white virgin beach littered with exotic shells and driftwood, and on Shackleford Bank, wild ponies still roam freely.

Distinctly offbeat mainland seashore locales include: Hotel Engelhard at Engelhard bordering the untracked Mattamuskett National Wildlife Refuge where full room and board is only $55 each per week; and quiet oak-embowered Southport sheltered by jutting Cape Fear where shrimp boats land their catches and you watch river pilots scramble aboard.

For beauty, peace and contentment high in remote mountain eyries, try the Pisgah Inn, Box 375A, Route 1, Canton, N.C. 28786; or Snowbird Mountain Lodge, Robbinsville, N.C. 28771, fine rustic inns charging $20-$26 daily double with all meals.

If you're seeking the ideal college town for a quiet cultural spring and fall sojourn or permanent retirement, consider Chapel Hill, home of the University of North Carolina. Rimmed by cool woodlands, with charming gardens, huge shade trees and lovely homes, Chapel Hill is a Mecca for lovers, of beauty and learning. A writers' colony, it has been home for James Street, Betty Smith, Paul Green and many others. There are free lectures, forums, concerts and Sunday musicales and many first-class plays are presented at movie theater prices. Tourists are few, costs not high.

Three mountain resorts also offer a cultural background; Burnsville in a delightful setting in the Blue Ridge Mountains is known for its Fine Arts School and summer theater; Hendersonville is famed for its street and folk dances, concerts and theater, and gay festivals; and Brevard, another mountain-rimmed resort surrounded by waterfalls, stages a Music Festival throughout August with concerts and symphony. Popular, too, with artistic folks is Mount Toxaway Lodge in Sapphire, a few miles west.

Among small towns heavy with history and early-day atmosphere Edenton, Elizabeth City and New Bern are also first-class retirement towns with moderate costs. Bath, North Carolina's oldest village, also teems with historical atmosphere, old homes and churches.

Despite the heavy tourist traffic along the Blue Ridge Parkway you can find plenty of room to yourself at many cool, mountain-top campsites in the midst of superb scenery. Scores of others exist in neighboring National Forests. Among state parks is Morrow Mountain near Albermarle, amid superlative mountain scenery on the Pee Dee River; there are camping and cabins. At Mount Mitchell State Park, which includes the summit and slopes of mighty Mount Mitchell, highest mountain in the East, you'll also find splendid camping on Alpine slopes.

While traveling the Parkway, turn off at Asheville and take US19 north to Burnsville for a stay at its charming Nu-Wray Inn, a colorful but traditional hostelry with an enviable reputation for authentic mountain food. Another good spot for typical mountain fare is Sylva, west of Balsam Cap and west of

Asheville, where Sunset Farms serves traditional mountain meals.

More information: Department of Conservation & Development, Travel Promotion Division, Raleigh, N.C. 27602.

NORTH DAKOTA. Surprisingly few cross-country motorists stop to see Theodore Roosevelt National Memorial Park, which is something of a blessing in disguise for seekers of the unspoiled. For apart from good roads, development has scarcely touched this quiet badlands region. The country was made for riding and horses may be rented at Medora or from local ranchers. But you don't necessarily need a horse to take in the park's brilliantly colored table lands, buttes and conical hills, its vivid wildflowers and abundant wildlife, its prairie dog towns and burning coal veins. For there's plenty of automobile sightseeing too. You'll find adequate budget priced accommodation at the interesting old frontier town of Medora, a low cost retirement spot.

Another uncrowded natural wonderland is North Dakota's immense shoreline on Garrison Dam — 200 miles of winding, wooded shores with superb fishing. To find it, head for Garrison or Pick City, both with inexpensive accommodations and lakeside campsites.

More information: State Travel Department, Capitol Bldg., Bismarck, N.D. 58501.

NORTHWEST TERRITORIES. Few Americans are aware that you can drive your car for 700 miles north of Edmonton to the mining town of Yellowknife on Great Slave Lake. Made over the gravel-surfaced MacKenzie Highway from Peace River, Alta., this is a fabulous trip for anyone willing to turn his back on assembly line conveniences. (You may also reach Yellowknife by regular bus service of Canadian Coachways from Edmonton.) While Yellowknife is far outside the travel horizon of most Americans, it is merely the jumping-off place for travel buffs headed for the high Arctic, the Eskimos' "Land of No Tomorrow."

Four times a week, Pacific Western Airlines operates a flight for a further 600 miles north, to Canada's Western Arctic and its model capital of Inuvik. Lying 150 miles within the Arctic Circle, Inuvik was built at a cost of $50 millions to demonstrate that life can function normally in the Arctic. Its MacKenzie Hotel provides comfortable lodgings and you'll enjoy visiting the igloo-shaped cathedral and seeing such unique features as the utilidor, a surface pipe which, at a cost of $200 per foot, transports water, sewage and heat.

Don't expect bargain prices. Air fare is $172 roundtrip and living costs are not low. But you *will* see lots of Eskimo and Indians and, if you like, you can fly a further 90 miles north to Tuktoyaktuk, a true Eskimo town on the Arctic Ocean near the Dewline early radar warning system. Here, over 400 Eskimo live by hunting seals and caribou and dogsleds are widely used all year. The Igloo Inn provides hospitality. If you like, you can hire an Eskimo and his dog team for an expedition over the sea ice and your guide will build you an igloo for sleeping. Another Eskimo town easily accessible by air is Aklavik, where Steffanson spent the winter.

Anyone is free to go to Canada's Western Arctic but it's wise to have confirmed hotel reservations in advance.

More information: Northwest Territories Office, 400 Laurier Avenue West, Ottawa 4, Ont.

OHIO. Escaping tourists during the summer heat is something of a problem in this populous Midwestern state. But here are some suggested locales. Try: 1. Pike Lake State Park, with beach, in the beautiful rugged hills of Pike County; cabins are $60 a week. 2. Lake House Park in the scenic Zaleski State Forest; or Hueston Woods Park amid primeval forest near Oxford; both have cabins at $60-

$75 a week and Hueston Woods also has a splendid lodge. 3. The uncrowded lakes in Muskingum Conservancy District around New Philadelphia, where the lodge on Atwood Lake is especially recommended. 4. The colorful Amish country around Wooster. 5. The many farms in restful southeast Ohio which offer weekly board at $45. 6. Pundersson State Park near Newberry in Geauga County with its splendid Manor House Lodge. 7. Burr Oaks State Park with its luxurious housekeeping cabins and attractive lodge.

Worth consideration, too, are Ohio's Wine Islands in southern Lake Erie. The two largest, Kelleys and South Bass, have been discovered but are quite enjoyable after Labor Day. Middle Bass, with fewer accommodations, is as yet unspoiled. Together with Canada's Pelee Island, the group forms a stepping stone chain of islands across Lake Erie. These are green islands dotted with vineyards, surrounded by rugged cliffs, rock formations, and gently shelving beaches. Clustered round the main islands are islets with curious names like Mouse, Starve, Green Ballast, Rattlesnake and Sugar.

Kelleys, the largest, is carpeted by beautiful vineyards and acres of woodland; on the north shore are two miles of Ohio's finest beaches and the east shore is lined by picturesque flat rocks. Thirty-three miles of scenic road bring you to Indian heiroglyphics and the famous glacial carvings. You'll find excellent camping on the eastern shore, cottages elsewhere average $75 a week in season. Several large religious groups camp on Kelleys in summer and considerable real estate development is under way. But there is no Coney Island atmosphere yet.

On nearby South Bass Island is Perry's monument commemorating the battle of 1813, the resort community of Put In Bay, and similar scenery to Kelleys. Notwithstanding its commercialism and night spots, you can still bike down shady lanes to caves and old wineries and visit the hydrobiological laboratory on craggy Gibraltar Island in the harbor, where Jay Cook's old mansion peeps above the tree tops. But its proximity to the mainland (4 miles), stock car and boat races do make South Bass touristy till Labor Day. The Rendezvous Hotel charges $4-$10 daily for two, meals extra, and cottages average $75-$85 in season.

Middle Bass, 1½ miles from Put In Bay, is site of the famous fort-like Lonz winery, sandy beaches, vineyards, and deep wine cellars. Here you can still enjoy a peaceful midsummer vacation. At Buckirene Lodge summer cottages including a 14 foot boat rent at $60 a week for four; similar cottages are available from M. Ashley, James Brentz, and Dale Willey, all at Middle Bass Island, Ohio. Little Bass offers much the same thing but lacks accommodations and among the islets, Rattlesnake's private club is the sole place to stay. However, Pelee Island in Canadian waters has a variety of cottages and lodges at similar rates to the Ohio islands and trading posts selling British textiles and china.

All the islands are served by frequent car-carrying ferries from Port Clinton, Sandusky or Marblehead, Ohio, and by an airline using the famous "Tin Goose" Ford Trimotor planes from Sandusky and Port Clinton. For more information, write the CoCs at Kelleys Island and at Put In Bay, Ohio.

Ohio has three historic towns with atmosphere. Granville resembles a New England village, has scores of stately old homes, historic St. Lukes Church and the picturesque campus of Denison University. The inn serves excellent meals and is a hideaway for honeymooners-in-the-know. Besides its old homes and yesteryear atmosphere, Lebanon boasts the fine old Golden Lamb Hotel, where Charles Dickens once stayed. Oxford with its two colleges, cultural activities and many homes dating from the early 1800's is also attractive. All three towns would be fine for retirement.

More information: Development

Dept., Box 1001, Columbus, Ohio 43216.

OKLAHOMA. The Sooner State has two state parks of more than usual interest. Lake Tenkiller State Park on the blue man-made lake of the same name lies among the rugged Cookson Hills, home of the Cherokee Indians. There are good bass fishing, islands and coves to explore for driftwood, and a score of historic sights to visit nearby. Many old timers living on the lake came over the "Trail of Tears" and can tell you about the James, the Starrs and others. Strictly modern air-conditioned cottages rent at $53 a week. Only January and February are wintery and this big lake is fine for retirement. Comfortable retirement cottages can be built on the shore for $4,500.

For the ultimate in unusual resort lodges, try the lodge at Sequoyah State Park on a lake known for its natural beauty and colorful history. Special low rates apply at the park lodge September 15th to April 16th with an additional discount if you stay Sunday through Wednesday plus a further 20% off if you remain for 7 days or more.

More information: Oklahoma Industrial Development and Park Dep't., Room 500, Will Rogers Memorial Bldg. Oklahoma City, Okla. 73105.

ONTARIO. Within a few hours of Detroit and Toronto, the Bruce Peninsula jutting out into Lake Huron is not entirely untouristed. But outside popular Sauble Beach and Tobermory, you'll find uncrowded and unspoiled villages where no one is in a hurry and you can enjoy the colorful artistry of lakes, cliffs, beaches and forests in complete serenity. In spring the peninsula is a naturalist's haven. Hundreds of enthusiastic observers arrive every weekend to view the rare orchids, mosses and ferns.

Especially recommended are: Barrow Bay and Hope Bay, flanked by towering cliffs and idyllic vistas; Colpoy's Bay, a quaint tree-shaded bayshore village; Lion's Head—rugged grandeur, wonderful lake views; Pike Bay, where inns and tourist homes overlook the beautiful bay and beach; Red Bay on a beautiful island-dotted bay; Wildwood Lodge, with cabin and meals provided for $60-$80 double a week; and Stokes Bay, a picturesque shore village. If you don't mind fellow tourists too much, Tobermory at the cape's tip, is a gem of a fishing village. Boats leave from here for the various islands of Georgian Bay Islands National Park. There are campsites on some. For more information on this region, write Bruce Peninsular Resort Association, Wiarton, Ont., Canada. All costs are very reasonable; housekeeping cottages average $40-$45 a week. There are also numerous campsites on the peninsula.

Excepting for the built-up south and southwestern areas of Ontario, getting away from it all presents few difficulties in this huge province. And rates average 10%-20% lower than in the United States. Head north up any of Ontario's highways and within hours you're in a jewelled maze of virgin forests, lakes and rivers in an unbroken setting of solitude and peace far from the humdrum world.

For instance, you'll find numerous fishing camps and lodges on Lake Temagami, with cottages from $40-$50 a week, ideal for family fun and relaxation as well as fishing. Then there is enormous Algonquin Provincial Park, 2,720 square miles of escapist lakes and woodlands with numerous camp-sites and several comfortable lodges. The Algoma area north of Lake Huron is another almost untouched wilderness of rockbound lakes, streams and rivers among primeval pines. Practically every one of its comfortable accommodations is a perfect escapist retreat. Another off-the-beaten-path region you'll like is the Highlands of Haliburton—rugged beauty and sandy beaches which include part of Algonquin Park; all its hideaway resorts are inexpensive.

Any part of Georgian Bay, dotted by a galaxy of 30,000 islands, could be a paradise but you'll particularly enjoy the

French River and Huronia areas. Parry Sound in the former is jumping off place for the wild rugged coast and hundreds of islands; Point au Baril is another gateway to getting away from it all. Typical rates for full board at resorts and fishing camps are $45 weekly, 10% less off season. Try the homelike Canada Camp on Lake Nipissing near Lavigne; its island setting ensures welcome freedom from pesky black flies. Huronia (the area around Midland, Collingwood and Honey Harbor) is similar, with an historical background and numerous small resort villages with beautiful beaches. Good accommodations and camping sites are numerous. Worth special mention: informal L-shaped Royal Hotel on a piney rock islet at nearby Honey Harbor, $75-$100 weekly for full board; Deer Horn Lodge, farther north on tiny Sans Souci Island; and The Outpost on Lake Jobamageeshig north of Thessalon on Lake Huron.

Lake of the Woods in northwestern Ontario, a fisherman's Mecca studded with 16,432 islands and hundreds of smaller lakes, is virtually one big chunk of paradise. Rates are a bit higher but you'll pay no more than in the United States. The Land O'Lakes area is also unfrequented.

Restful simplicity is the keynote at many camps and resorts on the Muskoka Lakes. And around Red Lake in northwestern Ontario you'll find numerous fishing camps in a frontier, bush-country alive with deer and moose.

If you have a boat and a trailer, you can voyage in your own boat to one of the dozen islands comprising St. Lawrence Islands National Park in the Thousand Islands of the St. Lawrence River. Camping is permitted at most. But you must have your own boat or rent one. The Sudbury and Lake Nipigon areas in northern Ontario also abound in comfortable fishing camps in the virgin outdoors.

Settled by Loyalists in 1784, Quinte's Island in Lake Ontario remains strongly pro-British. Its three villages of gingerbread adorned homes are named for the daughters of George III, its ferry is the *Loyalist,* its hotel the Royal. There are beautiful cliff-lined beaches and dunes, ancient cemeteries and picturesque villages like Waupoos to explore. Get there from Kingston via Route 33.

Not far away in Ontario's Thousand Islands, too, is the idyllic retreat of Wolfe Island, reached by ferry. Here you can stay at the 130-year-old Hitchcock House, with magnificent balcony views, for $10 a day. Then, too an easy drive north of Toronto are the Kawartha Lakes where such resorts as Elim Lodge on Pigeon Lake are satisfactorily remote, and farther north, Almaguin Highlands is an inexpensive region of unspoiled northwoods rivers, hills and forests grouped around Burks Falls.

When writing for more information, specify the areas in which you are interested. Besides literature, you will receive accommodations listings.

More information: Department of Tourism & Information, 185 Bloor Street East, Toronto, Ont., Canada.

OREGON. Here are five areas of unsurpassed scenery with comfortable backwoods-style resorts made for relaxation.

You'll discover a wealth of scenery and unequalled fishing in Oregon's McKenzie River section. Lodges start from $35 weekly for two, meals extra.

The Metolius River country is one of the few real wilderness areas left in the Northwest. Through gorge after gorge the Metolius and Deschutes Rivers drop down through the rugged Deschutes National Forest, past lakes teeming with rainbow trout and secluded housekeeping cottage resorts with rates averaging $55 per week.

Up in northeastern Oregon where sixty gem-like lakes nestle under the dramatically carved Wallowa Mountains, you can vacation away from it all in the West's last real frontier. Spectacular scenery lies on every hand: perpetually snow-capped mountains, timeless glaciers and grim granite peaks. There are modern lodges averaging $7-$12 double daily and numerous camp-grounds. You'll get completely away from stray strangers at the Wallowa Horse Ranch, accessible solely by pack trail or light plane.

Near Bend, beneath the forested Cascades, many little known lodges offer ideal hideaway settings outside the hunting season.

Equally colossal is the scenery of the Rogue River country in southern Oregon, a primitive paradise of green forests carpeting the Siskiyou Mountains. Along the river and on lakes are plenty of cozy, isolated camps and there are fine lodges at Prospect, Trail, Ashland and historic Jacksonville, a well-preserved, early-day, goldmining town.

For an old fashioned country inn vacation in cowboy country, drive south from Burns to lovely Frenchglen Hotel.

More information: Travel Information Division, Oregon State Highway Department, Salem, Ore. 97310.

PENNSYLVANIA. A sizeable bit of Americana is offered in southeastern Pennsylvania Dutch and the somberly-attired Plain People—Amish, Dunkard and Mennonite farmers. With its barns bright with hex signs—"just for fancy" these days—and its bearded farmers and sunbonneted women, merry blacksmiths and woodworking shops, this unique area lures summer tourists by the thousands. The best place to learn a lot about this horse and buggy country is, for its size, New Holland, closely followed by Bird-in-Hand, Intercourse, Blue Ball, Ephrata and Lititz. You'll also see the Plain People in the larger communities of Belleville, Kutztown and York and Lancaster. Owing to religious meetings inside homes we are informed it is rather difficult to experience living with the Plain People through obtaining room and board with a family. But such room and board can be obtained with Lutheran or Moravian Pennsylvania Dutch families and if you know anything of their cooking, you know your vacation will be memorable in more ways than one.

An enchanting old canalside village is New Hope near Washington Crossing State Park. Here beside the Delaware Canal, a colony of writers, artists, painters and craftsmen work year around, and in summer there are Broadway productions at the Playhouse. The local inn offers good accommodations.

To escape tourists, Gilbert Love of the *Pittsburgh Press* suggests sampling a few days at an inexpensive country hotel in a typical western Pennsylvania small town. Suggested small towns are Mercer, Waynesburg and Greencastle. Similar places along the Allegheny River include Tionesta, Tidioute, East Brady, Kittaning, Port Allegany, and Coudersport, a popular deer hunting center. Quiet picturesque communities along beautiful Susquehanna River, most in delightful natural settings, are Clearfield, Renovo hemmed by rugged hills, Lock Haven, Athens bowered by shade trees, Towanda, Wyalusing—famed for its panoramic views, Tunkhannock, Danville, the attractive river islands at Selingsgove, and Millersburg. Also attractive are State College, a mid state mountain community with cultural roots; resort town Bedford; and in off season periods, Eagles Mee. Many more scenic spots and offbeat hill hamlets are virtually unknown until you come within a 10-25 mile radius, sometimes even less.

More information: Vacation and Travel Development Bureau, State Department of Commerce, Harrisburg, Penna. 17120.

QUEBEC. Almost anywhere in Quebec one can find the typical church-spired French village, often with a small hotel serving delectable French cooking at inexpensive rates. Undeniably, however, the one best place to enjoy the simpler life and untouched charm of a French Canadian village at its finest is along the Gaspé Coast. Until 1925, French speaking Gaspé was accessible only by boat and today it still remains an unspoiled treasury of Breton fishing villages and Norman farms.

One thing you must know. In July and August its coastal highway is packed with cars, its villages are crammed with tourists. Only after Labor

Day does Gaspé come back into its own. From then until the warm days end in mid-October, spectacular autumn beauty is your bonus to scenery ranging from grandiose to picturesque.

The best scenery is from Percé north. The best scenery is from Percé north. Here are bald capes and great headlands where dog carts and horses and wagons take the place of summer's cars.

Clockwise around the perimeter, here are some idyllic villages; all have inexpensive accommodations and French cooking. Ruisseau Castor, Ruisseau Arbour and Rivière à Claude are picturesque villages; at Gros Morne the village church lies atop a cape; Petite Madeleine, L'Anse à Valleau and Petite Riviere-au-Renard are attractive villages; for real rugged coastal scenery stay at Cap des Rossiers; Cape Gaspé, tip of the Gaspé Peninsula, is a fishing village where few tourists go and families offer room and board; Anse à Beaufils is another pleasant little seaport; at Barachois, a village over two centuries old, you'll be thrilled by unsurpassable seascapes.

Finally there is Percé, larger but the jewel of the entire Gaspé coast, dramatically situated among sheer cliffs and magnificent land and seascapes with the immense bulk of Bonaventure Island just offshore. In early fall, most hostelries are budget priced.

Other escapist retreats include: the restful Ile aux Grues near Montmagny, Ile Vert near Riviere du Loup and other St. Lawrence River shore islets like Ile aux Pommes, Ile aux Basque, Ile du Bic, Ile St. Barnable and larger Anticosti Island, privately owned by the Consolidated Paper Corp., in Montreal. Quebec's huge Laurentides and Gaspesian Parks are also confirmed hideaways for lovers of the outdoors.

You can drive to Sept Iles on the north shore of the St. Lawrence, but from here to Labrador stretches a roadless 400 miles of rockbound coast dotted with isolated fishing villages. Though each village has electricity and a Hudson Bay store, life resembles that of a New England village of a century ago. Crime and tension are unknown. You'll find a small hotel at Havre St. Pierre and a guest house at Blanc Sablon but families at most other villages take guests. From Sept Iles, you can fly to the villages by Les Ailes du Nord Airline or you can go by the passenger steamer *Jean Brilliant*.

If you've discovered how beneficial yoga can be and if you're serious and enthusiastic about it, you can spend a wonderfully healthful vacation at the Sivananda Ashram Yoga Camp, 8th Avenue, Val Morin.

For a painting vacation among fellow artists, a rare discovery is Le Vieux Moulin Art Centre at St. Pie de Bagot, in the Quebec countryside 40 miles from Montreal. Studios and accommodations are in five century-old mills, rich in reminders of the nostalgic past, and the food is excellent.

More information: Information Division, Department of Tourism, Fish & Game, Tourist Branch, Parliament Bldgs., Quebec, P.Q., Canada.

RHODE ISLAND. Try Prudence Island in Narragansett Bay. Remote from mainland crowds, there's little to do except swim, go fishing, and propel a rocking chair. Fewer than a hundred people live on the island year around, and none but old jalopies and hot rodders stir up the dust on the island's unpaved roads. Summer visitors are increasing. But after Labor Day cottages are inexpensive. Since there's no central information center, ask Captain Sousa, skipper of the Prudence Navigation Company ferryboat, to post your request for information on his bulletin board, where the islanders will see it. The ferry operates regularly from Bristol.

Everyone knows that Newport is a busy summer resort of plush estates and expensive cottages. But what few people know is that after Labor Day you too can live on one of the opulent estates—at reasonable cost. From mid-September through June 1 it may be possible to rent a gatekeeper's cottage or a beautifully remodelled stable at one of the estates lining Ocean Drive. Rents are

$110-$135 a month and these are charming places within a few minutes' walk of the sea. Uncrowded fall, with its fine weather until mid-October, is the best time to enjoy Newport's colonial atmosphere, antique shops, scenic Cliff Walk, fishing, country auctions, bicycling, beachcombing, piano sings in taverns, and the free clams and oysters. If you prefer, you can rent a luxurious beach cottage for $100 a month, a small furnished home for $85 or stay at a guest house for $85 double monthly.

Rhode Island has its share of New England villages such as Kingston, Little Compton and Portsmouth, all hoary with history, colonial homes, ancient churches and graveyards. Inn and cottage rates here are also low in fall. Jerusalem, Wickford and Galilee are other favorite spots for artists.

More information: Rhode Island Development Council, Roger Williams Bldg., Providence, R.I. 02908.

SASKATCHEWAN. Truly different from the surrounding prairie country is Cypress Hills Provincial Park in southwest Saskatchewan. At a cool 4,300 feet, high among pine forests alive with deer and elk, the park has relatively few visitors. You can ride, drive through the hills, or play golf for just $3 a week. Cabins rent from $4-$10 and camping costs $1 a day.

Greenwater Provincial Park 28 miles north of Kelvington is another not-too-frequented park among forests of poplar and spruce. Here is the best fishing of any Saskatchewan park, and swimming, riding and dancing after dark. Cabins are $4-$6 per day, camping $1.

Far off the main highways in northwest Saskatchewan, the Lac La Plonge country brims with beauty spots that stagger the imagination. Walleye and deer are plentiful. Meadow Lake and Nipawin are two barely developed wilderness parks practically unknown to tourists.

Lac La Ronge, studded with over 1,000 tree-grown islands, is another fishing paradise far from the beaten path. You can stay inexpensively at a small fishing village carved out of the wilderness or at somewhat higher rates at one of the new motels. Hundreds of Indians live around the lake. Deer, moose and beaver are always seen and here you witness the colorful phenomenon of the aurora borealis.

Like an eyrie, the Moose Mountains rise from southeastern Saskatchewan's limitless rolling plains to provide an oasis of inspiring scenery and cool relaxation. Azure lakes attract bathers, boating groups, and fishermen and there's an 18 hole golf nearby. Chalet rooms are $3.50-$5 a day, cabins $5-$10 a day, motels $7-$8.

Another fabulous pioneer area now open is the Hanson Lake Road, winding and weaving 225 miles from Smeaton, Sask., to Flin-Flon on the Manitoba border. Here scenic lakes, fabulous fishing and wilderness camping make for a memorable vacation.

More information: Tourist Branch, Department of Industry & Commerce, Power Bldg., Regina, Sask.

SOUTH CAROLINA. Charleston's thirty blocks of historic old town provide an atmospheric background for a vacation or longer stay in fall, winter or spring. You'll discover much of the aristocratic, traditional Old South in Charleston's brick plazas and old churches, among its ancient churchyards and porticoes, antique houses and lacy iron grillwork. Spires and slate roofs overlook formal Old World gardens ablaze with color in spring and there are numerous drives to the nation's largest and finest gardens nearby.

Charleston, noted for its inexpensive yet sophisticated entertainment, offers Broadway plays, fine restaurants, and art classes.

Inland are Camden, Summerville and Aiken, small cities whose grace and Southern charm are enjoyed among historical sites and peaceful surroundings.

An untouristed yet interesting and highly scenic area for a spring vacation is South Carolina's "Up Country," its three most westerly counties of Oconee, Pickens and Anderson. Here, in spring, massed blooms of rhododendron and mountain laurel transform the roads into flower-lined corridors while the scent of apple orchards mingles with the pine flavored air of primeval forests. Driving around, you'll discover historic homes galore, waterfalls, 3 covered bridges, beautiful Table Rock State Park, historic old Pendleton, and an unspoiled hill folklore famed for its original mountain music.

More information: State Development Board, Box 927, Columbia, S.C. 29202.

SOUTH DAKOTA. Notwithstanding summer's tourist crop, you'll find scores of quiet, off-beat camp-sites where you can relax and enjoy the best of the Black Hills. After Labor Day and until November 30, three other outstanding Black Hills beauty spots are less crowded. Here they are:

Huge granite cliffs enclose three sides of enchanting Sylvan Lake. At over 6,000 feet this beautifully clear, spring-fed mountain lake produces magnificent reflections. It's a fine center for exploring the 70,000 rugged acres of Custer State Park, where among the most imposing scenery in the Black Hills—huge granite monoliths and mountains—you'll see wild sheep, goat, deer, elk and bison grazing. You can camp at the lake or stay at Sylvan Lake Resort for $8-$17.50 double without meals.

Spearfish Canyon in the northern Black Hills is 17 miles of enthralling beauty sandwiched between towering thousand-foot cliffs and dense green woods. You can camp near waterfalls or stay at several inns and lodges. Cabins range from $35-$95 a week (average is $50) and full room and board for two can be had for $110 weekly.

To observe everyday life among the Hutterites, approach the community leader at any of the colonies along the James River. Permission to set up camp on property owned by the sect is readily given.

More information: Publicity Division,

Dep't of Highways, Pierre, S. D. 57501.

TENNESSEE. Le Conte Lodge, a rustic retreat at the top of Mount Le Conte in Great Smoky Mountains National Park, is accessible only by foot or horse trail. You get there by a hike or horseback ride of about 5 hours from Gatlinburg and if you prefer, you can camp instead of staying at the lodge. At 6,000', often above the clouds, the lodge overlooks spectacular panoramas of wooded mountains while a variety of hiking trails offers walks of an hour to a day through the highest peaks of the Great Smokies. Confirmed reservations are essential. Write: Le Conte Lodge, Gatlinburg, Tenn.

More information: Division of Tourist Promotion, 2611 West End Ave., Nashville, Tenn. 37203.

TEXAS. Big Bend National Park beside the Rio Grande on the Mexican border does not draw the crowds of the big Western parks. In its wild, rugged mountain and desert scenery you are looking at the last real frontier wilderness in Texas. There are several campsites and also cabins.

Not many people outside Texas have heard of Palacios, a pleasant shrimp-fishing village on the Gulf of Mexico. The climate is agreeable all year and you can fish, swim and sail in a labyrinth of adjacent bayous. Farther south is Rockport, where for more than a decade an art colony has flourished.

An unexpected German culture still persists at New Braunfels on U.S. 81, a serene farming center with a bright green tropical park. New Braunfels was founded in 1845 by a German Prince and its *Neu Braunfelser Zeitung* has been continuously published ever since. A similar outpost of quaint German folklore and old stone houses is Fredericksburg, founded in 1846. A few older traditions linger, notably brass band concerts, folk dancing, and songfests in bravado Teutonic style.

Eighty-mile-long Padre Island National Seashore is free of all commercial developments and is a perfect escapist spot for campers.

A few miles southeast of El Paso, tucked away down Farm To Market Road 258 beside the Rio Grande, are a string of missions founded long before the pilgrims reached America. At San Elizario, the Presidio Chapel stands as it did two centuries ago, overlooking a tree-shaded plaza and bandstand that are straight out of Mexico. Artists haven't discovered this purely Mexican village yet but living here would be an utterly different experience. The crumbling adobe jail, still in use, held Billy the Kid and few buildings around the plaza are less than a century old. Just down the road lies Socorro Mission, its adobe walls 3 feet thick. Every Easter sees a re-enaction of the Cruxifixion while Mexican style bazaars, mariachi bands and brightly decorated food stalls surround Socorro plaza and remind one of a country fair of 50 years ago. Lacking many modern amenities, these Rio Grande pueblos are not for everyone. Yet here one can literally live in a Mexican village without leaving the U.S.

For a winter sunshine vacation close to nature, head for the Sea Gun Sports Inn, Route 1, Box 85, Rockport, Texas. The inn is center for exploring Aransas National Wildlife Refuge, where the largest list of birds ever tallied in the U.S. in one day was made.

More information: Travel and Information Division, Texas Highway Department, Austin, Texas 78701.

UTAH. Bluff in southeastern Utah is probably this state's best example of a town that looks the same today as it did 50 years ago. You'll find excellent rock hunting and outstanding opportunities for geology study and exploring old Indian ruins.

Hanksville is another real frontier town. Zane Grey stayed here with the Ekker family while writing many of his Western novels. You can still meet the Ekkers.

Moab, known for its 3-D scenery, is dramatically situated among the deep red canyons and mesas of the Colorado River. A health resort and locale for shooting Western movies, Moab is neither unknown nor untouristed but you'll find it full of interesting people and its canyons, covered with thousands of Indian petroglyphs, are certainly a photographer's paradise. Some twenty points of interest nearby include Arches National Monument, Canyonlands National Park, and scenic Monument Valley. Cabins and motels charge $6-$12 double daily and men can stay inexpensively at private homes.

St. George in southern Utah's Dixie is also an interesting Mormon community with an extremely mild winter climate.

Other good off-beat sojourning spots are: Escalante, a picturesque cow town; Bear Lake; Blanding; the Mormon village of Pine Valley in the heart of the Dixie National Forest, one of the state's most attractive hideaway locales for campers; North Fork Guest Ranch overlooking the yawning canyons of Zion Park; Red Canyon Lodge on the turbulent Green River; and the revitalized mining town of Park City near U.S. 40, which may become another Aspen.

More information: Utah Travel Council, Council Hall, Capitol Hill, Salt Lake City, Utah 84114.

VERMONT. Finding a "dream" village or a secluded lake-shore hideaway is not difficult in this scenic, history-filled state. Simply by turning off main highways on to winding country back roads you'll discover a wealth of untouched countryside and magnificently unspoiled white villages such as Charlotte, East Poultney, Mount Holly, Plymouth or Weston. Alternatives include Craftsbury Common, Waterford, Lyndonville, Morgan Center, Peacham, Greensboro and East Thetford. There are no large cities at all, little or no commercialism, and even billboards are strictly controlled. Nor are rates high but when prices drop during the still warm October days, there are real bargains to be had. For anyone who enjoys a true old fashioned winter, Vermont's villages were made for retirement and all costs, escpecially for older properties, are exceptionally low.

One of the most overlooked scenic treats in New England is Lake Champlain, its spindly 120 miles bordered by two high mountain ranges. Along hundreds of miles of undeveloped shores are scores of secluded coves and tree-lined beaches. Small hotels, cabins and motels tucked away here and there charge rates today like those most other places charged several years ago. Particularly delightful and untouristed is the Grand Isle Peninsula stabbing down the middle of the lake from Canada. You'll find it full of unsuspected beauty spots, vacant beaches and quiet coves. Isle La Motte, still less frequented, can be reached by connecting road. Other enticing lake locales are island-dotted Lake Memphremagog; scenic Lake Willoughby; and relatively little known Caspian Lake.

Better known but uncrowded in fall is Woodstock, a storybook New England village. All the charm of bygone days is reflected in its old homes, trim village green and elm-dotted streets. For only $8-$12 per day, meals included, you can enjoy congenial family living at neighboring farm homes and you are automatically invited to all the friendly neighborhood activities without the necessity of becoming acquainted. You'll find Woodstock a cosmopolitan community and there are frequent concerts, lectures and recitals at both Dartmouth College and Hanover nearby. Wallingford, also in the Green Mountains, is another typical, unspoiled New England village. Bennington exudes historical fascination.

Dorset with its writers and artists colony and summer theater draws the culturally minded as does Manchester, which stages art exhibits, lectures and concerts during summer. Also of interest are Marlboro, and the Goddard College live-in program at Plainfield and the Fletcher Farm Craft School at Ludlow.

More information: Publicity Director, Dept. of Development, Montpelier Vt. 05602.

VIRGINIA. Virginia abounds with historical atmosphere. One place where you can combine history with culture is Abingdon, home of the unique Barter Theater. Throughout the year, Abingdon's centuries-old streets and colonial mansions echo the life and color of the theater. During the Virginia Highlands Festival held August 1-15, you can go backstage, dine with actors at the Barter Inn, and attend classes in drama, music, arts and crafts creative writing.

Or if you'd prefer to combine history with a magnificent display of daffodils, head for Gloucester in April. Surrounding this historic tidewater village, hundreds of acres of daffodils form a fragant backdrop to its fine old estates, ancient courthouse, debtor's prison and other relics of colonial days.

Waterford, near Leesburg in Loudoun County, is another truly quaint community which attracts artists and craftsmen. Tucked away in a ravine with an old brick mill dating from 1733 at the lower end, Waterford still teems with the flavor of colonial days. Of course, you'll also find plenty of history in Alexandria, Charlottesville, Fredericksburg, Richmond and Williamsburg if you don't mind the tourists. Smaller flavorful centers are: Warrenton in hunting country; friendly Culpeper; Appomattox; and Charles City, adjacent to riverside plantation homes. An out-of-the-way establishment still operated in the traditional manner is the Orkney Springs Hotel. Fewer persons know about quaint old Warm Springs where you can stay at the atmospheric Warm Springs Inn, and enjoy the fine French cuisine prepared by a famous chef.

Two typical East Shore fishing villages, catering more to sports fishermen than tourists, are Chincoteague and Wachapreague. Chincoteague is home of wild pony bands which are rounded up and penned each July. Near Wachapreague and reached by boat are superb untouched beaches on neighboring islands.

Probably the finest camp-site in Virginia is at Big Meadows high in the Blue

Ridge Mountains in Shenandoah National Park. Short walks in the vicinity take you straight into a page of Americana, to mountain farms with zigzagging rail fences and pioneer homesteads.

More information: Virginia State Travel Service, 911 E. Broad St., Richmond, Va. 23219.

WASHINGTON. Not too many people outside western Washington and Oregon know of Washington's fabulous Driftwood Coast. On both sides of Aberdeen, secondary roads lead north and south to a beachcomber's paradise of long hardpacked sands littered with amusingly-twisted driftwood, big glass fishing floats, and semi-precious stones and shells. Clamming, crabbing and salmon fishing are superb.

South of Aberdeen, Route 13A leads to windblown Westport, a sports fishing village on a sand reef; to North Cove—a treasury of driftwood—and to Grayland, a Finnish village renowned for razor clams. Then at the end of the road, on a lonely peninsula overlooking placid Willapa Bay, lies unhurried Tokeland. All are ideal for a beachcombing vacation, all have inexpensive accommodations.

North of Aberdeen, Route 9C, the Clamarama Drive, winds up the Driftwood Coast, through lush green forests, sparkling lakes and streams to more villages such as Ocean City, Pacific Beach, and Copalis Beach. These too are ideal for a quiet, inexpensive beachcombing holiday; razor clams abound.

But really to get away from it all you should go farther north, to the dense rain forests and tumbled peaks of the Olympic Peninsula. Three spur roads from U.S. 101 lead down to the sea. One, from Sappho, takes you to Neah Bay and Cape Flattery with its dramatic seacoast, huge blow holes and caverns. Another branch of this same road leads to Ozette Lake and reached by trail, an abandoned Indian village on Cape Alava, a truly wild, shipwreck-dotted coast and a beachcomber's dream. The third, near Forks, takes you down to the Indian village of La Push on a spectacular coast

guarded by lofty, spired islands. All three places have inexpensive cabins and are uncrowded outside the salmon fishing season.

A more accessible continuation of this same coast parallels U.S. 101 between Ruby Beach and Queets. Kalaloch has a good lodge and a National Park campground. Winter rain is heavy on this coast but summers are delightful.

Most flavorful of the offbeat waterside communities found on byways in the Puget Sound area are Poulsbo, known as "little Norway" for its Scandinavian air; and La Conner, opposite Whidbey Island, where many Indians live.

A freak of political geography left a 9-square mile chunk of the United States surrounded by Canada. Thirty minutes south of Vancouver and accessible only by crossing into Canada, Point Roberts is a United States enclave surrounded on three sides by water and on one side by British Columbia. The nearest large American city, Seattle, is 150 miles away. Unique for its Victorian appearance and friendly mien, Point Roberts boasts a dry climate, three general stores, clean beaches abounding with giant clams, driftwood and gemstones, high cliffs where bald eagles nest, a variety of summer cottages, two motels, two beer joints which jump with Canadian patronage at weekends, and a small permanent population, many of whom are of Icelandic descent. The salmon fishing is outstanding and apart from summer weekends, it's an ideal place to get away from it all.

Known only to local residents are: 1. beautiful Baker Lake, lying below Mount Baker, with excellent fishing and a very inexpensive cottage resort (Get there from Mount Vernon on I-5, via paved road to Concrete, thence 30 miles of Forest road); and 2. Spirit Lake below Mt. St. Helens, where the lodge lies across the lake and you summon the boat by ringing a cowbell (for information write the CoC at Castle Rock, Wash. 98611.) Both are full of interesting features and recommended for an untramelled family vacation of a week or more.

How about staying at a derelict but charming mining town hidden at high altitude among spectacular granite peaks far from the coast? Then set out for Monte Cristo. This former boom town is almost totally forgotten by the rest of the world. Even the paved road peters out before you arrive. Yet there's plenty to see in the old town and winding trails take you to a number of rather awesome open mine shafts among the clouds. An unpretentious lodge, once a mine cookhouse, has rooms from $3 nightly and cabins for $4-$7.50 per couple, less by the week. Home cooked meals are also available.

Another offbeat area is the 19th Century county of Skamania in the Columbia River Gorge. Scenery is spectacular, people are few, life moves slowly, there are no stoplights or parking meters and accommodations are economical. Write the CoC at Stevenson.

More information: Washington State Department of Commerce and Economic Development, General Administration Bldg., Olympia, Wash. 98501.

WEST VIRGINIA. Charles Town's pari-mutuel race track draws betting crowds but otherwise, this small, quiet town dozes and dreams of its associations with the John Brown trial. First laid out by George Washington's brother Charles in 1786, Charles Town became home for several branches of the family and today, one out of three residents bears either the Washington name or claims relationship. Streets are named for family members and you'll see beautiful examples of colonial architecture in the various Washington family mansions. There are outstanding views of the Blue Ridge Mountains.

Another peaceful West Virginian community, chartered in 1776, is Berkeley Springs. Once a fashionable spa, it still offers mineral water baths at reasonable rates. The town is ringed by well wooded hills convenient to river and lakeside recreations. Nearby Cacapon State Park furnishes lodge rooms and cottages.

Another fine historic college town in the Eastern Panhandle, between Berkeley Springs and Charles Town, is Shepherdstown. Founded in 1732 and rich in Revolutionary and Civil War landmarks, Shepherdstown is full of ancient stone and brick buildings over a century old. It's a splendid spot for retirement.

More information: Dept. of Commerce, Travel Development Division, State Capitol, Charleston, W. Va. 25305.

WISCONSIN. No review of North America's beauty spots would omit Wisconsin's rugged Door County Peninsula. Even in midsummer it is not over-commercialized, there are no carnival concessions and rates are not hiked in mid-season. But if you don't mind an occasional nip in the air, consider a vacation here in uncrowded spring or fall. For in May the peninsula bursts with cherry blossoms, and only in September and October can the true beauty of its northwoods setting be experienced. During both periods as well as in June, rates are reduced from the summer average weekly level of $60 for a cottage or $75 single with meals.

Washed on one side by Green Bay and on the other by Lake Michigan, the peninsula is a scenic medley of cliffs, islands, bays, coves, harbors and trim villages. The Green Bay shore is more rugged: its limestone headlands and white cliffs are broken by bays and snug sheltered coves. Among villages on this shore, you'll like Egg Harbor, scenically situated on a forest-clad bluff; Ellison Bay with its artists paradise, the "Clearing," site of a vacation art school; and Ephraim, a picturesque Norwegian village of white buildings and spires, home of the Peninsula Art Association. Most dramatically placed of all of this coast's villages, however, is Fish Creek, which nestles below a massive weather-beaten cliff. It is home of the August Music Festival and the Peninsula Players. Sister Bay near the tip, is despite its modern business district, a quaint village with a view of the seabird-crowded Sister Islands.

On the gentle Lake Michigan shore, among sand dunes, forests and long crescent beaches, are: Bailey's Harbor, an older village surrounded by wildflower meadows; Jacksport, a fishing village with a magnificent beach; and Gill's Rock, another friendly, picturesque fishing village at the peninsula's tip, where fishermen welcome company on their daily trips.

Inland, Hayward in the beautiful Namekagon Valley is a typical old logging town with a genuine lumberjack flavor and Chippewa Indians and mackinawed loggers on the streets. Heart of 200 top ranking muskie lakes, Hayward offers plenty of elbow room for a hideaway vacation. Rustic cabins rent for as little as $35 a week with a boat thrown in, modern ones $55 also including a boat. Typical of the logging camp atmosphere here are the all-you-can-eat meals served at the Northwest Logging Camp Museum. Besides unlimited maincourse helpings of prime ribs, roast turkey and chicken, you get a whole home-baked loaf, a pound of butter, a gallon of milk, a tray of pastries, and more if you want it.

In the old part of Prairie du Chien, an historic Mississippi river town on an island under high, forested bluffs, you'll discover a wealth of lore and legend. In this uncommercialized area, you can visit the great mansion Villa Louis, Egyptian lotus beds which flower in August, and a number of Indian mounds.

An interesting foreign background is supplied in Westby, where over 90% of the population are Norwegian speaking and movies show films with dubbed Norwegian dialogue. Monroe and New Glarus are primarily Swiss cities, worth visiting at festival times, when Swiss dress and customs can be seen.

Several outstanding state parks for camping include Peninsula and Potawatomi Park on the Door County peninsula and Devil's Lake and Interstate Parks inland.

More informations: Travel and Vacation Service, Wisconsin Conservation Department, Box 450, Madison, Wis. 53701.

WYOMING. To sample life in a real Western town, drive to Dubois, a typical mountain frontier settlement surrounded by the cattle ranches of the Wind River country. Another genuine Western cow town in the Wind River Mountains is Pinedale, on the western slope.

Two ghost towns you can add to your collection, or live in if you like—both are still inhabited—are South Pass City and Atlantic City nearby. Both have been crumbling away since all but a few stalwart families abandoned them in 1875.

The western slope of the cool, green Big Horn Mountains is an off the beaten path locale that merits attention for both vacations and retirement. Here, Western tradition lives on in an unspoiled cattle country of scenic trout streams, lakes and mountains, all in a climate that is surprisingly balmy throughout the year and boasts an extremely low wind velocity.

For about $85 a week, or slightly more, you can vacation in true western style at a choice of genuine cattle ranches that take a few summer guests. And for retirement in a nonconformist cowtown setting, the two centers of Buffalo and Sheridan emanate a great deal of charm.

More information: Wyoming Travel Commission, 2320 Capitol Ave., Cheyenne, Wyo. 82001.

YUKON TERRITORY. North America's wide variety of unusual settings can satisfy any taste. If you'd like to spend some time in either of two former Klondike Gold Rush towns that are still very much alive, you can reach them by driving up the Alaska Highway. Both are still typical frontier towns of Canada's Far North.

Dawson City, reached by a branch road from the Alaska Highway, was center of the Klondike Gold Rush and you can still visit Robert Service's cabin, the old Palace Grand Theater, and the gigantic gold dredges which displaced the pioneers.

Whitehorse, still rich with memories of the 1898 gold rush, is a bustling frontier town and capital of Canada's Yukon. It lies on the Alaska Highway. Immediately south is Miles Canyon where the Yukon foams and swirls through a rugged gorge. Scores of '98ers perished while shooting these rapids.

More information: Department of Travel and Publicity, Whitehorse, Yukon.

OTHER HARIAN BOOKS

HOW TO TRAVEL—
AND GET PAID FOR IT

There's a job waiting for you somewhere: on a ship, with an airline, in overseas branches of American firms, in foreign firms overseas —even exploring if you're adventurous.

The full story of what job you can fill is in Norman Ford's big book **How to Travel and Get Paid for It.** Whether you're male or female, young or old, whether you want a lifetime of paid traveling or just hanker to roam the world for a short year or so, here are the facts you want, complete with names and addresses and full details about the preparations to make, the cautions to observe, the countries to head for.

You learn about jobs in travel agencies (and as tour conductors), in importing and exporting concerns, with mining and construction companies. Here's the story of jobs in the Red Cross and the UN organizations, how doctors get jobs on ships, the way for a young girl to land a job as airline hostess, the wonderful travel opportunities if you will teach English to foreigners, and the fabulous travel possibilities for those who know stenography.

"Can a man or a woman still work his or her way arround the world today?" Norman Ford asks in this book as you might ask today. He replies in 75,000 words of facts, "The answer is still a very definite yes!" $2.50.

FABULOUS MEXICO—WHERE
EVERYTHING COSTS LESS

The land of vacation and retirement bargains — that's Mexico.

Where you can build a modern home for $4,500 and an American retirement income looks like a fortune. It's the land where your vacation money can buy double or more what it might back home—provided you know where to go for Mexico's best values.

Norman Ford's big book **Fabulous Mexico— Where Everything Costs Less**—tells you exactly where to get all of this country's best vacation and retirement values, where you can live like a prince on what you might just get along on in the U.S.A.

Norman Ford knows Mexico from north to south, from east to west, and he takes you to vacation and retirement areas that look more like the South Seas than Tahiti itself; to whole sections of just perfect weather where it's like June all year round; plus resort after resort, towns, cities, spas, and what not else where you'll have a vacation to remember at a cost so low it could seem unbelievable.

If you want a delightful retirement area with plenty of Americans around to talk to, he leads you to all the principal retirement towns, as well as dozens of little known, perhaps even more delightful areas, where costs are way far down, there's plenty to do and meeting people is easy. Always, he shows you modern, flower-bedecked hotels and Inns that charge hardly half of what you might expect to spend in even such a land of vacation and retirement bargains as Mexico.

There's a great deal more besides: everything from exploring ancient pyramids as old as Egypt's to finding fabulous hunting and fishing. If you might want to share in the high interest rates Mexican banks pay or to buy equally high-earning real estate or start a business of your own, this detailed guide to a fabulous land tells you what you must do to start your money earning so much more than in the U.S.

Fabulous Mexico—Where Everything Costs Less opens up Mexico to you. It's a big book, yet it costs only $2.

AMERICA BY CAR

This big book is your insurance of seeing all the four-star sights in whatever corner of the U. S. or Canada you drive to (and it even covers Mexico as well).

Day by day, **America by Car** tells you where to go from Alaska to Mexico. Whether you're visiting New England or California, Florida or the National Parks, the Great Lakes, the Mississippi, the East, the South or the Southwest, the Indian country, etc., it tells you road by road the scenic way to go and it always directs you to the important sights along the way and in the cities.

In Niagara or Los Angeles, Washington or New Orleans, the Black Hills or Montreal, **America by Car** takes the guesswork out of travel. Of course it names hundreds upon hundreds of **recommended** places to eat and stay.

America is so big, you can easily overlook or forget important sights or make many a wrong turn. So get **America by Car,** the book that makes sure you'll see everything of consequence and aways travel right.

America by Car is fully 170,000 words in length (as large as 3 ordinary-sized novels). But it costs only $3.50 while it helps you see any part of America as you've probably never before explored this part of the world.

HOW TO ORDER: See your bookdealer, or if he cannot supply these titles, order direct from the publisher, enclosing remittance. (HARIAN PUBLICATIONS, Dept. D, Greenlawn, Long Island, New York 11740.)

OTHER HARIAN BOOKS

UTOPIA IS AN ISLAND

Right here in the U.S. there's many a transplanted Tahiti to which you can drive: many a coral island which rivals the South Seas; many a hideaway, many an off-beat, sun-warmed island gem in a sparkling bay; many an island paradise scattered off our coasts from Canada to Mexico.

And nearby are others to which you can drive most of the way: fabulous islands off Mexico, that country where your dollar buys so much more. Or off-beat gems in the brilliant Bahamas, just across from Florida. Or gems of staggering beauty in the West Indies to which a short airplane ride transports you.

If your eyes are upon Hawaii but you fear it would be too expensive, wait until you learn the corners which this book has discovered. See, too, whether you can resist those island paradises off in another direction where $50 a week means you and your wife can live like kings.

Altogether this book lets you choose among hundreds of other island paradises: Cozumel, Barbados, Tobago, Jamaica, Puerto Rico, the Virgins; Ibiza, Majorca, Capri, Crete, Madeira, the Canaries, and still more. It gives dollar and cents costs—for hotels, meals, your own apartment, food in the stores, entertainment, getting there, etc. Over 100,000 words long, yet it costs only $2.

HARIAN'S INVESTING FOR A SOUND 6%—AND MORE

Where to get 6%—8% and more

Harian's Investing for a Sound 6% and More names the seldom-known, and therefore higher paying banks and other places to put your money.

You learn about banks that actually pay 7% to 10% interest, government securities paying 7% to 9%, extra profitable ways to buy mutual funds, safe syndicates (often paying 12%), and many other ways to raise the rate you might normally expect.

You learn, too, about U. S. Government-guaranteed investments paying close to 6%, about British township obligations, leasebacks, unusual mortgages, finance companies paying 6% to 10%, and many other ways to start your money earning so much more. Although this book emphasizes the U.S., it also covers Canada, capital-short countries, Britain, and other countries where the going rates for interest and dividends top those in the U. S.

And there's still more: businessmen's investments like British warehouse receipts which often pay 20% a year, have tripled in value in 8 years; other long term, higher paying investments like timberlands; or the world's outstanding capital-short country, where banks, government bonds, and fast growing industries pay over twice as much as do similar U. S. investments. And it tells you many a way to enjoy a tax-free return on your money.

No matter how much you have to invest, it will pay you to learn how much more you can do with your money. By showing you so many more places to put your money, this book can be worth thousands to you.

But the book doesn't end there. It also includes the complete 7th Revised Edition of Harian's famous "How to Have Money to Retire On," the book that has shown thousands how to retire with a bigger nest egg. It details investment and insurance programs tailored to your needs, the outstanding U. S. income producers from the highest paying savings banks and s&l assns, on up the income producing ladder. Always too, it aims at helping you increase your present income.

$2.95 for this book could be one of the most productive investments you ever made.

BARGAIN PARADISES OF THE WORLD

How to double what your money can buy by vacationing or retiring in the most charming parts of all the world.

For that is what spending a few weeks or months—or longer—in the world's Bargain Paradises amounts to.

"Bargain Paradises of the World" proves that if you can afford a vacation in the U.S., the rest of the world is closer than you think. Author Norman D. Ford, honorary vice-president of the British Globe Trotters Club, shows that the American dollar is respected all over the world and buys a lot more than you'd give it credit for.

You read about pensions, inns, spas, and hotels where you can vacation or retire in a setting of magnificent beauty for as little as $4 a day. You learn where to spend a while in the fantastic West Indies, in South America, Mexico, Spain, the Canary Islands, the South Seas, the wonderlands of New Zealand and Australia, the marvelous Balearic Islands.

You read about the other fabulous "bargain counters" of the world for glamorous vacations and retirement, about cities and towns where it's always spring, about "Californias Abroad" and "Four Modern Shangri-Las," about mountain hideaways, tropical islands as colorful as Tahiti but nearer home, about modern cities where you can live for less, about quiet country lanes and surf-washed coastal resorts.

If you've ever wanted to travel but wondered how you could afford it; if you have a little income but wonder how you can live a happy retirement life on that; if you want a life of luxuries on what you'd get only necessities back home; if you want to see the most beautiful parts of all the world, then you want "Bargain Paradises of the World." Price $1.95.

188

OTHER HARIAN BOOKS

HOW TO TRAVEL WITHOUT BEING RICH

If you know the seldom-advertised ways of reaching foreign countries, you don't need fantastic sums of money in order to travel. You could spend $500-$1,000 on a one-way luxury steamer to Buenos Aires—but do you know you can travel all the way to Argentina through colorful Mexico, the Andes, Peru, etc. by bus and rail for just $179 in fares?

You can spend $5,000 on a luxury cruise around the world. But do you know you can travel around the world via deluxe freighter for only a fourth the cost and that there are half a dozen other round the world routings for about $1,000?

There are two ways to travel—like a tourist, who spends a lot, or like a traveler, who knows all the ways to reach his destination economically, comfortably, and while seeing the most.

Norman Ford's big guide, **How to Travel Without Being Rich,** gives you the traveler's picture of the world, showing you the lower cost, comfortable ways to practically any part of the world. Page after page reveals the ship, rail, bus, airplane and other routings that save you money and open the world to you.

What do you want to do? Explore the West Indies? This is the guide that tells you how to see them like an old time resident who knows all the tricks of how to make one dollar do the work of two. Visit Mexico? This is the guide that tells you the low cost ways of reaching the sights (how 76¢ takes you via 8-passenger automobile as far as those not-in-the-know pay $5.60 to reach). Roam around South America? Europe? Any other part of the world? This is the guide that tells you where and how to go at prices you can really afford.

If you've ever wanted to travel, prove now, once and for all, that travel is within your reach. Get your copy now of **How to Travel Without Being Rich.** It's a big book, with over 75,000 words, filled with facts, prices and routings, and it's yours for only $1.95. Even one little hint can save you this sum several times over.

ALL ABOUT CALIFORNIA—THE STATE THAT HAS EVERYHING

What can California offer you?

—**a vacation in Hollywood, San Francisco, Yosemite, elsewhere, all at a price you can afford?**

—**a place to retire on a small income? A home in the sun, with year-round spring-like days?**

No matter what you seek in California, this big book shows you city by city, town by town, road by road, everything you'll find in this big state.

There's not an important sight in all the state which you'll miss if you follow its detailed advice about all that's most worth seeing. You'll welcome the long lists of recommended restaurants, motels, and hotels where you can stop at the price you want to pay.

With well over 100,000 words and many maps, **All About California—The State That Has Everything** gives you the facts you need if you're looking for a home in the sun. With its help you'll find the California that appeals to you—whole regions with just the degree of warmth and sunshine you want, with houses and rentals priced within your means. You'll find the best places to live or raise a family or to retire on the money you have.

There's so much more in this book—the facts you need for trailer living in California, the best places to fish and hunt, what you'll pay in taxes, how best to find your own retirement or vacation paradise, etc. You probably wouldn't learn as much about California in months, even years, of traveling around the state as you can from this one big book. Yet it costs only $2.50.

WHAT YOU MUST KNOW WHEN YOU TRAVEL WITH A CAMERA

This is the one guide that really helps you take travel pictures you'll be prouder than ever to show to your friends. For it's not only a sound, basic guide to good photography anywhere, but it shows, page after page, the hundreds of easy tricks professional photographers have learned to make their travel photos look alive.

● **Do you know how to take pictures from an airplane in flight, the inside of a motor coach? Do you know the simple tricks for bringing out the picturesqueness of those many scenes that could be real treasures if you shot them right? Do you know how to take people so that they'll never know they're being photographed? Do you really know how to tell a complete photo story of your travels?**

But this book helps you do more than bring out all the colorfulness of the places you visit and the things you see. It leads you clearly all through the problems of foreign photography (equipment to take, getting good values overseas in films, cameras, etc.). There's hardly a question about such technical matters as loading, focusing, filters, lens, flashguns, cable releases, etc. which isn't answered.

Price only $1.50—less than you spend on just one roll of film and prints. But what a difference this book is going to make in the pictures you take!

OTHER HARIAN BOOKS

TODAY'S BEST BUYS IN TRAVEL

What's a "Best" Buy In Travel?

It could be a hotel with such unusual charm that it just about makes your trip. Or a restaurant where you dine graciously on little, yet get friendly, personal service and the finest in regional cuisines. These are the memorable discoveries you'd always be grateful for if a local friend recommends them to you.

Or a "Best" Travel Buy could be a guided tour that costs less than you'd spend on your own or unusual shopping buys or tranportation that slashes your overall costs. A really Best Buy never means spending a lot of money. Instead, it means getting the full travel riches that a trip should give you.

One book describes 10,000 such outstanding travel buys—each one so much more interesting and also so much less expensive than the ones you'd probably otherwise choose. For **Today's Best Buys in Travel** begins where the average guidebook leaves off:

> covering the world, it names the most exceptional values in hotels, restaurants, shopping, sightseeing, transportation, theaters, entertainment, and night life throughout the world. These are the Best Buys that really make your trip.

If you're headed for Europe, **Today's Best Buys In Travel** leads you to old English inns and flower bedecked Alpine hotels, to ivied chateaux and ancient castles, to many a little known place of genuine charm. If you're headed for Bermuda or Nassau or the West Indies, it leads you to guest houses or beachside resort hotels whose charm could never be duplicated in a gilded, tourist-jammed hotel at double the price.

Wherever else you go—Mexico, South America, Japan, the Bible Lands, etc.—it helps you visit them with almost a local resident's inside knowledge of what to see and do and thus have a richer travel experience than most tourists ever have. **Today's Best Buys in Travel** costs only $2.

NORMAN FORD'S FLORIDA
Where will you go in Florida?

If you want a vacation you can afford? Florida needn't be expensive—not if you know just where to go for whatever you seek in Florida. And if there's any man who can give you the facts you want, it's Norman Ford, founder of the world-famous Globe Trotters Club. (Yes, Florida is his home whenever he isn't traveling).

His big book, **Norman Ford's Florida,** tells you, first of all, road by road, mile by mile, everything you'll find in Florida, whether you're on vacation, or looking over job, business, real estate, or retirement prospects.

Always, he names the hotels, motels, and restaurants where you can stop for the best accommodations and meals at the price you want to pay. For that longer vacation, if you let Norman Ford guide you, you'll find a real "paradise"—just the spot which has everything you want.

Of course, there's much more to this big book.

If you want a job or a home in Florida, Norman Ford tells you just where to head. His talks with hundreds of personnel managers, business men, real estate operators, state officials, etc., let him pinpoint the towns you want to know about if you're going to Florida for a home, a job with a future, or a business of your own. If you've ever wanted to run a tourist court or own an orange grove, he tells you today's inside story of these popular investments.

If you want to retire on a small income, Norman Ford tells you exactly where you can retire now on the money you've got, whether it's a little or a lot. (If you need a part-time or seasonal job to help out your income, he tells you where to pick up extra income.) Because Norman Ford always tells you where life in Florida is pleasantest on a small income, he can help you to take life easy now.

Yes, no matter what you seek in Florida—whether you want to retire, vacation, get a job, buy a home. or start a business, **Norman Ford's Florida** gives you the facts you need to find exactly what you want. Yet this big book with plenty of maps and well over 100,000 words sells for only $3—only a fraction of the money you'd spend needlessly if you went to Florida blind.

ALL ABOUT ARIZONA
—the healthful state, where it's great to live and vacation

Just as a road map shows you how to reach your destination, Thomas B. Lesure's big book, **All About Arizona, the healthful state,** leads you to whatever you want in this fast growing state of sun and scenic wonderlands.

What do you want to know about Arizona?

Where's the best place to retire at low cost? Where are summers cool? Winters, sunny most of the time?

Where are the best areas for a job or a business of your own? For a home? What must a newcomer watch our for when buying land . . . or a home? How high are taxes? Is it true that living costs are less than in the East? What about salaries . . . schools for my children . . . my health?

Or do you want to tour this Grand Canyon State?

What's the best way to see Arizona by car (or otherwise)? What is really worth seeing along the roads and down interesting side

190

OTHER HARIAN BOOKS ▐█████████████████

roads? Or in the cities, the national parks, and the other four-star sights? What are those world-famous but relatively unknown four-star sights overshadowed by spectacular Grand Canyon? What is really the best way to see the Grand Canyon? The Indian reservations? The other canyons? Which are the best place to eat and stay along the way?

What are the sure ways to cut travel costs in this big state?

Filled with facts, over a hundred thousand words in length, **All About Arizona, the healthful state** almost brings Arizona to your door, answering these and a hundred other questions and giving you a richer, better picture of Arizona than many people have after living there for years.

To know all you should about Arizona before you go for a home, a job, a business of your own, retirement in the sun, or a vacation you'll always remember, read **All About Arizona, the healthful state**. Price, only $2.50.

All of Europe at Low Cost

THE GUIDE THAT RATES EUROPE'S CHOICE HOTELS BY PRICE

—**Because it emphasizes Europe's Low Cost Wonder Hotels, this is the way to get a perfect trip while spending little**

With this book, it takes only a glance to make a real discovery night after night. Because every hotel (and restaurant, too) is rated by price, you will never overspend, but you will always get the top values on the budget you've allotted yourself (which can be as little as $7 a day for hotels and meals). At all times, this is the complete guide to seeing Europe at LOW COST.

From one end of Europe to the other, it leads you to the towns and cities that have fascinated generations of travelers. It details what to see, the routings you're best advised to follow if you're traveling by rail, bus, plane, or local boats. There's a COMPLETE guide to motoring through Europe (and you'll use this whether you drive all the way or merely rent an auto now and then for local excursions). For every stop it names the choice hotels and restaurants at the price you want to pay.

180,000 words long, this in an enormous book, a complete guide to Enjoying Europe, with dozens upon dozens of absorbing, money-saving subjects. Just a sampling of the contents:

How best to cross the Atlantic by air, liner, or freighter.

How to make the Grand Tour of Europe for as little as $275.

What you cannot afford to miss in London, Paris, Rome, Vienna, Copenhagen, Amsterdam, Madrid, Lisbon, and a thousand other beckoning cities and towns in both Western Europe and the satellite countries.

The most interesting rail and bus routes through England, France, Holland, Belgium, Scandinavia, Germany, Switzerland, Spain, Portugal, Italy, and all the rest of Europe plus a COMPLETE guide to SEEING EUROPE BY CAR.

Only $3.75 for all this detailed help to get a perfect trip in Europe while spending only a little.

For adult travelers, the most helpful guidebook to low cost travel in Europe!

Sums up **Time Magazine** after comparing the 20 most populair guidebooks to Europe: "Norman D. Ford's **All of Europe at Low Cost** is a thorough, realistic guide to cutting corners as well as to good, inexpensive hotels and restaurants on both sides of the Iron Curtain . . . Excellent coverage of hotels, restaurants, and helpful hints to the tourist."

WHERE TO RETIRE ON A SMALL INCOME

Do you know where to find:

The greatest retirement bargain in Florida? The most beautiful town in California? The 3 top-notch retirement towns in the Southwest? The ideal island to spend a while in the South, with cool summers and warm winters? The most unspoiled paradise for retirement in the East? The most "cultural" small town in America, with a Little Theatre, art and music clubs, a cosmopolitan atmosphere? A spa, with wonderful facilities for recreation, surrounded by a national park? The top retirement towns in Texas, New Mexico, Arizona, along the Gulf Coast?

This book selects out of the hundreds of thousands of communities in the U.S. only those places where living costs are less, the surroundings are pleasant, and nature and the community get together to guarantee a good time from fishing, boating, gardening, concerts, or the like.

It covers cities, towns, and farms throughout America—from New England south to Florida, west to California and north to the Pacific Northwest. It includes both Hawaii and the American Virgin Islands. Some people spend hundreds of dollars trying to get information like this by traveling around the country. Frequently they fail—there is just too much of America to explore. This book saves you from that danger. Yet it costs only $2.

OTHER HARIAN BOOKS ▬▬▬▬▬▬▬

3 GUIDES THAT TELL YOU THE
WHOLE STORY OF HOW TO TRAVEL BY FREIGHTER

1. TRAVEL ROUTES AROUND THE WORLD
—the most complete guide to the world's
passenger-carrying freighters.

**Stop saying that travel is too expensive:
passenger carrying freighters are the secret
of low cost travel.**

Yes, for no more than you'd spend at a
resort, you can take a never-to-be-forgotten
cruise to Rio and Buenos Aires. Or through
the Canal to either New York or California.
Or to the West Indies or along the St. Lawrence River to French Canada. In fact, trips
to almost everywhere are within your means.

And what accommodations you get—large
rooms with beds (not bunks), probably a
private bath, lots of good food and plenty of
relaxation as you speed from port to port.

Depending upon how fast you want to go,
a round the world cruise can be yours for
as little as $300-$350 a month. And there are
shorter trips. Fast uncrowded voyages to
England, France, the Mediterranean; two or
three week vacations up and down the Pacific
Coast or elsewhere. Name the port and the
chances are you can find it listed in **Travel
Routes Around the World.** This is the book
that names the lines, tells where they go,
how much they charge, briefly describes accommodations. Hundreds of thousands of
travelers all over the world swear by it.
Travel editors and travel writers say "To learn
how to travel for as little as you'd spend at
a resort get **Travel Routes Around the World.**"

It's yours for just $1.50, and the big new
edition includes practically every passenger-
carrying service starting from or going to
New York, Canada, New Orleans, the Pacific
Coast, Mexico, South America, England,
France, the Mediterranean, Africa, the Indies,
Australia, the South Seas, Japan, Hawaii, etc.
There's a whole section called "How to See
the World at Low Cost."

2. TODAY'S OUTSTANDING BUYS IN
FREIGHTER TRAVEL—Norman Ford's
selection of the world's outstanding freighters
**What do you want when you travel by
freighter?**

● A real buy in a short trip?
● A longer journey via many exciting ports?
● Would you like to "island hop" around the
   Caribbean or the South Seas or to explore
   the Mediterranean? Would you like to wander ashore at half a dozen West Indian
   islands or at Tahiti or Bali, or at the enchanted Spice Islands of the East?

For real value in freighter travel, Norman
Ford, America's top travel expert, picks out
for you in his big book **Today's Outstanding
Buys in Freighter Travel** just those freighter
trips which top all the others for comfort,

good food, low cost and the like. (Ask any
traveler who's gone by freighter, and he'll
tell you there simply is nothing else to
compare with this informal, lower cost way
of seeing the world!)

**Today's Outstanding Buys in Freighter
Travel** is a book of well over 85,000 words,
jammed with facts about the ships, their ports,
prices, etc. Because it names names, tells
which are the world's outstanding freighter
trips, it's your buyer's guide to getting your
money's worth whenever you travel.

● Would you like an exciting winter cruise at
   perhaps half of cruise liner fares? Or a
   journey completely around South America?
   Or to all corners of the Orient? Or would
   you like to know how you can actually find
   a good, recommendable combination of
   services to show you almost every continent
   on earth?

Remember, freighter travel is a real discovery, and it can save you real money.
Wherever the world might be calling you—
Europe, the Mediterranean, South America,
the Orient, or elsewhere—get the real help
of **Today's Outstanding Buys in Freighter
Travel.** Yours for only $2.50, a very small sum
for the whole new world this book opens to
you.

3. FREIGHTER DAYS—HOW TO TRAVEL
BY FREIGHTER—Your guide to life
aboard your freighter
FREIGHTER DAYS—The guide to how to
travel by freighter—tells you everything you
want to know about your life on a freighter
from the moment you cross the gangplank
to your last day on board, when you're won-
dering how much to tip and who gets a tip.

You learn who does what on the ship, what
the ship's flags are saying, what the bells
mean, etc. FREIGHTER DAYS details the
preparations to make to get the most fun
from your trip, and it describes everything
from dozens of ways to spend your days
aboard the ship to such marine lore as what
might be the names of those huge birds who
fly above the ship when far out to sea, how
to win the ship's pool for the daily run, and
enough other facts to make you an "Old Salt."

So don't even think of boarding your ship
without FREIGHTER DAYS, the guide that
tells you how to travel by freighter. Many,
many drawings, yet it costs only $1.50.

**HOW TO ORDER: See your bookdealer,
or if he cannot supply these titles, order
direct from the publisher, enclosing remittance. (HARIAN PUBLICATIONS, Dept. D
Greenlawn, Long Island, New York 11740.)**